*Women
in the
American
Theatre*

Yale University Press

New Haven and London

Women in the American Theatre

ACTRESSES & AUDIENCES

1790 — 1870

Faye E. Dudden

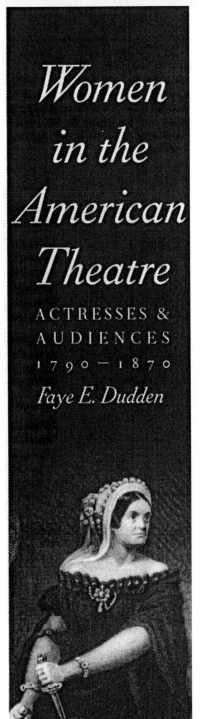

In order to keep this title in print, this edition was produced using digital printing technology in a relatively short print run. This would not have been attainable using traditional printing methods. Although the reproduction of this copy may not appear the same as in the original edition, the text remains the same and all materials and methods used still conform to the highest book-making standards.

Publication of this book was assisted by a grant from Union College.

Designed by Nancy Ovedovitz and set in Fournier type by Marathon Typography Service, Inc., Durham, North Carolina. Printed in the United States of America by Lightning Source

Library of Congress Cataloging-in-Publication Data

Dudden, Faye E.

Women in the American theatre : actresses and audiences, 1790–1870 / Faye E. Dudden.

    p. cm.

    Includes bibliographical references and index.

    ISBN 0-300-07058-6

    1. Women in the theater—United States—History—19th century.   I. Title.

PN1590.W64D84 1994

792'.082—dc20   93-40780

ISBN-13 978-0-300-07058-3   CIP

A catalogue record for this book is available from the British Library.

The paper in this book meets the guidelines for permanence and durability of the Committee on Production Guidelines for Book Longevity of the Council on Library Resources.

Contents

Acknowledgments

I could not have written this book without the generous assistance of others. I wish to thank the National Endowment for the Humanities and the American Council of Learned Societies for fellowships that gave me time to research and to write. Thanks, too, to the American Antiquarian Society for fellowship assistance and to Union College for faculty development grants. Members of the history department at Union were always supportive; I am particularly grateful for their cheerful willingness to redistribute teaching duties when I had released time. Special thanks are due to my former chair Donald Thurston, who encouraged me a number of years ago to develop a course on American popular culture. That course turned out to be the first step toward this research and this book. And I am grateful to my students, who wanted to understand the force of popular culture in their lives, and who made me learn some of the dimensions of performance.

My research benefited from the gracious assistance of many librarians and archivists. I want to thank the staff at the Harvard Theatre Collection, the American Antiquarian Society, the New York Public Library at Lincoln Center, the New-York Historical Society, the Library Company of Philadelphia, the Historical Society of Pennsylvania, and the Folger Library. Special thanks are due to Joe Keller of the Harvard Theatre Collection and to John Hench and Nancy Burkett at the American Antiquarian Society.

Colleagues and friends read my work, listened to my ideas, and asked probing questions that helped me to refine my analysis and focus my narrative. Some passed on research leads, shared unpublished work, and helped me to find my way in the complex world of theatre history. Others offered words of encouragement and generous hospitality on research trips. They all made this book, and my life, better. I want to thank Jean-Christophe Agnew, Sari Biklen, Janet Bogdan, Richard Butsch, Adrian Frazier, Rona Gregory, Carol Groneman, Anne Higgins, Graham Hodges, Mary Kelley, Ann Lane, Bruce McConachie, Barbara Sicherman, Ruth Stevenson, Christie Sorum, and Nancy Tomes. The Berkshire Conference of Women Historians provided an ongoing sisterhood of scholarship within which I have been glad to work. Chuck Grench and Cynthia Wells at Yale University Press were unfailingly professional and made the manuscript better in innumerable ways. And I owe special thanks to Joan Brumberg, to whom I could take drafts far too rough to be shared with anyone else. She has been the best kind of historian and friend. My husband, Marshall Blake, knows that books steal time from other things, but he never questioned the worth of this project and often urged me on when I might otherwise have faltered. He has my gratitude and my love.

Women
in the
American
Theatre

Introduction ·
Acting Female

My grandmother once told me, with an air of considerable importance, that *she had seen Ellen Terry.* I was an upstate New York farm girl, perhaps ten years old; I had never heard of that famed Victorian actress, and my family did not encourage youngsters to interrogate their elders. Many years later I was awarded the Ph.D. and installed in front of a college classroom full of eighteen-year-olds. I was thoroughly frightened, but somehow I realized that I must not let them see it, and so I began to *act like* a professor. Raised to be a farm wife, I was in the process of becoming a professional woman. Part of me became the thing I enacted, and eventually I was not afraid anymore. I was ready at last to remember my grandmother's boast and to consider what Ellen Terry might have meant to Sarah Haynes Dudden.

My grandmother was the eldest of eleven children of an English factory worker. She was probably working as a domestic servant when she saw the actress. Perhaps, unable to afford a ticket, she merely glimpsed Terry in the street. Perhaps she sat high up in the cheap seats to wonder at Terry's magnificence in one of Sir Henry Irving's London productions of Shakespeare. By the time I knew my grandmother, she had traveled thousands of miles, adopted a new country, and converted herself into the matriarch of a farm family—a formidable woman in an era when women were supposed to be meek and deferential. Grandma was no theatre buff; nor am I. But I am interested in what the theatre holds for women.

Because "all the world's a stage," the stage is a way to understand the world. Particular historical moments and human conditions provide special focus for the stage's revelatory powers. For example, in early modern England the stage reflected and modeled the social relations of the emerging market economy.[1] My interest grows out of the fact that theatre has never been able to ignore gender. Like religions that revere incarnated gods, theatre must show itself within and through the human body. Players come before audiences as male or female; even ambiguity and cross-dressing cannot help but draw attention to the "identity" they propose to evade. Channeling all its representational fictions through the human body, theatre is always asking not only, "What is true and what is false?" but also, "What is male and what is female?"

"Acting female" is what traditionalists and reactionaries prescribe for women, but an "acting female"—a woman who plays roles—reveals the possibility of escaping that imperative. Whenever a women enacts a part she implicitly threatens the prevailing definition of womanhood: she shows she can become someone else and make you believe it. The very project the actress engages in undermines assumptions about the fixity of identity, and throughout Western culture theatre has been associated with both falsehood and the female. In the words of film critic Molly Haskell, "Acting is role-playing, role-playing is lying, and lying is a woman's game."[2]

An acting, "changeling" woman may in fact seem threatening; her performance hints that supposedly meek, mild, domestic woman might really be quite the opposite—tough, vengeful, or even demonic. No wonder that for centuries men forbade the stage to women and enlisted boys to play their parts. With the sure instincts of a confirmed misogynist, Rousseau condemned the theatre because it gave power to women. The effect of plays and players was, he said, "to extend the empire of the fair sex, to make women and girls the preceptors of the public."[3] Thus the discrepancy between seeming and being that is intrinsic to theatre whispers to women about transformation, self-creation, even power. This is theatre's revolutionary normality, its secret-out-in-plain-sight.[4]

There is, however, a problem. Ever since women first appeared onstage they have been associated with sexuality and immorality. The actress has been equated with the whore so persistently that no amount of clean living and rectitude among actual performers has ever served to cancel the equation. Acting is linked to sexuality because it is an *embodied* art—in contrast to the relatively disembodied business of writing, or the decorative arts so long associated with women. To act you must be present in the body, available to be seen. The woman who acts is thus inherently liable, whatever her own intent, to become the object of male sexual fantasy and voyeuristic pleasure. Acting is a particularly acute case of the general phenomenon of woman being reduced to sexual object. The theatrical enterprise thus contains two divergent possibilities for women: transformation and objectification. Theatre may enable women to rehearse the most radical projects of self-creation or may reduce them to bodies and present them as objects.[5] Theatre may do either of these, or both, or neither:

it depends on the conditions under which theatre is conceived, produced, and received. It depends, that is, on history.

The story of the American theatre's two standing offers to women is deeply intertwined with the history of modern women and of public life. Theatre is a quintessentially public activity, and traditionally the public sphere belonged to men. In early America, women were confined to the privacy of home and family, and the only "public women" were, as slang neatly indicated, prostitutes. Yet beginning in the late eighteenth century a few women began to realize that the public realm was where economic resources were divided and decisions about social policy were made: the penalty for failure to present oneself in public was powerlessness, poverty or dependency. And so modern women's history revolved around women's struggle to enter public life on terms equal to men — to win the vote, to win access to higher education, to challenge employment discrimination. But women's problems did not end when they breached the barriers and entered these realms. The continuing problem of a woman in public, on the street and in the workplace, is the same as the problem of a woman on the stage: she must be there in the body. To be present in the body carries with it the inherent risk of being taken as a sexual object against one's will — in sexist deprecation, in sexual harrassment, in physical assault. Theatre thus exemplifies a general problem for women in public, what we might call the "body problem."[6]

Yet the nineteenth-century theatre also presented a historical opportunity. When actresses showed themselves in public, women had a chance to imagine new ways of acting and being. For although gender is deeply implicated in our identities, it is also performative — that is, it is actually achieved or constituted through our actions: we are born with sex, but we must learn to "do" gender. Gender only seems natural: it is in fact assumed or enacted — as sociological talk of "roles" and "scripts" suggests. Routinely permitting women to play male "breeches" parts, the nineteenth-century theatre made this insight potentially available — in a simple-minded way — to anyone who attended. In a major performance like Charlotte Cushman's legendary Romeo, where a woman dressed, talked, and acted like a man, it hit the audience in the face.[7]

Today we live in a society in which one of theatre's two possibilities has won out, especially in its technological descendants, film and television. While live theatre harbors a fringe of avant-garde "gender bending" and feminist performance art, the mainstream of film and TV conducts a multibillion-dollar business involving the commercialized display of the female body, and the pornography industry accounts for billions more. The body problem is perhaps greater today than ever, for we live and work relentlessly surrounded by images that cater to male sexual interest, making it impossible for women to be unaware of their objectification. The ubiquity and verisimilitude of modern popular entertainments, together with their kin in the advertising industry, constitute a hall of mirrors that can rob women of any authentic sense of self. As the art critic John Berger writes: "Men look at women. Women watch themselves being looked at. This determines not only most relations between men and women but also the relation of women to themselves."[8]

The social history of American theatre helps to account for this troubling contemporary problem by charting the origins of the modern entertainment industry from the earliest years of the republic to the days just after the Civil War. This chunk of theatre history explains how entertainment first became a business, how it came to be so thoroughly controlled by men, and how it began routinely to display women's bodies for visual pleasure. The way that theatre evolved exacerbated the body problem by making male visual pleasure and the sexualized image a routine element of commerce and hence of public life. Women were not only objectified but also commodified. *Women in the American Theatre* examines why and how that happened, for the change was neither natural nor inevitable yet it was freighted with enormous consequences for modern women's lives. In charting the significant historical developments, I look at all the ways women were involved in the American theatre, not only as performers and audiences, but also as managers and as characters in plays. I pay special attention to the nature of the "business" and the predominance of commercial concerns. The antebellum theatre's turn toward one of its two inherent possibilities, objectification, provides a critical case study in the relationship of gender, popular culture, and American capitalism: women's bodies became products in the entertainment marketplace of nineteenth-century America long before there were "mass media."

I have written about a particular time in American history when each of the stage's seemingly contradictory possibilities was realized. In the early and middle decades of the nineteenth century in the United States, the theatre first reached out to a mass audience, and in that same time and place the first organized women's rights movement in world history emerged. Between 1790 and 1870 entrepreneurs came to realize that entertainment could be produced and sold like other mass-consumption items, and they eventually found that one of theatre's two possibilities was significantly more profitable than the other: exposing female bodies brought in large audiences. Yet the other, more liberating, possibility of theatre for women was never squelched and often was flaunted, for women were always present onstage, often appeared in male roles, frequently took on theatre management, and constituted an increasing segment of the audiences, all while the "woman question" was before the nation as never before.

This book blends biography with analysis and narrative. The story is arranged in rough chronological order, but I organize most chapters around vivid theatrical personalities of the era. I begin by exploring the contradictory possibilities that the early theatre offered women, the powers and dangers they might enjoy or suffer in the public space of the playhouse. American theatre in 1790 was marginal, provincial, and disreputable—a craft in the first stages of becoming a small business—but it also offered women a rare opportunity to combine remunerative work with marriage and a family. And because the playhouse was a political forum, actresses enjoyed a unique chance to take part in political debate. Actresses—and I will use this now increasingly outdated term—took part in the respected art of elocution.[9]

Because theatre was an essentially aural experience, there was more attention given on stage to women's voices than to their bodies in the years between 1790 and about 1830. The woeful reputation of the early theatre as a place of sexual dissipation was in effect confirmed by the presence of prostitutes in the third tier of boxes.[10] Nevertheless, respectable women did attend the theatre, although they were outnumbered by men. In doing so they stepped into a public space and made it at least partly their own by taking advantage of active audience dynamics that granted all attendees the right of demonstrative disapproval. The early playhouse was thus a contested arena where men were dominant but never in control, where women found the cultural authority of audience members, the economic independence that came from the actress's work, and even a limited entrée into politics.

In the 1830s one actress, Fanny Kemble, broke the impasse between the theatre's penalties and its possibilities. Aided by talent, family connections, and literary powers, Kemble was raised by the star system to such heights that she became larger than life, an exception that challenged rather than proved the rule about actresses and immorality. Kemble won widespread acclaim for her accomplishments, earned large sums of money, and shone as a heroine in an age given to hero worship. She seems to have influenced important nineteenth-century feminists such as Margaret Fuller and Elizabeth Cady Stanton, who were young women at the time of her star tour in 1832–34. Although she shortly afterward retired from the stage, Kemble remained in the public eye as a writer and Shakespearean reader, and her highly publicized divorce again revealed the financial and personal independence that the stage might afford to women.

But the 1830s also saw contradictory developments. The Bowery Theatre manager Thomas Hamblin pioneered a more self-consciously commercial theatre by reaching out to a mass audience with a low-price, high-volume strategy. Hamblin emphasized visual effects in spectacular plays because he saw that visual entertainment offered better profit margins. The shift to the visual at this time occurred in large part because images made better commodities than words; they were cheaper to produce and easier to consume. But social change reinforced the shift, for in the same era when theatre was organized as a capitalist enterprise and feminism was organized as a social movement, "looking" was in effect organized as a male privilege in the modern city. Urbanization expanded the public realm; daily life was lived more and more in fleeting contact with strangers. Sexual expression was affected by these new conditions, for anonymity facilitated certain sorts of sexual adventure, including the pleasures of looking at but not touching the faces and bodies of strangers. The expansion of public life in the nineteenth-century city encouraged male sexual pleasures that had nothing to do with intimacy, and the invention of photography at the end of the 1830s reinforced this cultural shift. Theatre took a critical "turn toward the visual" in these years, not least because society as a whole was doing the same.[11]

The new emphasis on visual rather than aural pleasure put women performers at increased risk. Hamblin himself profited by exploiting young women performers and playwrights both sexually and professionally; the new conditions of commercializing theatre penalized ordinary players but benefited theatre managers, who claimed new powers, including those of the casting couch. Simultaneously, Hamblin sought greater profits by tapping the underrepresented market of women theatregoers. He pioneered the new genre of melodrama, which, I argue, offered a great deal to women precisely because it thematized male sexual villainy and economic domination.

The radical potential of the nineteenth-century theatre was most fully realized in the career of Charlotte Cushman, the greatest American actress of the century. Her success reflected the growth and influence of the female sector of theatre audiences, for by the 1840s middle-class theatres in particular sought to appeal to a wider audience, especially women, by banishing prostitutes, alcohol, and bad language from their premises and their plays. Cushman's greatest parts all broke the romantic, happily-ever-after mold, and some of them evoked the uncanny power of woman as sybil, Cassandra, seer, or witch. Her Romeo was acclaimed one of the greatest of the century by *any* player, male or female. In this role she took on the body problem directly. At least some women were receptive to Cushman's implicit challenge of gender roles, though others surely understood her Romeo as a simple display of virtuosity. Cushman reached the furthest limits of what the stage permitted, and she won extraordinary acclaim and financial reward in doing so. Yet she failed to alter the terms of commercial theatre, and she accepted the limitations inherent in converting one's self into a commodity — an object for sale. Cushman's obvious genius may have made it difficult for other women to imagine how they might emulate her success.

By the late 1840s theatre was increasingly fragmented, as part of the segmentation of the entertainment market. Separate theatres addressed audiences differentiated along race, class, and gender lines. Just as "Mose the Bowery B'hoy" was central but "Lize," his girlfriend, was marginal to a series of "Bowery B'hoy" plays, women were underrepresented in working-class theatre audiences. In middle-class theatres, by contrast, women constituted about half the audience by 1850. Like another group that lacked social independence and market clout—African-Americans—women could not sustain a theatre of their own. There was, however, a men's theatre: beginning in 1847, the "model artist" shows offered men a chance to ogle the bodies of women dressed in tights and standing motionless in imitation of classical statuary. At the same time as the segmentation of commercial entertainment came changing audience dynamics that undercut women's powers as active audience members.

In the 1850s and 1860s the career of Laura Keene, an actress who became a theatre manager, testified to the limitations of the power of the female manager and the female audience alike. Keene succeeded in the crowded New York market. Her middle-class theatre appealed especially to women, through a vein of melodrama that spoke to their interests and took a female point of view. But Keene was handicapped in the intensely competitive entertainment marketplace: as a woman she faced extra problems in gaining access to capital, countering legal challenges, and getting a fair shake from the new corps of professional drama critics—who were always men and often were hostile toward female entrepreneurs. The need to make a profit drove Keene to produce spectacle plays, and starting in the early 1860s she used a plentiful display of women's legs to recapture male audience members lost to the competition of the model artists and their successors, the "concert saloons." Eventually fed up with this sort of expediency, Keene quit New York theatre management. She toured as a manager and a star and tried to start a magazine that would influence women of the upper classes to support a different, noncommercial, theatre. But she failed, because she had no elite connections and lived an unorthodox personal life.

The formula Keene pioneered in the early 1860s was picked up by male competitors and in 1866 yielded *The Black Crook*, a spectacular "leg show" that combined ballet and scenic wonders. It became the first million-dollar Broadway hit, and spawned a host of imitators. The key innovation of *Crook* was its strategy to titillate the male audience with a show of leg (to mid-thigh, encased in tights) without excluding the female audience, which found other sources of interest in the dancing, music, and scenery: having it both ways created the basis for record profits. Behind *The Black Crook* lay Keene's earlier experiments and the actress Adah Isaacs Menken's exploits in *Mazeppa*, where she was clad in tights and tunic to thrill male audiences. As the 1860s ended, the actress and feminist Olive Logan sounded the alarm, pointing out that the leg show imperilled what had formerly been a good job for women. Had her vision been larger, she might have seen a cultural opportunity slipping away as well.

The triumph of the visual, the ascendancy of a more powerful and increasingly all-male management, the pacification of theatre audiences, the redefinition of the public realm by commercial entertainments sold primarily to male-dominated markets, the elevation of female stars who could do and be what ordinary women could not—all these were in place by 1870. No one had planned it that way. In fact, absorbed in the traditions of the players' craft and the customs of an aural stage, theatrical entrepreneurs had been relatively slow to recognize that the embodied character of theatre presented profit opportunities in the display of women's bodies. The same commercialization that took the stage to a mass audience pushed the objectification inherent in stage representation a step further, into commodification. It converted women's bodies into a realizable asset. The early history of the American theatre helps us to understand the cumulative and interactive ways in which social conditions and profit opportunities gave rise to an industry that has often shaped Americans' fantasies but seldom shaped them to women's advantage.

1 · Power and Danger at the Theatre

Susanna Haswell Rowson took her first bows on the stage in 1792 because her husband William's hardware business in London had failed. Both Rowsons could sing and dance and play various musical instruments, and so they joined a theatrical company. Susanna and William Rowson performed in Edinburgh during the 1792−93 season, then left for the United States, where they appeared in Philadelphia, Annapolis, Baltimore, and finally at the Federal Street Theatre in Boston. By 1792 Susanna Rowson was already the author of what would become one of the great trans-Atlantic best-sellers of the era, a novel called *Charlotte Temple: A Tale of Truth*. But writing books, even best-sellers, did not yield a living income in those days. Acting did.[1]

In her novel Rowson created a passive, sentimental heroine, but on the stage her imagination took quite a different turn. She not only performed but also wrote several plays, including one called *Slaves in Algiers* (1794), in which women helped to solve the American foreign policy dilemma of the day. At the time the Barbary pirates were seizing and holding Americans for ransom. In Rowson's play, a woman captive becomes a virtual missionary of republicanism to the North Africans, and her teachings on liberty extend to matters of gender. "It was she who nourished in my mind the love of liberty, and taught me, woman was never formed to be the abject slave of man," says an Algerian harem dweller. "She came from that land where virtue in either sex is the only mark of superiority. —She was an American." The result of such talk was, of course, a grand mutiny of all the slaves, women and men together. After the final curtain of *Slaves in Algiers*, Rowson emerged to deliver an epilogue which began, "Well, ladies, tell me, how d'ye like my play?"

9

and concluded with the playful suggestion that *men* were born to "adore, be silent, and obey." Rowson's protofeminist theatrical gestures were so pronounced that they drew fire from the gadfly essayist William Cobbett, then in an arch-Tory phase. Cobbett complained that Rowson had asserted "the superiority of her sex" in so spirited a manner that Congress might, at this rate, soon be composed entirely of women.[2]

Susanna Rowson knew from experience how few employment options existed for women. She had learned as a girl that the failure of a male breadwinner obliged a woman to find work when her father, a revenue agent for the British

Fig. 1 Susanna Rowson. Nineteenth-century lithography enabled engraved images to be reproduced inexpensively. This portrait of Rowson, done after she left the stage to become a schoolmistress, fittingly emphasizes the head rather than the body. Harvard Theatre Collection.

Crown, had seen his fortunes ruined by the American Revolution. Young Susanna Haswell went out as a governess, leaving service in 1787 to marry William Rowson. In her day the great majority of women who worked for pay were domestic servants; other jobs open to women, such as needlework, seldom paid a living wage. Acting was virtually unique in offering the chance for an adequate income to women and men alike. Susanna Rowson did not mind hard work: during her five-year stage career she appeared in 129 different parts in 126 different productions and also wrote at least two original plays. But it was wearing and worrisome to engage in a business that so many considered immoral. At the time Susanna and William Rowson were performing in Boston, for instance, a well-to-do Bostonian learned of his son's theatrical ambitions and in a letter predicted the young man's "ruin," declaring that among actors and actresses he would find no "respectable gentlemen or female virtue."[3] When the Federal Street Theatre closed in 1797, Susanna Rowson concluded that it was time for another career change. She opened a female academy, which prospered. Rowson successfully assumed the role of a schoolmistress (fig. 1), having judged correctly that the new nation sustained a more reliable, more respectable market for education than for theatre.[4]

Susanna Rowson's stage career reflected the opportunities and the limitations for women of a career in acting in the early republic. Both the disapproval of moralists and the dispersion of population in a rural nation kept American theatre audiences small and confined to the seaboard cities and towns. Yet this marginal and stigmatized craft offered women who had to work a rare welcome, with relatively good wages and the chance to combine marriage and motherhood with their profession. And as Rowson was quick to see, the American stage even offered a chance for women — for white women at least — to air bold talk about gender and republican politics.

THEATRE WORK, 1790–1830

Like Susanna Rowson, many other women went onto the stage alongside their husbands. Eighteenth-century American theatre companies could be accurately described as several men "and their wives": player lists were studded with married couples such as the Rowsons or Edgar Allan Poe's parents. The most prominent performers of the American stage in the 1790s — the Hallams and the Hodgkinsons — were couples who worked together. So common was a woman's continuing to perform after marriage that players shook their heads regretfully over one actress who retired temporarily from the stage after her wedding and thereby "lost six or seven years of profitable and unrivalled engagement." A married actress might not enjoy much real independence—not when her husband pocketed one combined salary for them both or made the decisions about her career—yet she still had more potential power, in her earning ability, than the vast majority of American women of her day.[5]

Actresses found work in residential stock companies, where they engaged to work a theatrical season from fall to spring. Plays were presented three or four nights a week, and an actress worked only on those nights when she was cast in the scheduled entertainment. Like a preindustrial craft, acting was arranged around hierarchies based on age, experience, and skill. Each player in a stock company assumed a particular "line of business"—leading lady, "walking lady" (principal supporting actress), old woman, low comedian, and so on. Rank newcomers began as supernumeraries ("supes") or "ballet girls" and moved up to speaking roles and, if they performed well, to larger parts over a period of months or years. Talent consisted in knowing one's lines and delivering them well. Because the playbill changed nightly, it was no small task for an actress to be "perfect" in her part. Theatrical memoirs refer frequently to great feats of memorization, and the prompter who "gave the word" when a performer "stuck" was an indispensable part of the early company. In the early republic residential stock companies were located in all the larger cities and a good number of smaller ones, such as Baltimore, Washington, Richmond, Savannah, Albany, and Providence. Soon after the turn of the nineteenth century, a few theatrical companies set out into the hinterlands, but having to travel via stagecoach, flatboat, or keelboat stymied most early attempts to tour.[6]

Acting was a familial business. Actresses could arrange fitful work schedules to accommodate childbearing, and they raised their youngsters in and around the theatre, often recruiting them early into children's roles. Some families became theatrical "dynasties," their distinction spanning generations. Naturally it was a busy life, and according to one performer, "any lady in the theatrical profession who has a young family" could not be expected to indulge in much socializing. Some actresses even took on theatre management, as widows seeking to carry on a husband's business. The best known was Anne Brunton Merry, who made her American debut in 1796 and after the death of her husband managed the Chestnut Street Theatre in Philadelphia between 1803 and 1805.[7]

In the 1790s the structure of the theatre business began to change. Initially stock companies were often organized around shares of responsibility and profit: each player took a share of the profits depending upon the importance of his or her part, with some extra share or shares allotted to a performer who agreed to manage—that is, to handle matters of scheduling, publicity, and overhead. But over the course of the decade the manager began to assume new authority, orga nizing the stock company and hiring the other actors and actresses on weekly salaries. No longer just one of the troupe, the manager leased the playhouse, selected and cast the plays, supervised rehearsals, and—when the play was successful—pocketed the profits. Still, purely capitalist motives were rare, for most managers were actors who continued to perform while managing. In fact, one reason actors aspired to management was to secure the juiciest leading roles for themselves; they hoped to make profits if possible, but at all events aimed to cover expenses and keep performing.[8]

Although hired by the manager on a weekly salary, players retained some control over their compensation via "benefits," special, end-of-the-season performances from which they pocketed part or all of the proceeds. Major actresses and actors chose favorite roles to encourage their admirers to swell the audience, while minor players divided the proceeds of a popular play. The profits of benefits, which might amount to one-third of a player's annual salary, in effect made merit pay a matter negotiated directly between audiences and performers themselves.[9]

Actresses found theatrical pay scales relatively generous, especially given that working women's alternatives were so few and so poorly paid. Anne Brunton Merry earned $100 a week in New York in 1801, and in 1814 Agnes Holman Gilfert was paid $200 a night, the most ever paid at that time to an actress. Good pay enabled actresses to support themselves and others as well; Sarah Ross Wheatley, for example, returned to the stage to maintain her several children and an aging mother. The good wages reflected a favorable situation for all players in the early decades of the nineteenth century; even the lowest utility players seem to have been relatively well paid. It was a matter of supply and demand, one actor recalled:

> As yet the supply of talent was not beyond the demand, and consequently incomes maintained a fair level. . . . If an actor were unemployed, want and shame were not before him: he had merely to visit some town in the interior where no theatre existed, but "readings" were permitted; and giving a few recitations from Shakespeare and Sterne, his pockets in a night or two were amply replenished. This easy resource, in rendering the actor independent, compelled the manager to be generous.[10]

No less a theorist of the marketplace than Adam Smith agreed. In his *Wealth of Nations* (1776) Smith had explained that what he called the "exorbitant wages of players" were due to the "public opinion or prejudice" which kept more people from pursuing the occupation. Unless they were born into theatrical families or married actors, women may have been especially loath to work in a morally questionable realm. In Pittsburgh in 1815 a manager found it impossible to recruit female extras for a crowd scene: "Seamstresses and shoebinders would have as soon thought of deliberately walking into Pandemonium as to have appeared on the stage as 'supes' or 'corps de ballet.'" In the early theatre, good money was thus partial compensation for ill repute.[11]

SPEAKING UP

Although a pretty face and comely figure were appreciated, early actresses were told they really needed good enunciation as well as "retentive memory." The quality of one's voice was as important as or more important than physical appearance. The voices of the best actresses of the period were described as "thrillingly expressive" or "soul-subduing." About one actress it was said, "When she spoke a little thrill went through the assemblage. It was one of those low, round, sympathetic voices that stir you, and its articulation was so perfect that every shade of vocal meaning reached your ear." The noted actress Anne Brunton Merry's voice had a "magic sweetness," and when she began, the words "Hush! she speaks!" ran through the audience. "Despite the disadvantages of a short and corpulent figure," a minor actress named Mrs. Barnes had a career of more than twenty-five years on the Providence stage. Another, Mrs. Whitlock, who appeared in 1813, "had become very large, but in spite of her corpulence had sufficient talent to force admiration of her acting from every spectator." A prominent leading lady in tragedy, Mrs. Melmoth, was quite heavy—"far beyond the sphere of *embonpoint*," as one contemporary put it. These early nineteenth-century actresses built long careers on their speaking skills, and since stage makeup could hide many marks of age, youth was not at a great premium. When young Clara Fisher was breaking into the stage in the 1820s, she found every leading lady "seemingly old enough to be my mother." A number of prominent actresses in the early decades were described as too tall, heavy, plain, or old, and yet they kept on playing.[12]

Actresses participated in one of the most highly respected elements of American public life—the art of elocution. The love of excellent public speaking pervaded politics and held Americans spellbound in crowds of fifty thousand for two or three hours at a time to hear an orator like Daniel Webster. It also took them, some pocketing their qualms, to the theatre. When the tragedian George Frederick Cooke played in Providence in 1811, for example, all of the lawyers and most of the pastors in town attended because Cooke's pronunciation was so faultless: "None could appreciate the beauties of the language until he heard it from the lips of Cooke." Even the enemies of the stage conceded that the actors' eloquence was a powerful argument in its favor. One pamphleteer explained: "As elegant speaking and chaste pronunciation are accomplishments of the first importance in enlightened society, and as these may be cultivated in the theatre, it is inferred that the want of this source of oratorical instruction and speaking rightly, would be a public evil and a real loss to the world."[13]

Since the formal beauties of the human voice were not considered intrinsically masculine, women found an opening. Although they could not hope to present themselves as political candidates, pulpit orators, or lawyers, their performances in recitations, declamations, and readings, as well as in drama itself, amounted to a kind of aural inclusion. For example, in the summer of 1818, one attraction at the Pavilion Theatre in New York was "little Miss McBride," only nine years old, reciting choice items such as "Dr. Warren's Oration on the Boston Massacre." If such a performance lacked the solemnity of the original recitation, so did many instances of male oratory, for antebellum popular speaking could be humorous as well as solemn. As one historian has pointed out: "Popular declamation of the 30s and 40s has often been considered as bombast when it should be taken as comic mythology."[14]

Love of the spoken word crossed boundaries of class and condition. According to one story, James Murdock, a prominent actor and elocutionist, retired to a farm in Ohio and had a quantity of calfskins to sell.

> Driving to the tannery, he met the proprietor, of whom he enquired, "What are you paying for calfskins today?" The tanner, to whom Murdock was an entire stranger, took a huge chew of tobacco, thrust both hands in his pockets, and replied with a lazy air that he "didn't know—he wasn't sure that he wanted any calfskins at all." Murdock's anger was at once considerably aroused with the fellow's mixture of impudence and indifference. Straightening himself into an acting attitude, he delivered a splendid piece of vituperation from one of Shakespeare's plays. The tanner was a very ignorant man, but Murdock's oratory and Shakespeare's words had completely transfixed him! When the "piece" was finished, the tanner reached out his hand saying, "Who are you, Mister? If you'll only say that 'ere speech over again, I'll give you a dollar a pound for your calfskins!"[15]

Here oratory literally functions as currency, undercutting the mutual suspicion of the marketplace. Like Stephen Vincent Benét's "The Devil and Daniel Webster," a 1936 short story romanticizing the antebellum age of great talkers, the story of Murdock and the calfskins—quite possibly apochryphal—turns upon the vitality of the spoken word and reflects a society fascinated with its seemingly limitless power.

Within such a context, Americans conceived of acting as an *aural* art, like the New York mayor who, laying the cornerstone of a new theatre in 1826, anticipated delights in store for "the enchanted Ear." The bare stage of the early theatre, with its generic sets, minimal props, and scant attention to costume made clear that its appeal was to "auditors," not spectators. Like orators, actors and actresses stood alone to create their effects with unaided expression, posture, gesture, and above all with the voice. Looking back, Henry James would wonder how the early stage could work its spell "in such a material desert, in conditions intrinsically so charmless, so bleak and bare."[16]

For men, theatrical elocution was closely linked to the other professions that traded in public speech—law, politics, and the ministry. Talented young men moved from one line of oratorically based work to another, or solaced themselves for making more respectable career choices by indulging in amateur theatre. The embarrassing kinship between preaching and acting provided actors the means to discomfit their clerical critics. When Charles Booth Parsons, a former actor, condemned the stage from his pulpit in the Methodist church in Louisville, an old theatre associate present at the services was amused to detect Parsons in his favorite melodramatic part, Roaring Ralph Stackpole: "It was Roaring Ralph all through the sermon, the prayer, the benediction." The veteran actor and theatre manager Sol Smith twitted the Reverend Lyman Beecher for attacking the stage: "One would suppose, doctor, to hear you, and such as you, speak of actors and actresses, that in *your* profession there is no *acting*." Dickens covered this ground and played it for laughs in *Great Expectations* (1860). Wopsle, the parish clerk with a deep voice who always "punished the Amens" in Pip's hometown, leaves the church to take up playacting. Joe Gargery accompanies Wopsle to London and sees him play Hamlet, "continiwally cutting in betwixt him and the Ghost with 'Amen!'"[17]

Excluded from the bar, the pulpit, and the political arena, women found that the only professional work to which an actress might effect some partial transfer of her speaking skills was teaching. Ex-actresses leaned upon the arts of oratory and recitation when they moved into education. Mrs. Melmoth, for example, ran a school on Washington Street in New York City in the early 1820s. Susanna Rowson's students recited poetry, dialogues, and addresses that she composed for them at annual public exhibitions beginning in 1802.[18]

All the professions associated with oratorical skills laid some claim to the public exposition of social or spiritual truth, but only the stage countenanced women's voices. As Wopsle's comic inability to disentangle the words of the church service from the words of his part suggests, a performer came close to assuming a role of social and cultural authority when he or she spoke from the stage. When audiences heard and applauded an actress, she entered for a brief interval into a semblance of public power then unknown to the rest of her sex.

PLAYHOUSE POLITICS

At the playhouse women moved in a realm that was not only public but often explicitly political, a forum where issues of power and public policy were routinely aired. The Revolution had forcefully injected politics into the American theatre: in Boston, for example, the British staged *The Blockade of Boston*, and an anonymous patriot, possibly Mercy Otis Warren, responded with *The Blockheads, or, The Affrighted Officers*. At least one play, *Cato*, was staged at Valley Forge, and apparently the plans of the Continental Army's officer corps for further productions prompted the Continental Congress to issue its famous prohibition against plays.[19]

After the Revolution, American audiences continued to assume that the play was both a social event and a public political dialogue. In the 1790s, for example, the Chestnut Street Theatre in Philadelphia was "nightly the scene of noisy rivalry between the Federalists and the Democrats." A new theatre was built in Boston in 1797 because some citizens found the existing Federal Street Theatre too Federal*ist* in its politics. In New York a play called *Tammany*, which opened in 1794, sparked controversy about its excessively democratic sentiments: depending on their politics, contemporaries considered *Tammany* either "genius of the first order" or "a tissue of bombast." Disapproving Federalists called it a "worthless" piece, and described its audience as "the poorer class of mechanics and clerks."[20]

In New York in 1794 many of the men in such an audience would have been without a vote, just as all the women were, but early playhouse politics demanded only an opinion and a voice, not formal enfranchisement. Expressing one's politics at the theatre yielded demonstrations that were taken so seriously they could spill over into riot. Mrs. Trollope saw that intensity about politics at the theatre in Cincinnati in the 1830s: "When a patriotic fit seized them and 'Yankee Doodle' was called for," she wrote, "every man seemed to think his reputation as a citizen depended on the noise he made." In some sense, it did.[21]

Actresses occasionally were central participants in playhouse politics: delivering curtain speeches or writing plays gave them a chance to make explicit political statements. When *Tammany* opened in 1794, a rumor spread that Mrs. Melmoth had refused to speak the epilogue because she objected to the politics expressed. Hostile public opinion flared: "The *people* resent her impertinence," said one outraged contributor to a journal.[22] In the world of the theatre, an actress's political opinions mattered. The prologue to Susanna Rowson's *Slaves in Algiers* (spoken by an actor) claimed politics as Rowson's purpose:

Some say—the Comic muse, with watchful eye,
Should catch the reigning *vices* as they fly,
Our author boldly has revers'd that plan,
The reigning *virtues* she has dar'd to scan,
And tho' a woman, plead the Rights of Man.[23]

Women exploited the political opening the theatre offered by writing a number of early plays, including *Tammany*, the controversial political piece of 1794. Perhaps the best known female playwright of the era is Mercy Otis Warren, who had never seen a play before she wrote several in the 1770s in order to excoriate the British and their Tory associates. Although many of her plays were issued anonymously and circulated as pamphlets or in newspaper extracts rather than being performed, the fact that Warren chose to present her opinions in dramatic form reflects the conviction of the times that a play was the most public, most social of the arts, and the playhouse a place of civic debate.[24]

In 1790 Warren published the play *The Ladies of Castile*, which explored the implications of republicanism for women by contrasting two women of different temperaments caught up in a revolutionary civil war. The delicate Louisa, who cares nothing for politics, is torn apart by conflicting passions when her lover goes off to fight against her brother's side. The strong, resolute Maria gives all her loyalties to the political insurgency and even after her husband's death is firm enough in purpose to rally the troops. As the historian Linda Kerber explains, the message of *The Ladies of Castile* is clear: "The Louisas of the world do not survive revolutions; the Marias—who take political positions, make their own judgments of the contending sides, risk their lives—emerge stronger and in control."[25]

Judith Sargent Murray, an early feminist author, wrote two plays for the Boston stage. She did not involve women in politics as explicitly as did Rowson and Warren, but both plays include episodes commenting on the public behavior allowed to women. Murray's *The Traveller Returned* (1796) featured an intriguing colloquy between two young women about publicity. One young woman is terribly fearful of having something bad written about her in the newspapers. The other dismisses such fears as "irrational," arguing that one might take criticism as a kind of compliment, since envy always aims "its most envenomed shafts" at true merit. In this dialogue, which seems all the more conspicuous because it is tangential to the plot, Murray rejects the idea of fleeing from the public realm because someone might say something hostile. Indeed someone probably will, but Murray's spirited young woman assumes that she is not just an object to be talked of but one of the talkers, too, and more than able to hold her own in public give and take. In *The Medium* (1795), Murray includes an additional comment on women's situation in her portrait of an independent single woman of some wealth, Matronia Aimwell. Miss Aimwell visits a Mr. Maitland on a matter of financial business and realizes afterwards that that conceited fool supposed she was there to advance a marriage proposition. She laughs and exclaims that hers is an "Unhappy sex! whose ways are environed with peril," when innocent behavior can be so misconstrued. Here, men's false ideas—their reading of sex into everything—are seen through the eyes of an independent woman and can be firmly rejected, even laughed at.[26]

Given the access to political discourse allowed women on the stages of the early republic, it is not surprising that the pioneering feminist and socialist Fanny Wright at one point turned her hand to a play. But it is significant that a play was the first means Wright employed to express her ideas in public. When her *Altorf* was produced in New York and Philadelphia during the 1819–20 theatre season, she had not yet written *Views of Society and Manners in America*, nor thrown in with the causes of antislavery and communitarian socialism at Nashoba and New Harmony. A *succès d'estime* rather than a popular hit, *Altorf* was revived in 1829 in New York, published by Mathew Carey, and reprinted in London. The circumstances of its first production underscore how the stage offered women definite but compromised access to public activity: to placate her family and friends, Fanny Wright had agreed to keep her identity as playwright a secret and so had to sit quietly while the New York audience called loudly for the author.[27]

Altorf is set in Switzerland, where the Swiss have just defeated and expelled the hated Austrian tyrants. Like Warren, Wright uses the device of two contrasting women, here arrayed on either side of the hero, Altorf, a captain in the Swiss army. Altorf had loved Rosina, daughter of the archroyalist Count de Rossberg, but with the revolution he cast his lot with the rebels and married Giovanna, a good woman of firm republican loyalties. Giovanna understands quietly that he has no passion for her; she loves him anyway, asking only confidence and friendship, and steadiness in his country's cause. But Rosina, romantic and desperate, comes in disguise to the mountains to find Altorf and reclaim his love. Unlike Giovanna, Rosina thinks nothing of politics: "Altorf's love is all I seek. . . . I know but little of these public quarrels." Meanwhile her father, the scheming count, is also in the mountains in disguise, and he contrives to use Altorf's meetings with Rosina to make it appear that Altorf has turned traitor to his people. Rosina finally realizes that her father has used her—"Have I been made the tool in such foul dealings?"— too late for her to do anything but commit suicide. Altorf, whose weakness and vacillation encouraged Rosina, is shamed by his patriotic father's dying curse, and takes his own life as well. De Rossberg is captured and the Swiss remain free, but the lovers are dead. Only Giovanna, the woman who understood that republican politics are part of women's lives as much as men's, remains to mourn them. Such dramas were never among the most widely popular of the era. But since women were admitted to so few aspects of public life and were excluded so thoroughly from politics, the fact that these plays were written and sometimes produced has a different significance: with dramas like these women counted themselves into republicanism.

Male playwrights offered women a bit of unexpected help in the same project. They did so in responding to the English clergyman and writer Sydney Smith's famous taunt, "In the four quarters of the globe, who reads an American book or goes to an American play?" Because British imports and French and German translations were the most popular plays of the period, Americans fretted about their cultural provincialism, and American dramatists strove to create distinctively American themes and characters. Eventually they invented a number of stock characters that were supposed to stand for quintessential American qualities; one of the earliest of these was the American Girl. Versions of the witty, coquettish, and enthusiastically tomboyish heroine repeatedly romp through early American drama—from Louisa Campdon in James Nelson Barker's *Tears and Smiles* (1806) to Diana Headstrong in Robert Montgomery Bird's *The City Looking Glass* (1828). "The passive sentimental heroine," writes one critic, "was simply an inadequate type for native dramatists, largely because she could not personify the essence of American independence." For example, in Mordecai Noah's *She Would Be a Soldier*, which premiered at the Park Theatre in New York in 1819, the theme is national and patriotic, focussing on the recent struggle against the British. The plot, however, revolves around the heroine's successful masquerade as a man in order to enlist in the army and keep an eye on her lover. Noah drew upon a long European tradition of popular tales about women who passed as men to become soldiers, but in weaving it into the War of 1812, he made the disguise emblematic of the American spirit of boldness and action. Such heroines were not capable of conveying the self-conscious assertiveness of Rowson's creations, but they were both unconventional and popularly successful. [28]

Thus the theatre extended a rare invitation to the otherwise for-men-only world of oratorical panache, public authority, and political controversy to women—but only to *white* women. African-Americans made a bid to participate in professional American theatre in the 1820s and were violently rebuffed. The first black professional theatre company in America, the African Company, began in New York City in 1820 or 1821. The players acted Shakespeare, and they were good at it: the great black actor Ira Aldridge would go on from the African Company to a distinguished European career spanning several decades. The African Company also presented original plays, including the first American drama by a black playwright, *King Shotaway*, about the insurrection against the British on the island of St. Vincent. It was too much: white rioters, perhaps encouraged by the jealous management of the Park Theatre next door, descended upon them, the police arrested the performers, and the company was disbanded by 1824. There would not be another such professional African-American theatre for many decades to come.[29]

ACTRESSES AND MALE DESIRE

All the theatre's promises were limited by the fact that women's presence in the play or at the playhouse took place under a moral cloud. Ever since their initial appearance on the English-speaking stage in the Restoration, actresses were associated with sexual immorality. The women who made their living performing on the stage worked in uncomfortably close proximity to the "public women"—slang for prostitutes—who crowded the third tier. The ways in which participation in or mere presence at the theatre tended to subject a woman to male sexual advances are revealed in a novel written by one of the American theatre's founding fathers, William Dunlap (fig. 2).[30]

Dunlap's novel is set in New York City in 1811. He suggests to the reader that his novel is closer to truth than fiction by choosing an autobiographical title, *Memoirs of a Water Drinker*, and by incorporating as characters some real actors under their own names, including George Frederick Cooke and Thomas

Fig. 2 William Dunlap, the "father of the American stage" and manager of the Park Theatre in New York. Harvard Theatre Collection.

Abthorpe Cooper. Although he does not use a first-person narrator, many of the lesser characters and incidents are clearly drawn from Dunlap's own experiences as manager of the Park Theatre.

The hero, Zebediah Spiffard, is a young man from Vermont who has thrown over his legal studies for a career as an actor. The novel opens with a scene in which several actors, including Cooper, talk of an actress named Mrs. Trowbridge and wonder about Spiffard's attentions to her. "He cannot certainly think of marrying her. . . . Her mysterious conduct in regard to Trowbridge, both before and after his death, is too notorious to allow of such an alliance with a man of Spiffard's correct way of thinking." When Spiffard joins them, he is ribbed by his companions, who seek to warn him of Mrs. Trowbridge's reputation by exchanging whispered confidences: "Does she not . . . ?" "It is more than suspected . . ." Spiffard finally stops them by revealing that he has recently married her in secret. They assure him that they were only joking, but he leaves deeply worried about having married on so short an acquaintance.[31]

In this opening scene, as in the novel as a whole, a woman is defined by men's assessment of her sexual behavior. The men are leeringly eager to assume the worst, and the pervasive double standard is the most important rule of public conduct. There are no good women of the theatre in the novel. Spiffard's mother-in-law — a veteran actress who lives with her daughter — is a superficial, unreflective hypocrite. The men of the stage, by contrast, are portrayed rather sympathetically, even though they spend most of their time tippling and devising an elaborate hoax. Mrs. Spiffard herself is evasive when her husband asks about her past, and she takes an occasional drink. Although these are her only missteps, the reader is clearly meant to believe that she merits her bad name; her pangs of guilt serve to confirm but in no way to mitigate her "sins." Mrs. Spiffard represents the gravest ills the stage was charged with: sexual immorality and dissembling. She begins to drink more heavily and finally commits suicide. At the end of the novel, Spiffard is released from doubt and anguish, and resolves on a new career in the ministry.

In Dunlap's novel the infection of the stage even extends to a woman who is not an actress. His heroine, Emma Portland, is seventeen. As an orphan, she has come to live with her cousin, Mrs. Spiffard, and her aunt. Emma is all "purity and truth — piety and love," naive, artless, and confiding. She has at first no "fastidious notions" about the theatre and accompanies her cousin and aunt backstage to help them dress. But when she is accosted by a strange man in a dark passageway in the rear of the Park Theatre, Emma quickly decides that the theatre is a terribly wicked place. When Emma tells her aunt and cousin that she will never set foot in the theatre again, she first cites "objectionable passages" in the play, then confesses what really happened. To their protests that this is an isolated incident, she replies that it is, on the contrary, representative: alone backstage she is unprotected from insult by the supernumeraries and others who are "not proper persons for a young and unprotected female to be placed so near, as to be within hearing of their jests and ribaldry." Assaulted by looks and talk and finally by groping hands at the playhouse, she flees (1:23–24, 28, 34–36).

But though Emma scrupulously avoids the theatre, she is not out of danger. The man who accosted her there continues to stalk her in the streets. She is trapped by him when she ventures forth on a classic errand of mercy, visiting a poor sick woman. He explains, "I saw you with—and apparently dependent upon people whose profession—and as the world says—but I will not offend ..." (2:87), whereupon she calls him despicable and cries loudly for help. Fortunately a rescuer, a noble young man, is close at hand: these two will later marry, for a happy ending. Thus Emma Portland only narrowly escapes the fate of Mrs. Trowbridge—becoming what men think she must be. In her case the reputation is based simply on her presence in a theatre and her association with actresses. By acting on his assumptions, her attacker very nearly renders them self-fulfilling.

At one level Dunlap's plot argues that the problem with the theatre for his hero, Spiffard, is that it contains bad women. A reading centered on the heroine, Emma Portland, however, discloses a very different problem with the theatre: it exposes women to men's roving eyes and nasty assumptions. The men may act upon what they think they see, mouthing coarse jests or threatening outright physical assault. Dunlap's advice is that a good woman should flee into domesticity and the arms of a male protector, and yet he cannot quite justify the double standard he announces. Dunlap explains, "It is in vain to deny or endeavor to conceal from the actress that the very circumstance of publicly exhibiting for hire, that person and those talents, so admired and applauded, has degraded her in the eyes of the world. Be it just or unjust, *so it is*, and, perhaps, so it ought to be. That this is unjust, in some instances, is certain" (1:166). As Dunlap's language indicates, the problem with the theatre for women is that their very presence makes their bodies available to men's eyes—"the eyes of the world"—eyes prepared to read them as sexual objects. Yet the egregious waffling of this passage also reflects Dunlap's real ambivalence, for as a dramatist and a manager he knew he needed women—women as actresses, as dramatis personae, as audience members.

Although in his novel Dunlap seemed to assume that the "baser" elements of the playhouse experience would override all others, he knew that was not the case, especially for women in the audience. The women who attended could avoid, reject, or ignore what they did not wish to countenance. Theatregoing was a mixed experience, but at least some women found it worth the candle.[32]

AUDIENCE DYNAMICS

The early nineteenth-century stage has been called a performer's theatre, for playwrights had little authority and the modern director was unknown. But acting meant continuously consulting the audience's pleasure. What happened onstage was largely the product of lively interaction between players and audiences that were knowledgeable, assertive, and spirited. Both rich and poor attended. With liquor to drink and peanuts to munch, convivial and often rowdy audiences sat down to enjoy a long evening's entertainment. The price of admission entitled them to a full-length five-act play *and* a shorter afterpiece, plus songs, dances, music, animals, stunts, and freaks exhibited between the acts. Since all this would last four or five hours or more, and since the house lights could not be extinguished during the performance, audience members gave the stage full attention selectively, each waiting for the parts of this mixed fare he or she liked best, and otherwise beguiling the hours by socializing.[33]

According to the customs that governed behavior at the playhouse, audience members had a right to express themselves freely about everything that took place. Because theatrical repertory leaned heavily on old favorites, audience members could and did detect it when actors transposed a few words or blew a line. Shakespeare, which accounted for perhaps as much as one-fourth of the repertory before 1830, presented especially acute problems: many knew the plays by heart before they ever entered a theatre, and they quickly learned that they were entitled to respond to errors with jeers and hisses. By the same token, audience members would freely interrupt the stage action to cheer, applaud, and demand encores when they were pleased. They also injected themselves into the performance via groans, animal noises, missiles thrown at the stage or other parts of the audience, and witticisms shouted out at opportune moments. When the performance onstage dragged, the antics in the seats provided laughs. Writing as "Jonathan Oldstyle," Washington Irving declared that the gallery at the Park Theatre in New York in 1802 sounded like Noah's ark and described "a discharge of apples, nuts and gingerbread on the heads of the honest folks in the pit." Irving reported he had been "saluted aside of my head with a rotten pippin."[34]

Women were present, although not as numerous as men, in these lively theatre audiences. Harriet and Maria Trumbull, for example, at ages fifteen and seventeen, attended the theatre in New York City in 1801 in large family parties. Margaret Fuller, aged eleven, went to see *Bluebeard* with her aunt, uncle, and cousins in Boston in 1821. In Richmond in 1811, a Mrs. Gibson, who kept a boarding school for girls, got up a theatre party consisting of several of her young students. The same performance was viewed by another group consisting of a husband and wife, their three children, and the wife's female friend, while else-where in the house an older woman attended in company with her son and his fiancée. Catharine Sedgwick attended the theatre in New York at age eleven in 1805, and continued to attend as an adult, recalling her youthful playgoing with delight. These women knew that the theatre contained questionable elements, but, sitting with family and friends in boxes, they were able to ignore them. In Boston in 1833 Eliza and Anna Quincy and other members of their family enjoyed seeing Fanny Kemble, even though the adjoining box held two drunken gentlemen whom they found mildly annoying. Anna Quincy con-cluded that the theatre was "certainly, even at the best, no fit place for 'an elegant female!'" And yet there she was, misgivings and all, and more to the point she returned subsequently.[35]

No one in the theatre audience expected to pay attention to the whole evening's entertainment, much less to like it all: selective inattention was the nor-mal mode of audience behavior. Such inattention, sometimes combined with demonstrative disapproval, enabled women who attended the theatre to overlook or reject objectionable persons or behaviors. They ignored the third tier. They lit-erally turned their backs when something offensive occurred onstage. They did not attend the opening nights of a new play, waiting to hear reports of its suitabil-ity. And in case of serious rowdyism or riot, they left.[36]

Men went to the theatre by themselves or with male companions, while women went within groups of family and friends, male and female. Those men who attended the theatre alone or with other men may have scanned the mixed situation looking for a racy, permissive atmosphere or even intending to visit the third tier and find a prostitute. The point is that such interests and perceptions were not necessarily shared by women.[37]

Eliza Southgate, a proper young woman of the middle class, provides the best example of how women sifted what they saw and heard at the theatre. After she saw a play in Portland in 1801, she wrote to her cousin discussing the players:

> Mrs. Powell as Miss Blandford delighted us all. How I admire that woman! She is per-fectly at home on the stage, and yet there is no levity in her appearance; she has great energy, acts with spirit, with feeling, yet never rants; her private character we all know is unexceptionable. . . . As for Mrs. Harper she is my aversion—for, as Shakespeare says, she will "tear a passion to tatters, to very rags," and she is too indecent ever to appear on the stage.[38]

Eliza Southgate was well-informed about the "private character" of the actresses and while rejecting one as "indecent" could admire another freely. Although she relied implicitly on her male relatives for the price of her ticket and protection against the offer of insult, her theatregoing experience was one of choice, taste, and authority. She did not assume that being exposed to what was indecent must affect her; she judged for herself, approved or condemned.

The selectivity and discrimination exercised by the women in the audience were in a sense reproduced onstage by performers. Actresses had to deal calmly and confidently with impudent audiences. They had to respond quickly to the audience's shifting moods; in fact, many players were in the habit of reacting immediately and visibly to gallery noises. Fanny Kemble spoke of performance as a mutual collaboration between actors and spectators, and she regretted an audience that was "unapplausive." Even when the silence of the audience was due to their unwillingness to interrupt a good performance, Kemble thought, the actor was "deprived by that very stillness of half his power."[39] A skilled player was one who had learned to ignore distractions and yet to draw strength and inspiration when the audience reacted warmly, playing *with* them, never despite them. An actress was always sorting what she saw and heard, deciding what to notice and what to ignore. Neither the woman performer nor the woman audience member had the power to censor or silence men, but each could use theatre customs of demonstrative disapproval and selective inattention to make this public space at least partly her own. Thus, although the early theatre was male-dominated, it was not male-controlled, and women found in it a heady mixture of possibilities and problems, penalties and chances.

2 · Starring: Fanny Kemble and the Actress as Heroine

Fanny Kemble stepped before the footlights on 18 September 1832 in New York City's Park Theatre and delivered a performance that stunned her audience. Philip Hone, a longtime New York theatregoer, had never seen an audience so "moved, astonished, and delighted." Everywhere Fanny Kemble went on her star tour the reaction was the same. A brilliant young Englishwoman then just twenty-one years old, she left an indelible mark on American theatre audiences and on American society. This "audacious girl" showed an entire generation what public accomplishment could look like in a woman.[1]

When she was seventy, Fanny Kemble tried to explain the phenomenon that she had been. The popular theatrical heroine of the day was, she wrote, "the realization of their ideal to the youth, male and female, of her time." That the theatre could stand for ideals and speak to young women had been in some substantial measure Fanny's own doing. Kemble severed the tie between the theatre's penalties and its positive potential, and she did so at the precise moment when the first stirrings of the women's rights movement could give all her achievements added resonance. More accurately than he could know, Philip Hone declared Fanny Kemble's American debut "such an exhibition of female powers as we have never before witnessed."[2]

Fanny Kemble was instrumental in the redefinition of the public woman because she was simply the finest actress who had ever appeared in this country; her wonderful quality of voice, mobile face, and electrifying stage presence set a new standard of excellence. With this glorious talent she had the power to normalize female public accomplishment, and in doing so to undermine deeply held assumptions about women's nature and capacities.

Her influence is nicely illustrated in a letter written by the author Catharine Sedgwick in February 1833. Sedgwick began, "We have had a droll time getting up a society in our Church. I do not think it is within a woman's prescribed destiny to do any public duty. We are, some of us, very ridiculous persons in full light." Despite the very considerable accomplishments of many women in church groups and other voluntary organizations, and despite her own fame, Sedgwick thus repeated the traditionally deprecating view of women as ridiculous in public. But she went on in the same letter to speak of Fanny, who was not ridiculous at all: "We are just now in the full flush of excitement about Fanny Kemble. She is a most captivating creature, steeped to the very lips in genius.... I have never seen any woman on the stage to be compared with her, nor ever an actor that delighted me so much."[3]

Fanny Kemble (fig. 3) performed in America for only two theatrical seasons, her career cut off by her marriage in June 1834 to Pierce Butler. Kemble's audience did not see her struggling to learn her art, nor did it see her fade and falter with age. Although she never again acted on an American stage, Fanny Kemble stayed in the public eye for another thirty years—as an accomplished author, highly publicized divorcée, Shakespearean reader, and trenchant critic of slavery. In all these roles she remained a public personality whose achievements both within and beyond the theatre cleansed the reputation of the actress. She not only lived in the public eye without loss of virtue, but also won acclaim for her genius and earned large sums of money by her own exertions. Standing on the public platform already granted to the actress, Fanny created a powerful new image: the female performer whose dignity was as undeniable as her talent.

STAR SYSTEM

Fanny Kemble had this powerful impact in part because the emerging star system in the theatre created the structural conditions in which great talent loomed larger than life. The "star system" began with George Frederick Cooke's very successful tour in 1810–11, which led the longstanding practice of occasionally importing prominent players, usually from Britain, to become regularized. Audiences in the 1810s were growing tired of the same old plays performed by a stock company, but good new scripts were hard to find, especially since the lack of copyright protection discouraged talented writers. Cooke demonstrated to managers that they could generate excitement and hefty ticket sales by bringing in stars to play leading roles. Rapid improvements in transportation soon made it feasible for star actors and actresses to tour the country, appearing for a period of from several nights to weeks in city after city. One observer attributed the emergence of the

Fig. 3 Fanny Kemble. This widely sold lithograph was based on a portrait sketch by Sir
Thomas Lawrence. Harvard Theatre Collection.

star system to a feeling that "we could annihilate time and space by the use of steam vessels."[4]

Initially star tours were more profitable for managers than stars, but by the 1820s the terms of advantage were reversed, as stars began to drive harder bargains. Because stars assumed the juiciest parts in favorite plays and pocketed more for a night than stock players earned in a week, their visits tended to demoralize the regular stock players. Ordinary players were reduced to taking supporting roles, and the hasty arrival and departure of the stars cut into rehearsal time and made effective ensemble playing impossible.[5]

Worse yet, because they now were paying large fees to stars, managers began to discharge members of their regular company and to cut salaries among those who remained: "To be able to procure stars, it was necessary to retrench in the stock company." The top to bottom pay ratio among players ballooned. Fanny Kemble saw the results: "The system upon which theatrical speculations are conducted in this country [the United States] is, having one or two 'stars' for the principal characters, and nine or ten sticks for all the rest." The logical response was to try starring oneself, and jokes proliferated about attempted "stars" who shone like two-penny candles. An American star tour was especially tempting to English actors whose careers had gone stale, for experience in London translated into prestige in the United States.[6]

The star system was harmful to the stock players, including the ordinary actresses, but it also had an important positive consequence for women. There had always been exceptions to the old rule that held actresses to be immoral. Susanna Rowson was one, the great tragic actress Mary Ann Duff another. But now the star system made an exception like Fanny Kemble loom so large as to change the rule.

DUTIFUL DAUGHTER

Kemble was able to resist the usual taint of her career in part through family connections, class associations, and the assistance of London prestige. Her father, Charles Kemble, was a famous actor and manager of the Covent Garden Theatre in London; her aunt was the legendary tragedian Sarah Siddons. The Kembles stood atop the ranks of English theatre for two generations and had a foot well in the door of upper-class society. Fanny herself had been patronized by titled families after her debut, whirling through a round of London balls and country house visits. Fanny's London acting debut in 1829 was a triumph; she played Juliet more than 120 times in an era when a nightly change of bill was normal and such long runs unheard of. Once in America, like other English performers, Kemble had to be careful to avoid any hint of condescension toward

Americans; touchiness on this account had led to a number of antebellum theatre riots. But initially Fanny could play her London credentials as a trump card.[7]

Fanny won additional respect for her poetry and blank-verse tragedy. She was described as the author of "many pieces of fugitive poetry lofty in their excellence." Her play *Francis the First* enjoyed a moderate success in production at Covent Garden, one critic calling it "the greatest work which was ever produced by any female at her age." The growing popularity of women writers by the 1830s magnified such praise and prepared the ground for Kemble.[8]

Most decisively, Fanny Kemble stood apart from the iniquities of the theatre because she never wanted to be an actress. Her girlhood ambition was to be a writer; as late as 1828 this was "meat, drink, and sleep" to her.[9] But then her father's management of Covent Garden fell into deeper and deeper trouble. Desperately hoping to avoid bankruptcy, Charles Kemble scheduled a family production of *Romeo and Juliet*, with nineteen-year-old Fanny as Juliet, himself as Mercutio, and Fanny's mother, returning to the stage after an absence of twenty years, as Lady Capulet. Fanny had never appeared in any role. To start in a starring role with stakes like this was madness; to do it and succeed was magic. Opening night, 5 October 1829, found Fanny weeping in fright backstage. At her cue she was almost literally pushed on, and promptly ran to the shelter of her mother's arms. She spoke her first lines softly but soon began to catch fire, until at last the audience roared its approval (fig. 4).

Kemble's stage career was effectively marked by this melodramatic story of pure motives, great risk, and brilliant success. To her London audience Charles Kemble's financial embarrassments were a matter of "painful notoriety," and in this country too, as Fanny toured in company with her father, the story was repeated. In an extended biographical sketch appended as front matter to an American edition of *Francis the First*, the biographer detailed her father's financial woes and praised "the sacred motive which prompted her appearance in public." Readers might have recognized this highly formulaic material, for it paralleled the self-justifications offered by a new group of women novelists then achieving success, and they in turn inscribed it in their fiction, which so often featured young women reluctantly thrown upon their own resources. Charles Kemble's insolvency meant that, far from seeking publicity, Fanny was "as it were *sacrificed* unto fame."[10]

Fanny's convictions fit neatly into the tale of the young woman forced reluctantly to go to work, since she deprecated acting. Poetry she adored, but in the theatre poetry was covered by "wretched, tawdry, glittering rags, flung over the breathing forms of ideal loveliness." "How I do loathe the stage!" she wrote in a journal kept during her American tour. She later declared, "My

Fig. 4 Fanny Kemble as Juliet. A poor-quality lithograph like this one could do little more than remind the viewer of Kemble's triumph as Shakespeare's heroine; the artist scarcely catches her likeness. Harvard Theatre Collection.

going on the stage was absolutely an act of duty and conformity to the will of my parents."[11]

Kemble spoke to her audience in two ways, through her own story and through the parts she enacted, but as usual in actresses' lives these two tended to become intermingled. They were so particularly in one of Fanny's most popular roles, that of a dutiful daughter named Julia in Sheridan Knowles's *The Hunchback* (fig. 5). This part was written especially for Fanny, and the play became extraordinarily popular. Julia, who has never known her father, is watched over by an agent of her mysteriously absent parent, a hunchback named "Master Walter," whom she has learned to regard with filial affection. (As in many such plays, the mother is simply absent, presumably long dead.) In a fit of youthful pique, Julia throws over the fiancé Master Walter has carefully chosen for her, a sterling fellow named Clifford, and engages herself to marry a heartless cockscomb, the Earl of Rochdale. Julia must learn to curb her waywardness. After Clifford loses his title and all his money, Julia begins to soften toward him, and finally realizes she loves him. She begs Master Walter to help her gain release from her promise to Rochdale, but he is adamant: having been capricious before, Julia must now honor her word at all costs. He demands her obedience, and against all inclination, she finally assents: "See thy Julia justify thy training, and lay her life down to redeem her word!" Whereupon Master Walter reveals himself to be in fact her father *and* the real Earl of Rochdale to boot. Julia is restored to Clifford, and all ends happily, her self-denying obedience being precisely the price she must pay in order to get her wish after all.[12]

Tragedy and popular melodrama of the day often portrayed intergenerational tensions over issues of duty, love, and money played out between fathers and daughters. The dutiful daughter sought above all to honor and obey her parent;

Fig. 5 Fanny Kemble as Julia. Portraits in oils could capture a rich likeness but could not be reproduced for a mass market. This 1833 painting by Thomas Sully depicted Kemble in a favorite role. Rosenbach Museum and Library, Philadelphia.

the errant daughter who disobeyed her parent must, on the other hand, suffer and repent. Still, it was not easy to be dutiful. When, for example, a father would, for reasons of policy, force his daughter to marry a villain, melodramatic plot devices would have to intervene to secure a happy ending. Duty to the father was thus enjoined, but wisdom usually was seen to lie in the young woman's heart. The dramatic representation and resolution of intergenerational tensions probably had a particular resonance for early nineteenth-century audiences, living in a time when social change was opening great gaps between the experiences of parents and their children.[13]

Although Fanny played the dutiful daughter, her own story turned on a capacity—female earning power—which had no part in the tales dramatized on stage and had only begun to intrude into the novel. Her dutifulness consisted in pursuing activity beyond anything envisioned in drama, and yet it was in assuming the role of yielding passivity that Fanny placed her foot in the new territory of female stardom. She was Julia the obedient and Fanny the willful and powerful; each made the other possible. Kemble could represent the conventional formulas of women's lives, but she also ran beyond their reach. She was both familiar and unprecedented, comprehensible yet incomparable.

HEROINE

Fanny Kemble came to the United States in an age given to hero worship. American politics of the era were being reorganized around Andrew Jackson, a master politician nicknamed "the Hero." Jackson, who was quite capable of judicious self-dramatization to further his political purposes, became the center of the Democratic Party while the anti-Jackson forces rallied around strong personalities like Henry Clay and Daniel Webster to create the Whigs. It was a time for heroes because it was a time of dizzying social change. The quickening pace of the market, the extension of political democracy, the decay of social deference, the restless geographical mobility, the clambering rise of new men with new money—all these made for anxiety. And one antidote to social and cultural vertigo seemed to lie within the extraordinary individual like Jackson who could master events through sheer force of personality.[14] The focus on the hero infected intellectual life as well as politics, with examples ranging from the Byronic heroes of the Romantics to the meditations of Carlyle and Emerson. Heroic men seemed to hold the answers to the intellectual and philosophical problems of the age. Ralph Waldo Emerson wrote of "representative men," who "have a pictorial or representative quality and serve us in the intellect." Such men were, he declared, "lenses through which we read our own minds."[15]

Women were not supposed to be heroines: *their* answer to the accumulating stresses of the public sphere, articulated in the 1830s by the likes of Catharine Beecher and Sarah Josepha Hale, was "true womanhood." Let the male, public world degenerate into a greedy, disorderly scramble, they argued: the true woman would counteract it all from within the private world of home and family. Domestic, dependent, self-denying woman would be the keeper of the softer Christian virtues, the guarantor of a haven in a heartless world. This powerfully appealing ideology, proposing no radical changes and yet seeming to promise women real power, exerted extraordinary force in the lives of most middle-class women. Fanny Kemble eluded its grip and stood for something almost entirely different — neither domestic nor sexual, escaping the limitations of public and private through triumphant, undeniable genius. Kemble's career helped to move the definition of "public woman" away from sexuality, replacing one set of connotations with others that were different but equally vivid.[16]

She had to be a heroine to mixed audiences, since women characteristically attended the theatre in the company of men, and men still constituted the largest part of the theatre audience. Men were enthusiastic: Kemble was hemmed in backstage by "troops" of them and accumulated packets of letters sent by lovesick young admirers. Henry Lee recalled being one of a crowd of "youths and maidens hanging round Tremont Place to see her mount Niagara — a horse I rode henceforth, on holidays, and in vacations, because she had been on his back." Walt Whitman saw her repeatedly and credited her (along with Junius Brutus Booth and two figures in Italian opera) as "the first part of the influence that afterwards resulted in my *Leaves of Grass.*"[17]

Many stories link Fanny Kemble to the famous public men of her day. In Washington, Daniel Boone, Daniel Webster, John Quincy Adams, and Henry Clay came to admire Fanny's performance. Even President Jackson, usually inclined to spend his leisure at the horseraces rather than the theatre, felt obliged to see Fanny perform, and later to meet her. Backstage or in the drawingroom Fanny was handsome rather than pretty, strikingly animated, fearlessly witty, and completely unabashed by eminence. When President Jackson remarked that "scribbling ladies" were the real cause of the recent "southern disturbances," Fanny did not know enough about American politics to catch what may have been an allusion to the Peggy Eaton affair, but she confidently hazarded that the ladies must have "scribbled to some purpose." This exchange between the president and the actress betokened a new kind of female presence in the public sphere. Peggy Eaton's notoriety was the product of a supposed affair while her husband was at sea. She had violated the old rule whereby a woman's name should appear in print only three times in her life — at her birth, marriage, and death: publicity could only mean sexual misconduct. But Fanny and the scribbling women authors Jackson linked her with were not confined to the alternatives of domesticity or sexuality; they had opinions and an impact of their own.[18]

Chief Justice of the United States John Marshall and Associate Justice Joseph Story went to see Kemble in *The Stranger*, an old warhorse of a drama first translated by William Dunlap in 1798. Kemble played Mrs. Haller, a benevolent lady who devotes herself to good works in a melancholy effort to expiate guilt, for she is "a woman with a past." Having married at sixteen, she was young and foolish enough to fall prey to a seducer who, assisted by forged letters and the treachery of a servant, convinced her that her husband no longer loved her and induced her to run away. The action of the play occurs when a misanthrope known only as "the Stranger" is revealed as her long-lamented husband. A terrific scene of recognition and repentance brought the curtain down; it was not quite clear whether the pair would be reunited in this world, or only in a better one. That Fanny could make this story believable, indeed moving, was testimony to her powers, for the play was sentimental, predictable, and doubtless tediously familiar to every member of the audience. Yet somehow she touched them all, made them feel the pain of irreparable personal loss. Both Marshall and Story were, according to Story's letter to his wife, reduced to tears.[19]

Anecdotes testifying to Fanny Kemble's impression on prominent men often are clearly apocryphal. For instance, supposedly John Quincy Adams attended one of her plays in company with a Kentucky politician who was at a loss to express the depth of his admiration. Evidently it was difficult to find the right terms of praise for female public performance: according to the story, the Kentuckian finally spluttered, "By Heavens, Adams! She's a horse! She's a horse!" Fanny's influence on Justice Story also seems to have entered the realm of apocrypha. When Story was teaching at Harvard Law School, another tale goes, a student had the temerity to ask how the professor could reconcile his Puritan heritage with his delight in Kemble's performances. He is said to have replied, "I don't try to. I only thank God that I am alive in the same era with such a woman." Precisely because they are of doubtful veracity, such stories offer testimony to the magnitude of Fanny Kemble as a public phenomenon: the men who admired the actress acknowledged her power and even embroidered it.[20]

Women found their own means to indicate their admiration. Adoring girls left bouquets at Kemble's door. Young women adopted the Kemble curls or the Kemble cap and took up horseback riding for exercise because she had. Fanny found admirers among women from all social backgrounds; at least one was described by Kemble as "poor and obscure, the sister of a tailor." Women who did not themselves see Fanny Kemble perform could have seen her likeness in cheap lithographs (fig. 6) and heard "the affecting phrases of the idolized Julia . . . repeated on every corner."[21]

Fig. 6 Fanny Kemble is here shown in a cheap "penny plain" sheet of figures meant to be used in a toy theatre. Harvard Theatre Collection.

Some young women went further and saw in Kemble the inspiration for a career. Charlotte Cushman, who would go on to become the greatest American-born actress of the century, was merely an aspiring young woman when she walked for hours in Tremont Street just to get an opportunity to see Fanny pass from her hotel to the theatre. "I believe seeing Fanny Kemble act was the foundation of whatever style I may be said to have in acting," Cushman later wrote. Anna Cora Ogden, a young miss in her early teens who never visited the theatre because she had learned in Sunday School of its wickedness, made an exception to see Fanny as Julia; she went on, as Anna Cora Mowatt, to become a distinguished performer and a playwright of some note.[22] To still others Fanny Kemble was an examplar of freedom, achievement, self-confidence. While male heroes strode the world cloaked in political power, female "heroism" had been to this point largely confined to a vein of European literature beginning with Madame de Staël's *Corinne* (1807). Corinne was a poet, a dancer, and a great tragic actress, and reading the novel as a young woman, Kemble had conceived "a wild desire for an existence of lonely independence." But her eventual career was no novel. Fanny's triumphs were real, and her claims to genius palpable.[23]

Margaret Fuller was probably moved by Fanny's example. Fanny's tour coincided with a crucial moment in Fuller's life. The young men of her age had gone on to college or career, and she was left at home to survey her limited options. Her father had withdrawn the family to a rural existence in Groton, Massachusetts, and she was contemplating life as a schoolteacher or an old-maid help to the family when Kemble came to Boston. Fuller saw her perform twice. The first time she was distracted from the play by overidentification with Fanny: "Thought all the while of Miss K——how very graceful she was, and whether this and that way of rendering the part was just." The next night, however, "all my soul was satisfied," and she declared Kemble had "genius, which could give such life to this play [*The Stranger*]."[24]

What did Kemble mean to Fuller? Perhaps the Mariana story contains some clues. Fuller's *Summer on the Lakes* (1844) included the tale of a girl named Mariana, described by Fuller as someone she had known in boarding school. A high-spirited girl with a taste for costume and an eccentric flash of genius in all she does, Mariana becomes restless in the narrow routine of the school until she finds an outlet as a fine performer in school plays: "For a time she ruled mostly, and shone triumphant." But after the last production, Mariana continues to apply her stage makeup occasionally. The bright dots of rouge on her cheeks excite the resentment of the other girls, and they conspire to humiliate her one night by all appearing at dinner with identical spots. Mariana is devastated, retreats into a shell, and ultimately suffers an emotional breakdown, from which she is rescued only by the intercession of a sympathizing adult.[25]

The editors of Fuller's *Memoirs* and her biographers have tended to agree that the Mariana story was in some degree autobiographical. Certainly something traumatic seems to have happened while Fuller was a student at the school run by the Misses Prescott in Groton. In the Mariana story theatrical performance expresses impatience with quotidian routine and reveals the wish to shake free of reality as given. But, like the dots of rouge, this urge can become offensive if carried outside the boundaries of the play. Mariana suffered for her display of nonconformity, but Fuller found in Kemble an example of a woman who successfully carried a bold persona offstage, who did not fear the censure of conventional society.[26]

As Margaret Fuller struggled to invent her own career and to analyze woman's place in the world, Kemble's example of fearlessness in public could have been steadying. When she embarked on her famous "conversations," Fuller's activities were likened to performances. "Had she been attracted to the stage," Horace Greeley said of Fuller, " [she] would have been the first actress America has produced." Fuller knew she was no actress and said in connection with her conversations that she dreaded the feeling "of display, of a paid Corinne." But she also knew and valued what young people saw in performers: "So materialistic is the course of common life, that we *ask daily* new Messiahs from literature and art." Fuller sent a copy of her feminist classic *Woman in the Nineteenth Century* to Fanny Kemble and more than once expressed a desire to meet her. They never did meet, but if they had, Fuller might have said to Kemble what she did in fact say to George Sand upon their first meeting in Paris: "Il me fait de bien de vous voir." [It does me good to see you.][27]

As the Mariana story suggests, a woman of the theatre like Fanny Kemble might provide practical examples of new female behavior, since the theatre was a public realm in which women already spoke and worked alongside men as their acknowledged peers. So in *Woman in the Nineteenth Century* (1845) Fuller cited the stage as an example of women's speech and presence in public life. "We should think those who had seen the great actresses, and heard the Quaker preachers of modern times, would not doubt that Woman can express publicly the fullness of thought and creation." Similarly she claimed women's right to move about outside the home by reference to "balls, *theatres*, meetings for promoting missions, revival meetings" they already attended. By pointing out how women were already participating successfully in the public realm, Fuller could reassure as well as persuade, balancing her more radical suggestions, such as the famous "Let [women] be sea captains, if you will."[28]

This line of reasoning proved so appealing that it appeared in the Declaration of Sentiments issued by the first women's rights convention held in Seneca Falls in 1848. The declaration resolved that complaints about woman's addressing public audiences came "with a very ill grace from those who encourage, by their attendance, her appearance on the stage." The instigator of the convention, Elizabeth Cady Stanton, would later recall having seen Kemble on her tour, and as late as 1870 she served up the same line of argument in defense of coeducation. When Goldwin Smith warned that coeducation might arouse a feeling of rivalry between men and women, Stanton retorted, "Who objects to women in the theatre or opera lest a feeling of rivalry might spring up?" At the historical moment when women's roles were first subject to systematic question, Fanny Kemble and performers like her offered a trope for rethinking the plot and the action of women's lives.[29]

COMMODITY

Fanny always understood that her stage success was not simply the effect of her own brilliance, and she considered her American tour an example of "the manufacture of public enthusiasms." The elements that comprised this "manufacture" included not only her performances but also the newspaper notices, the lithographs in store windows, the plates and saucers and handkerchiefs (fig. 7) printed with her likeness. The public knew her largely and increasingly through intermediaries—self-seeking men who promoted her for their own profit. Engravers, for example, executed miniatures of her because they could sell multiple copies and pocket the entire profit, since there was no copyright protection. Fanny thought it one of the many nuisances of being a "public character" that "one's likeness may thus be stolen, and sold or bought by anybody who chooses to traffic in such gear." Strangers having possession of her portrait made Kemble feel as if her "whole life was only a confused dream!"[30]

Journalists were the most powerful and therefore dangerous of these intermediaries. Fanny was horrified by the casual affrontery with which the press seized upon her as a choice commodity. Shortly after their arrival, a New York journalist called on her father, declaring, "My dear fellow—if your bella donna is such as you describe—why we'll see what we can do—we will take her by the hand." At this point Fanny ran out of the room in disgust. Sensational doings sold papers, so journalists had reason to help make her not just an excellent actress but a phenomenon, especially if, in return, they received free tickets and flattering attention. It was all part of "that nauseous ingredient in theatrical life, puffery."[31]

Mutual back-scratching between press and stage was long-established, but it was about to become much more problematic with the emergence of the "penny press" in the 1830s. Covering entertainment, crime, and human interest more broadly than ever before, the penny press had a persistent nose for sensation. Fanny could not stand the "press gang" but Charles Kemble seems to have done what he had to do, and coaxed her to play along. She spent at least one day trying to "scribble something for the *Mirror*, at my father's request."[32]

It would not do to ignore or snub the press, lest they lend themselves to the hostile purposes of rival actors or theatre managers. An actor named Keppel proved so incompetent in the male leads opposite Fanny at the Park Theatre that he was dismissed. Keppel promptly began to write to the papers, Fanny reported, "to convince them and the public that he is a good actor, at the same time throwing out sundry hints, which seemed aimed our way, of injustice, oppression, hard usage." A friend advised Fanny's father to handle Keppel's

Fig. 7 Fanny Kemble as Belvidera. The images of many public figures were reproduced on portrait china. Photograph by permission of J. and J. May Antiques Ltd., London.

charges carefully, so as not to appear arrogant or unfair. Even the audience in the playhouse was liable to manipulation by rivals. In October 1832, Fanny's father received an anonymous letter informing him that a cabal was being formed by "the friends of" two native-born actresses, Naomi Vincent and Josephine Clifton, who were appearing at Thomas Hamblin's rival Bowery Theatre. The cabal promised to hiss the Kembles off the New York stage if possible, and if not, to send people in every night to create a disturbance. It is likely that "the friends" were organized by Hamblin, who had the two actresses under contract and had lost business to the Kembles. Mr. Kemble did at one point go to see Miss Clifton at the Bowery, but Fanny's journal does not indicate the purpose of his visit.[33]

The problem was inescapable: either one arranged for a favorable reception and coverage, or left the field open to rivals who might do all they could to create a hostile reaction. At one point Fanny's career was nearly destroyed. In

Washington she went out for a ride on a borrowed horse and exchanged some chaffing pleasantries with its owner, a grandson or nephew of Robert Fulton. Subsequently a letter arrived informing her father that she was rumored to have insulted the young man and spoken derogatorily of America and Americans. If Mr. Kemble did not make explanation and apology, the letter advised, his daughter would be hissed off the stage that evening. The show went on without incident, but on the following night, Kemble noted, handbills were thrown into the pit "professing to quote my conversation with Mr——— at Washington and calling upon the people to resent my conduct in the grossest and most vulgar terms." Her father stepped before the curtain to assure the audience that the charge was a falsehood. As it turned out, people then crammed the playhouse to show their support and approbation; "so much for the success of the handbills." But to resist a hostile publicity ploy, was to fall under suspicion of having engineered a favorable one. "I heard that a man said the other day that he should not be surprised if *my father had got the whole of this up himself.* Oh, day and night! that such thoughts should come into any human being's head."[34]

Fortunately for Fanny, her father seems to have acted as a buffer between her and the press, patiently cultivating good contacts and rebutting false stories. Fanny's casual candor could not otherwise have survived. Her father's tact, aided by the brevity of her stage career, protected her from the central reality of the emerging marketplace in entertainment: her talent was to be sold, and if she did not make her public self into a commodity, others would do it for her.

AUTHOR

In June 1834 Fanny Kemble married Pierce Butler (fig. 8), a Philadelphian who stood as heir apparent to a vast fortune. Although Fanny did not know it at the time, much of the Butler fortune lay in the form of sea-island plantation property in Georgia and hundreds of slaves who worked it. Pierce's idleness while he lived on his expectations enabled him to travel about pursuing Fanny as she toured in different cities. Within a matter of months it was clear that the marriage was a disaster.

It is not easy to say how Fanny came to make such a mistake. Perhaps she was disgusted with the commercialized stage and sensationalistic press. Certainly the role of dutiful daughter had begun to pall. In a letter from Philadelphia in October 1832 she confided to her dearest friend, Harriet St. Leger, "I do not think that during my father's life I shall ever leave the stage; it is very selfish to feel regret at this, I know, but it sometimes seems to me rather dreary to look along my future years, and think that they will be devoted to labor that I dislike

Fig. 8 Pierce Butler. Library Company of Philadelphia.

and despise." Marrying a man of great wealth would permit her to retire from the stage with her husband's fortune as guarantor against her parents' falling into want. Perhaps sheer physical passion had a lot to do with the marriage. If the plot of her *Francis the First* is any indicator, Fanny had some notion of the power of sexual desire. In a later letter to Pierce she would refer to "the sentiment which drew us together" as one "which can never long survive intimacy and possession."[35]

Conflict flared when Pierce set out to censor Fanny's writing. Fanny had kept a journal during her American tour, and had contracted with Carey and Lea of Philadelphia to publish it. Her original purpose in doing so was to raise a sum of money for her maiden aunt, but Aunt Dall died in the spring of 1834. Still the contract remained, and Fanny, at loose ends after her retirement from the stage, set to work, even completing a parallel contract with London publishers shortly after her marriage. Pierce took upon himself the right to control what she submitted for publication, and they fought about it.

The newspapers pirated excerpts, preparing the ground for a critical tempest when Fanny's *Journal* appeared in 1835. The New York *Commercial Advertiser* obtained a version untouched by Pierce's blue pencil. In it, Fanny had used the phrase "pearls before swine" to refer to a New York performance, and worse yet, had declared, "Next to a *bug* a newspaper writer is my disgust." Although the *Journal* as published contained neither of these howlers, the damage was done. In fact, except through absolute blandness—of which she was incapable—Fanny hardly could have avoided offending some American readers. Her memoir was published in the midst of an ongoing nationalistic literary brouhaha touched off by Mrs. Trollope and kept at a boil by publishers who knew that controversy sells books. Fanny's *Journal* appeared in the same year that Dickens' Tony Weller proposed sending Mr. Pickwick to America, so that he could "come back and write a book about the 'Merrikins as'll pay all his expenses and more, if he blows 'em up enough."[36]

Without any intention to "blow 'em up," Fanny did offend. She ventilated some English prejudices that did not look well on paper, for example, deploring so much sunny weather. She complained about mosquitoes, poor accommodations, and nasal accents. She was frankly skeptical about the great American sacred cow, equality: "These democrats are as title-sick as a banker's wife in England" (1:60). Above all, she did not bear fools gladly: editing left a sprinkling of asterisks and blanks for names but did not conceal her brisk judgmental capacity.

The *Journal* admits its readers into the company of a charming and companionable young woman who is in many respects high-minded and correct, but who has a great talent for fun. She reads her Bible and Dante; she embroiders, studies German, and writes poetry. But her high spirits bubble over in language and incident. She "cottons to" people (1:24) and "dawdles" after breakfast (1:7). She refers to the theatre as "lamps and orange peel" (1:27) and dubs an offending opera singer a "Squalini" (1:152). Thinking to break up a political argument at dinner, she bursts out with "Oh hang General Jackson!" and is rather wickedly astonished to find the Whigs welcoming the suggestion (1:35). Driven to distraction onstage by an incompetent Romeo who has mislaid the crucial property for the scene, she whispers, "Where the devil *is* your dagger, Mr——?" (2:27).

Having placed herself calmly but firmly in the company of eminent public men, she often proceeded to take their measure. Blanks substituted for names, but many readers could have made educated guesses. When Daniel Webster, seated next to her at dinner, made conversation by remarking that Knowles's *Hunchback* was not the equal of Shakespeare, Fanny responded crisply that Shakespeares did not grow on every bush (2:205). She was at a loss for words when John Quincy Adams, seated on the other side, launched into a critique of *Othello*. Years later she revealed that Adams had declared that Desdemona's troubles were "a very just judgment on her for having married a nigger."[37]

Fanny Kemble's buoyantly readable *Journal* carried the story of the young touring actress all over the country to readers who had been unable to attend a performance. Fanny thus found a way to speak over or behind her stage characters, apart from the theatre or the press, apart too from her actual presence. In print she was a voice and a mind rather than an inescapably sexed female body. As a writer she was both more and less than a player, but her subject was inevitably herself—the actress, and American and British readers alike made closer acquaintance with the hitherto-suspect figure of the performing woman. "Perhaps no book has, for many years, been looked for, long previous to its publication, with such intense curiosity," wrote Edgar Allan Poe in a review, observing that most of her readers would be unable to consider Kemble "the authoress" apart from Kemble the actress.[38]

If, as Kemble said, she was disgusted with the falseness associated with the stage, she more than compensated in print. Reviewers who were impressed with her prose nonetheless were disturbed by her artlessly frank observations and the bold, colloquial language in which she indulged. The *North American Review* detected "much indiscretion and bad taste, going, at times, to an extent which we hardly know how to excuse or account for." But it ran a thirty-five page review larded with lengthy excerpts and praising Fanny's style as "natural and colloquial . . . constantly enlivened by pointed and felicitous turns of language, and rising, when the subject requires it, into eloquence." The reviewer had to conclude that despite "some naughty language" the author was "upon the whole a favorite with us."[39]

Other notices were less kind. *Niles' Register* reprinted pans from the English press, including one from the *Athenaeum* that said, "It turns out to be one of the most deplorable exhibitions of vulgar thought and vulgar expression that it ever fell to our lot to encounter." Another English reviewer detected "FEMALE IMPERTINENCE." Edgar Allan Poe, although he praised Fanny's "vivacity of style," made the same observation in gentler language: "A female, and a young one too, cannot speak with the self confidence which marks this book without jarring somewhat upon American notions of the retiring delicacy of the female character."[40]

Readers on both sides of the Atlantic shook their heads and read on. The sixteen-year-old who would shortly become Queen Victoria found some "very fine feelings" in Fanny's *Journal* but regretted that it was "very pertly and oddly written," with "so many vulgar expressions." An American reader, Alicia Middleton of South Carolina, similarly found it "better than I expected" but with "slang and expletives anything but ladylike." Behind all the scandalized comments one senses how powerfully authentic her voice must have been. Years later Henry James described her style: "She wrote exactly as she talked, observing, asserting, complaining, confiding, contradicting, crying out and bounding off, always effectually communicating. . . . She uttered with her pen as well as with her lips the most agreeable uncontemporary, self-respecting English, as idiomatic as possible and just as little common."[41]

The fracas over the *Journal* was fed by knowledge of Kemble's substantial earnings. As Poe explained, the actress had been so "loaded with pecuniary rewards" that it seemed graceless to speak ill of her audience. A Washington journalist similarly denounced Kemble's "ingratitude": "Coming to this country without a dollar in her pocket, [she] made a handsome independence." From New York, Fanny's friend Catharine Sedgwick defended her: "The city is in an uproar: Nothing else is talked of . . . in the counting houses . . . and Wall Street . . . people seem to think that there never was such *ingratitude!*—that coming as the Kembles did beggars to this country & leaving the stage enriched, Mrs. B. should [not] dare to say a word against us—This is arrant nonsense."[42]

The importance of her earnings to her public audience was mirrored by its importance to Kemble herself. Fanny Kemble thought about money carefully before ever stepping on the stage. At nineteen she wrote to her friend Harriet St. Leger weighing writing against acting. She might, as a writer, be "the lioness of a season," she judged, her earnings a "useful auxiliary," but she feared that writing for a living was "to earn hard money after a hard fashion." On the other hand, she knew the stage could be "lucrative," and her father had been dropping broad hints to the effect that there was "a fine fortune to be made by any young woman of even decent talent on the stage now." All untried, Fanny worried about the "decent talent," but she calculated that by acting she might double the family income. Once Fanny's stage success had saved her family from ruin and yielded more personal delights, such as fashionable new dresses, she kept track of exactly how much she earned each week. She also thought carefully about marriage and money, having at one point a "long and edifying" talk with her Aunt Dall, who told her, "While you remain single and choose to work, your fortune is an independent and ample one. As soon as you marry there's no such thing." Her American tour enabled her to set aside $35,000, and at her marriage she made over to her father life interest on the sum to compensate him for her retirement from the stage.[43]

As for gratitude, Fanny thought about that, too, and wrote about it in her *Journal*. Did audiences attend the theatre in a spirit of self-sacrifice, or players perform out of self-indulgence? No, it was a free and fair exchange, she thought, and Kemble declared she had more than earned her rewards: "I individually disliked my profession, and had neither pride nor pleasure in the exercise of it. I exercised it as a matter of necessity, to earn my bread—and verily it was in the sweat of my brow. . . . I was glad the houses were full, because I was earning my livelihood, and wanted the money" (2:149).

For a woman who valued her ability to earn her own bread, Fanny Kemble made an odd choice in Pierce Butler. She was accustomed to a well-paid, active career, while he was unacquainted with self-support or indeed with exertion of any kind. Fanny soon came to realize that her husband was a lazy, indecisive creature whose lack of occupation was unrelieved by intellectual or cultural interests. He appears to have passed his time sporting and gambling among lowlife companions, and as soon as his inheritance fell into his hands, he dissipated it with astonishing rapidity. Less than a year after her marriage, Fanny understood her mistake, for she wrote to a friend who was newly engaged:

> Persuade your lover to embrace a profession. To be idle, objectless, useless, becomes neither man or woman. An idle man of pleasure is everywhere a sad specimen of *waste* in its worst shape. But in this country such a one is more to be pitied and disapproved of, I believe, I mean despised, than in any other one in the world. . . . His associates, pleasures, and pursuits must all be of an unworthy class, for the intelligent and cultivated are also here the laboring and idleness in this country can in no way be dignified, graceful or respectable.[44]

In an 1838 letter to Pierce she indicated that, although affection between them was dead, she remained bound to him by "utter dependence upon your means, and, therefore, upon your will." Such a bond, she thought, "must needs be irksome to one who has the least feeling or pride"; it was "doubly irksome" to her, because she "had and still have the means of perfect independence in my own power; in the exertion of a distasteful profession it is true, but, at all events unfettered by the very odious restraint of obligation without affection."[45]

Her disgust with Pierce was deepened by the fact that so much of his property derived from owning slaves. Before their marriage she had confided antislavery sentiments to her journal. Now questions of duty, honor, money, morality were all contained in this one issue. The months of residence on Pierce's Georgia plantations in the winter of 1838−39 were probably the coup de grâce for her failing marriage. One day a group of slave women pleaded with Pierce for a reduction in their duties, and as he stood sternly lecturing them on the necessity of fulfilling their appointed tasks, she turned away in "bitter disgust." When a slave woman was whipped and Pierce blandly turned aside her pleas for mercy, Fanny told him it was brutal and unmanly to do these things "to maintain in luxury two idle young men"—Pierce and his brother, the owners of the plantation. Pierce's idleness was bad enough, but to see it purchased at such cost in human misery sickened her.[46]

Fanny soon learned that Pierce, as her husband, had a legal right to her property and her income. The sale of *Francis the First* had yielded £420 in 1832, enough to pay for her brother's commission in the army. Her *Journal* brought in over $3600 for both British and American editions—to Pierce. Still she kept on writing, stubbornly trying to make money she could spend as she pleased. Once, when Pierce had sold her horse out of sheer spite, she scraped together a collection of her poems to make the money to ride again. In London in 1842 she translated a Dumas novel, prepared a ballet script, and set to work on a sequel to *The Stranger*, all in hopes of paying a milliner's bill for £97. She was chagrined when reminded that, for all her exertions, "Whatever I write is not my own legal property." Her experience as a well-paid, independent woman infected her marriage and made her loath to tolerate what another woman might have felt she had to ignore.[47]

DIVORCÉE

Discord hung over her marriage. Pierce dithered about where they should live, then set Fanny up in an isolated farmhouse outside Philadelphia while he spent most of his time in town, presumably in the pastimes of a bachelor. They moved by season between Georgia, to superintend the plantations, and cooler resorts. For years at a time they lived in London, but Fanny never knew when or where they might go, since Pierce was incapable of making plans. Their two daughters, born in May 1835 and May 1838, were the means by which Pierce kept a restive wife in hand. Periodically she would pack her bags and storm out of the house, but the children always brought her back. In 1842 a friend who saw them in London summed up her situation: "She has discovered that she has married a weak, dawdling, ignorant, violent tempered man, who is utterly unsuited to her, and she to him, and she is aware that she has outlived his liking, as he has outlived her esteem and respect."[48]

Fanny's friends, most notably the Sedgwicks of Lenox, Massachusetts, knew that she was high-spirited and counseled patience and compromise, but by 1842 she and Pierce had begun to live separately under the same roof. A crisis erupted in October 1843 when Fanny discovered some letters addressed to Pierce that convinced her he had had an affair "at an early and what to me had been a less unhappy phase of my married life." Fanny told friends she would sue for divorce on the grounds of adultery and gain custody of the children. The Sedgwicks, believing that Pierce had lied to them during their conciliation attempts, sided with Fanny. Pierce denied everything, assuming his wife would be unable to turn up legal proofs of his philandering. He seems in fact to have felt that he ought to be able to claim the benefits of the double standard, for he upbraided Theodore Sedgwick: "Even where the proofs of a husband's infidelity are undeniable, any honest lawyer and true friend would be anxious to soothe the indignant feelings of the injured wife." The credibility of Pierce's protestations of innocence, never very great, plummeted in April 1844 when an outraged husband called him out to a duel.[49]

Seeking to deflect attention from his own conduct and to put the onus on Fanny, Pierce began a sustained campaign to cut her off from contact with the children and to drive her from their home. Eventually she was reduced to following them about, taking rooms in nearby boardinghouses for the sake of seeing her daughters an hour a day. Exhausted, increasingly convinced the struggle was injuring the children, and without financial resources of her own, she sailed for England in 1845 to be taken in by family and friends. She traveled to Italy to stay with her sister, and then in 1847, lacking means of support, she returned to the stage after a thirteen-year absence, touring British provincial theatres. It was not a triumphant return. She had grown stout, unsuited to the ingénue parts managers insisted on, and her heart was not in it. But Pierce had accomplished his aim, and in 1848 he filed for divorce, alleging willful and malicious desertion.

The "Fanny Kemble Butler Divorce Case" immediately became front-page news. Just as her father's financial missteps earlier had put her in a position to play the dutiful daughter, now Pierce's tomcatting cast her as the wronged wife. Fanny resisted the divorce but asserted plainly, "His treatment of me was such, for a length of time, habitually, that I should have been warranted by the law of God and the land, to depart wholly from his house and never see him more, without incurring the charge of desertion or any other breach of my duty." No nineteenth-century reader could have failed to grasp her point: Pierce was guilty of adultery.[50]

Longer or shorter extracts from Fanny's lengthy and detailed response to Pierce's charges, which was presented in court by the brilliant litigator Rufus Choate, appeared in newspapers all over the country. Major metropolitan dailies like Bennett's *Herald* in New York gave it feature space, while Fanny's friends in Syracuse and Lenox found shorter clippings in their local papers. Though Pierce had his defenders, Fanny seems to have won the publicity battle. Still, she had to concede much in an out-of-court settlement negotiated the following year. Kemble came to realize that, although she could not produce legal proofs of Pierce's adultery, a divorce represented her only hope of keeping her earnings safe from his hovering creditors. In September 1849 the courts granted the divorce and Fanny had her freedom, but she paid a fearful price, for Pierce retained custody of the children. The settlement secured to her the proceeds from a mortgage on the Butler farm outside Philadelphia, and two months each summer with her children. She refused to accept the allowance, asking that it be set aside for her daughters.[51]

In the midst of all the divorce publicity, Kemble launched a new and successful career as a reader of Shakespeare. Equipped with only a lectern and an open volume, she read two-hour abridged versions of all of the major plays. Her reading of *Henry VIII* became a way to explain herself: Fanny Longfellow wrote, "Her Queen Catharine was most touching—so much her own story, a stranger resisting her husband's divorce. . . . She wept and everybody else." With her readings she conquered a new generation. Thomas Wentworth Higginson, for example, having heard her read *A Midsummer Night's Dream* in 1850 exclaimed about "the immense animal spirits, the utter transformation of voice, face, and gesture, with which this extraordinary woman threw herself into the comedy." Some combination of the divorce publicity and her wonderful readings endeared her to another generation of young women: a critic described her as "a goddess in the eyes of all young ladies who read Byron and think George Sand a 'dear.'"[52]

Well beyond midcentury Fanny Kemble (she had resumed her maiden name after the divorce) was the acknowledged standard of excellence in female elocution. In her readings she was able to exercise her dramatic talents without encountering what she had always considered the objectionable aspects of the theatre. She was immersed in the poetry of Shakespeare but not in its bodily enactment—and so was free to accept her own matronly girth (fig. 9). She made plenty of money, with no conniving managers, no jealous rivals, no incompetent supporting actors, no indifferent plays. As ever, she was an actress, yet much more than a mere actress—filling the category, transcending it, renewing and redefining it.[53]

Divorce had not destroyed Fanny's reputation. She went triumphantly on to new work, and remained well positioned to benefit from softening attitudes toward female celebrity by midcentury. Sarah Josepha Hale, editor of *Godey's Lady's Book* and a high priestess of true womanhood, certified Fanny's standing in a volume called *Woman's Record* in 1853: "We must, in justice, observe here,

Fig. 9 Fanny Kemble in 1862. Like many other prominent ante-bellum men and women, Kemble was only photographed late in life, but the verisimilitude of photography means we are likely to take these late images as the most "real." Harvard Theatre Collection.

that Mrs. Kemble's bitterest enemies have never charged her with the slightest deviation from the laws of conjugal fidelity; that her fame is spotless, and her position in society exactly what it ever was." Hale's volume, subtitled "Sketches of All Distinguished Women from 'the Beginning' to A.D. 1850," was itself a sign of a new willingness to celebrate public achievement in women, including actresses.[54]

Kemble also continued to be famous as a woman who made money, lots of it. In an era when most working women did not make a living wage and female self-support in fact mean penury, this was a remarkable achievement. Nineteenth-century women's dependency and domesticity were enforced by the fact that, barred from virtually all good jobs, they could scarcely earn their own way. Fanny broke the pattern not once but twice, for she survived a divorce—a moment of truth on the financial aspect of marriage—and went on to support herself again amply and cheerfully. The symbolism of the Pierce Butlers was all in Fanny's favor: she earned while he became a bankrupt; she was the exemplar and champion of free labor, he the idle slavemaster. And her earnings, like her differences with Pierce, were notorious.[55]

In 1863 Kemble published *Journal of a Residence on a Georgian Plantation*, a powerful description of slavery which dated from her sojourn on Pierce's properties in 1838–39. She brought it out to throw her influence, however slight, into the balance against the pro-Southern sentiment then current in some English circles. Pierce had by this time fallen into a spectacular bankruptcy and had been compelled in 1859 to sell more than four hundred slaves at auction to pay his debts. He was, however, an avid supporter of the Confederacy and had even been imprisoned briefly at the outset of the war under suspicion of helping to run guns to the South. Fanny was involving herself in the most serious public issue of the day, implicitly reminding readers of her early opposition to slavery and vindicating her quarrel with a slave-owning husband. Her continuing success as a reader was so solid that the *Galaxy* in 1868 predicted that although Kemble's "bright, brief [acting] career" was "one of the glorious memories of the stage," she would be longest remembered as an interpreter of Shakespeare. Her memoirs, published between 1879 and 1891, avoided any mention of her marriage but otherwise carried her story once more to the public.[56]

A WOMAN IN PUBLIC

Fanny Kemble made herself into a "heroine" and so escaped the typecasting that male sexual interest so often imposed on actresses. But she could not completely avoid being perceived through and judged by the body. As if in a kind of double bind, she escaped the status of sex object only to be criticized as "masculine." Sidney George Fisher, for example, a Philadelphia neighbor, confided to his diary: "She has a great deal of talent and a fine nature, impulsive, passionate, enthusiastic. This renders her very interesting, but too prononcée. She has besides a powerful physique, is accustomed to a great deal of exercise and her whole appearance and bearing are the reverse of feminine." In Fisher's eyes Fanny's talents seemed to slide easily into liabilities ("too prononcée") and her love of horseback riding rendered her so physically fit she was "the reverse of feminine." Charles Sumner, who met her in Lenox in 1844, described her as "peculiar, bold, masculine ... unaccommodating."[57]

What was it about Fanny's "bearing" that was masculine? It might have been her athleticism; it might have been her voice, whose lower registers she exploited for the male parts when she read Shakespeare. More probably it was a matter of the way she spoke to and dealt with men: there was apparently a want of deference, a dead-level quality in the way she presented herself to them which many men found unnerving. A woman who treated a man as her equal could only be labeled masculine. Sumner and Fisher came eventually to be Fanny's good friends, but some men were far too threatened for that to occur. Herman Melville, for example, met Fanny in the Berkshires and attended some of her readings of Shakespeare in Boston in 1848 – 49. In a poisonous comment that says far more about Melville than Kemble, he described her as "so unfemininely masculine that had she not ... borne children, I should be curious to know the result of a surgical examination."[58]

Such remarks remained private and individual; they were injected only once into the public press. N. P. Willis, editor of the *Home Journal* (fig. 10), suggested that Fanny set a bad example for the young ladies attending Mrs. Sedgwick's school in Lenox. Reprinting letters that had supposedly appeared first in local papers like the *Worcester Aegis*, Willis' coverage focused on Kemble's clothing and her horsemanship: "Mrs. Fanny Kemble is quite a topic in Berkshire at the present time. . . . It is her masculine costume when out on a hunting excursion and her skill in the management of a fleet steed, or in driving a pair of fast trotters, which attracts almost as much attention as her versatile genius in developing the mysteries of Shakespeare." Although Fanny had never appeared on stage in a "breeches" (i.e., male) part and always rode sidesaddle, she occasionally did don trousers for mountain climbing or fishing in the Berkshires. Willis slyly concluded that such behavior might set a bad example for other women: "Taking into account that the aberrations of genius, like the eccentricities of character, are apt to be sooner imitated than the most exalted virtues, I do not wonder at the difference of opinion which exists as to the impressions likely to be produced upon the delicate mould of the female mind. There is a philosophy, cherished in some select circles, which needs a little watching."[59]

Fig. 10 N. P. Willis, editor of the *Home Journal,* who inserted snide comments about Kemble's "masculine" manner into his paper. Harvard Theatre Collection.

Kemble never worried about such "watching," for she did not much care what people said or thought of her, even though her profession demanded that she "live to please and please to live," in Samuel Johnson's phrase. Pierce Butler himself told the story of how one day in Philadelphia Fanny was going riding, and said she would ride down Walnut Street to the Delaware River. Pierce told her not to go that way: "Ladies never went along the wharves" and there might be "great if not rude attention, . . . unpleasant remarks." He added, "She replied by a few disdainful words about my regard for what people said," and rode off to the river.[60] Fanny Kemble was neither worried nor frightened. Her frankness and fearlessness often got her into trouble, but they cut decisively across the traditional portrait that associated the theatre with posturing and falsehood. And they revealed to admirers and detractors alike the independence and authenticity the stage might grant a woman.

Triumphant in the public realm, Fanny Kemble saw little reason to cling to privacy. She once wrote: "Publicity is the safest of all protections, as in some sense freedom is also. Women, I suppose, will find this out, as the people are finding it out."[61] This line of thought was probably based on her own relentless honesty: if one had nothing to hide, there was nothing to be unmasked, no reason to be afraid. Envisioning a publicity that was benign, even "safe," she counted the abuses of publicity as akin to the errors of license that could accompany liberty. She thought she could glimpse a world in which life in the public realm—indeed, publicity itself—would be normal and natural, for women as for men. But she had forgotten the press gang and Willis' ability to vent his hostility. Her carelessness about publicity and public opinion was a luxury purchased by her own talents, by the brevity of her stage career, and by her versatility in turning to other means of self-support.

Kemble had, through a combination of good fortune and great talent, broken the narrow confines of both stage and womanhood, and set forth the lineaments of a public life for women that was not defined by male apprehension of the female body. But she had only brushed up against the emerging practices of commercialized entertainment. These were changing the conditions of theatrical work for women, redefining the content of their public presence in ways that would make it difficult to reproduce her achievement as a theatrical heroine.

3 .
Spectacles: Thomas Hamblin and His Women

The particular dangers for women of the newly commercializing theatre are revealed in the careers of Thomas Hamblin and the women who surrounded him at the Bowery Theatre in New York. Hamblin took over the Bowery in 1830 and turned it into a moneymaker by ignoring theatrical traditions and social niceties. Darkly attractive, with a classic profile and a "handsome head and features," Hamblin (fig. 11) had acted in England before his American debut at age twenty-five. He toured the country for several years as a star before entering management at the Bowery, where the previous manager, known for paying generous salaries, had gone bankrupt. Familiar with the benefits of the star system to actors, Hamblin was determined to avoid the financial strain it imposed on managers. Except for occasional absences in England and lapses imposed by theatre fires, he was connected with the Bowery (fig. 12) more or less continuously until his death in 1853. Unlike most theatre managers, Hamblin owned his theatre building outright; he took the full risks and profits. Despite many reverses, including the devastation of his theatres by fire four times with heavy uninsured losses, Hamblin possessed a fortune of over $100,000 at the end of his career.[1]

He profited as the first manager of a major New York theatre to discount the patronage of the wealthy and concentrate on expanding the size of the audience. Seeking the means to attract a mass audience, Hamblin turned toward the visual once he realized that spectacle was both alluring to audiences and comparatively inexpensive to produce. He exploited—both commercially and sexually— a succession of young women who worked at the Bowery. The careers of Thomas Hamblin and "his" women illuminate the pitfalls that

Fig. 11 Thomas Hamblin. This lithograph confirms
his "handsome head and features." Harvard Theatre
Collection.

the emergence of aggressively profit-oriented theatre held for women employed
in the theatre. Yet Hamblin's Bowery also nurtured melodrama, a popular new
genre that spoke to women in the audience and included women as playwrights.

CHANGES IN THE THEATRE BUSINESS

Hamblin's predecessors in theatre management in the early decades of the nineteenth century discovered that a mass audience for theatre was being created by
urbanization and the beginnings of the transportation revolution. Travelers
moving through cities for business or pleasure began to constitute some significant part of urban theatre audiences, and the numbers of urban residents also
were increasing rapidly. Managers sought to tap larger markets by increasing
the number of performances given each week, the length of the theatre season,

Fig. 12 The Bowery Theatre, New York City, in the 1830s. Harvard Theatre Collection.

and the seating capacity of theatre auditoriums. In the 1810s and 1820s weekly performances increased from three or four to six, and theatres experimented with summer seasons, so that open-air or garden theatres like Niblo's Garden in New York became popular. The 1820s also saw a boom in theatre construction in New York, Philadelphia, Boston, and Washington. After 1830, 2000 seats in a theatre would be merely average; 3000 was increasingly common. Seeking high volume, managers gradually and tentatively embraced low prices. In 1800 tickets cost one dollar for box seats, with pit and gallery seats at fifty and twenty-five cents; by 1850 prices had dropped to roughly half that.[2]

As in other ante-bellum businesses, entrepreneurs pursued profit by expanding output and cutting costs and prices. In workshops and factories, they undermined craft skills, mechanized or subdivided work to utilize unskilled workers, and found ways to force workers to produce more and faster. Skilled workers, formerly independent craftsmen, endured a painful and demeaning process as they faced an increasingly powerful management bent on cutting their wages or doing without them altogether. In the theatre, the same processes were at work, and although great stars could exempt themselves from such trials, ordinary actors and actresses suffered the same loss of autonomy and increasing work pace that workers in other fields experienced.[3]

Some performers tried to resist the new weekly schedules, which called for considerable increase in work without additional compensation. In New York

City in 1813, a group of performers from the Park Theatre who charged "ill usage and persecution" by the managers formed their own theatre company, calling it the Theatrical Commonwealth. In Philadelphia in 1830 similar sentiments seem to have launched a newspaper, the *Theatrical and Literary Journal.* The actor-editor blamed the troubled times on "speculating managers" who increased the number of performances while cutting the actors' pay. Managers, he wrote, had become "arrogant, insidious, and unjust," while actors were "cringing and submissive." Grasping after "casual, immoderate gains" in promoting stars, such managers supplied the places of established actors with "a muster of lubberly boys." Old-fashioned managers, who did not adopt the new methods and often ended bankrupt, also joined in condemning the enemy they shared with the common players—the new breed of managers who were "unprincipled speculators in acting."[4]

The transformation of theatre from a craft into a business was assisted by parallel changes in journalism, especially the rise of the new penny press in the 1830s which reached out to working-class and middle-class readers alike. Precisely because they were no longer underwritten by the political parties via publishing contracts or subsidies, the penny papers had to offer content with broad appeal; while they trumpeted their political independence, they lived and died on the bottom line and were quick to find out that sensationalism sold. Edgar Allan Poe wrote that the rise of the penny press had an influence on American life and letters that was "probably beyond all calculation."[5]

Certainly the press had an influence on the theatre. Early in the century what little dramatic criticism appeared in the papers tended to come from educated professional men who did not write for a living; they occasionally contributed critical pieces because they cared for the stage and wanted to see it elevated. Otherwise editors sent ordinary reporters to cover the opening of new plays or the appearance of stars, and they reported these events much as they might have a crime or a fire, confining themselves to plot summary and description of the reactions of the audience. Such reporters tended to pass over failures in silence and to overpraise mere competence, sometimes in a spirit of civic boosterism, sometimes because they took pay for "puffs." Yet egregious puffing was curbed by the newspapermen's habit of deferring to the opinions of the audience, especially the pit, and by managerial ethics as well. Managers in this earlier period deemed it unwise to be connected to journalists who wrote about the theatre, lest any negative comments appearing in print make the manager an object of suspicion to the players in his company. William Dunlap, for example, indignantly refused a man who applied "to officiate as the manager's salaried puff."[6]

In the 1830s, however, as a new breed of theatre managers set out to cultivate the press more deliberately, they found the penny press more than ready to cooperate. Charles Gilfert, Hamblin's predecessor at the Bowery, was the first manager to hire a press agent, and his theatre boasted a "cold cut room," where members of the press were offered food, beverages, and writing materials. James Gordon Bennett, editor of the influential *New York Herald*, was so ready to use his columns for profit or pique that his unscrupulous behavior made him something of a legend in his own time: he was repeatedly horsewhipped by those he had insulted, including Thomas Hamblin. It was said, however, that Bennett bowed to the lash willingly, knowing that the sensation would sell even more papers. Bennett, who hired a journalist to cover the theatre in regular drama columns but often employed his own editorial columns for the same purpose, reportedly demanded gifts and favors in return for good coverage when the dancer Fanny Ellsler toured the country in 1840. With no code of ethics to curb such behavior, intrusive and abusive press coverage and outright blackmail became woefully common. And yet as the cities grew and word of mouth became less reliable, newspaper coverage was more and more important to the success of theatres, plays, and players. Before long no calculating manager dared to be without "literary aids."[7]

HAMBLIN'S BOWERY

The Bowery audience was unique, even legendary, but its shirtsleeve style was emblematic of changes afoot all over the country as theatre managers tried to reach a mass audience. In Providence, for example, the taste for drama seemed to have declined among "the opulent citizens" by the 1820s; their departure left the audience so dominated by journeymen and apprentice shoemakers that the playhouse was dubbed the Shoemaker's Literary and Dramatic Society. By mid-century a veteran manager could declare that drama, "never more popular," was patronized by a different "class of persons" than it had been thirty years before. Hamblin's Bowery audiences were, according to one patron, full of "American-born mechanics"—"young shipbuilders, cartmen, butchers, firemen"—as well as, for some plays, a "more decorous and intellectual congregation." Another observer described the Bowery patrons as "young girls, factory hands, shop tenders, street walkers, . . . some few decent quiet family parties and many, very many little children! Nice little girls in white dresses and gay ribbons, little sleepy boys and babies!"[8]

Hamblin sought to appeal to this heterogeneous popular audience by playing on their patriotism. He had arrived in this country in the same year that the great English tragedian Edmund Kean was howled off a Boston stage for allegedly insulting the audience; Hamblin understood Americans' prickly sensitivity about English performers, and he boldly determined to exploit it. In his first season he informed his audiences of the Bowery's devotion to "native talent," restating his object in capital letters—NATIVE TALENT!—the following year when Fanny Kemble and her father offered him stiff competition at the rival Park Theatre. Hiring stars like the Kembles would be costly, Hamblin probably calculated, and, on the other hand, the opportunistic appeal to patriotism cost him nothing. Hamblin continued to harp on patriotism throughout his managerial days, and he may well have resorted to techniques like rumor-mongering and even riot to undermine English stars who appeared at rival houses.[9]

Hamblin tried to avoid paying star salaries by driving a hard bargain and by starring himself. By the 1830s the veteran tragedian Junius Brutus Booth had acquired a reputation for unreliability because of his alcoholism. Hamblin was therefore able to sign him to an eight-month contract at $120 per week for the 1832–33 season. When two of Booth's children died and he himself fell ill, Booth failed to complete the season. Undeterred by sympathy, Hamblin hauled Booth into court for breach of contract and extracted a settlement. Although Hamblin's own voice was marred by chronic asthma, he knew he could exploit his looks to take leading roles occasionally and thereby save money. "He had a large, shapely, imposing presence, and dark and flashing eyes," one young audience member, Walt Whitman, would recall. Hamblin appeared an average of more than twice a week during his first two seasons as manager of the Bowery.[10]

Hamblin also countered real stars with his own "manufactured stars." He realized that the public's belief in a player's merit was as important as talent, and the new penny press offered ready means to influence their views. Hamblin bound promising novices to long-term contracts with minimal salaries, then presented them in flattering lead roles and "puffed" them heavily in the New York papers. With their fame thus established, he could hire them out for star turns in other cities, pocketing the handsome fees they commanded.[11]

But Hamblin most consistently attracted audiences by means of plays rather than stars. His theatre became known as the "Bowery Slaughter House," because of its increasing concentration on blood-and-thunder melodramas, which gradually displaced other genres such as comedy. These popular melodramas put a heavy emphasis on action, costume, and special effects, while dialogue was pared to a minimum. Melodrama diminished the importance of acting skills. "Anybody can play Napoleon who looks anything like him," reasoned Hamblin, "and who does not with the dress on?"[12]

All Hamblin needed was a supply of new scripts, for which he relied on a succession of in-house playwrights. They adapted materials of proven appeal, including the popular novels of Sir Walter Scott and Edward Bulwer-Lytton.

"My pieces," said Hamblin, are "what I depend on." Paying his playwrights a small salary and granting them the proceeds of a benefit performance was much more remunerative than splitting his profits with an expensive star: "What a difference it is whether a *Piece* or a *Person* brings the money," Hamblin declared.[13]

Ever alert to profit, Hamblin did not scruple to take advantage of ordinary players. In the 1840s, aided by the depression, he attempted to hire players by the week rather than by the season. This practice threatened one of the only sources of employment security traditionally enjoyed by actors and actresses, the season-long contract. In 1851 one minor player gloated when Hamblin's retirement benefit turned out a complete failure: "I think there was little regret among the profession. Hamblin flooded the city with bills and notices for a month proclaiming his many virtues and his liberality to American actors and authors though it is well known that he never gave an actor 100 cents when he could get him for 99."[14] Hamblin lived to see many of his methods normalized. His reliance on newspaper puffing, his willingness to dispense with traditional practices, and above all his relentless attention to profit became standard practices in the theatre business, especially as the depression of the 1840s rendered profitmaking more problematic. A manager who took over a New Orleans theatre during the 1844–45 season described the Hamblinesque methods that brought him success: "I made a dash with bills—display—show—red fire—earthquake—and the devil knows what else." The "old-fashioned style of doing business," he concluded briskly, "does not answer."[15]

SPECTACLE

As Hamblin took command, American theatre was beginning to undergo a shift from a principally aural medium to a predominately visual medium. Theatregoers, commonly termed "auditors" early in the century, would later be designated "spectators," and only the term *audience* would remain to recall the early republic's "unalloyed fondness" for command of the language. Beginning in the late 1830s, journalists, players, and managers made the same sort of comments: the pleasures of the stage had "migrated from the ears almost entirely," there had been a shift to "entertainments for the eye rather than for the ear," audiences were "content with a recreation that appeals only to the visual wants." Edwin Forrest groused about the "gaudy kickshaws" of "scene painters' drama."[16]

Thomas Hamblin began the turn toward the visual by demonstrating its profitability. He increasingly emphasized spectacular effects in his new melodramas, with simulations of fire and water, live animals on stage, and lavish production values. Having seen that visual and special effects pleased his audiences,

Hamblin realized that it was worthwhile to produce elaborate sets and stage effects when a play could be presented not just once but a number of times. Since his audience lay among modest families and individuals who probably could not afford to attend the theatre every evening, it made sense to run the same play night after night so long as it continued to draw. Thus Hamblin was an early pioneer in what would come to be called the "long run," which at the Bowery in the 1830s might amount to some twenty to forty nights. Such runs were not quite the theatrical equivalent of mass production, but they did involve conceiving of the play as a product and recognizing that it was disadvantageous to try to produce and market a new product each day. Preferring to pay wages to stage carpenters, scene painters, costumers, and supernumeraries rather than split profits with great actors, Hamblin in effect based his operation on semiskilled rather than highly skilled, labor. His methods resulted in a diminution of skill among the players and an accumulation of power and profit in the hands of the manager. From the 1834–35 season he was reported to have cleared $30,000 by concentrating on "attractive spectacles without any great merit." The turn toward the visual was thus an integral part of the increased attention to profit. The image was cheaper to produce—and probably easier to consume—than the word.[17]

The turn to spectacle coincided with and was reinforced by social change, as Americans struggled to feel comfortable in an expanded public realm full of mobility and of strangers. The ideology of republicanism, like the rise of the nation-state and the spread of the capitalist marketplace, decisively expanded the occasions on which one had to deal with strangers. Urbanization, which proceeded apace after 1830, added considerably to the problem. Therefore, as Richard Sennett has pointed out, the nineteenth century was fascinated with appearances, and with the problem of "reading" others.[18]

The turn to the visual that began in the theatre of the 1830s for reasons that were both narrowly pecuniary and broadly cultural almost immediately received a significant boost from technology. In 1839 it was announced that Louis Daguerre, a former set designer and scene painter at the Paris Opera and other Paris theatres, had invented photography. Daguerre had tinkered previously with dioramas and panoramas in efforts to achieve compelling stage illusion. His invention helped to transform the theatre by promoting the assumption that visual representation was not just one element but the central core of the theatrical experience. By the 1850s shopkeepers displayed daguerreotypes of popular actors in their windows, and the stage could be described as "the daguerreotype of life," a metaphor that left little room for the rich aural culture of the early stage. By the 1860s theatre enthusiasts would be collecting carte de visite photographs of their favorite players as well as memorizing favorite lines.[19]

The new emphasis on the visual rather than the aural had important consequences for the theatre. Audience dynamics were implicitly affected, for spectacle is much more monologic than dialogic. The repartee that had been common when performers stood on a bare stage to speak their lines would prove out of place, or just inaudible, when audiences were confronted with onstage spectacles like a belching volcano or a steamboat in flames. The early performers' chief instrument—the human voice—had been potentially available to all; not so the manipulation of illusion and visual pleasure.

The implications for women were particularly grave, since they themselves were now liable to be taken as visual objects. The single criterion of appearance could create a large pool of potential "actresses" to be winnowed by the favors of the manager. The turn toward the visual thus emphasized what had always been the most problematic element of the theatre for women—its status as an embodied art. It had always been the chief risk of a stage career for a woman that she must be seen and that the male glaze could render her, without her consent, an object of sexual fantasy. If this process went a step further, and the fantasy object became a regular commodity, the conditions that made acting good work for many women would be undermined. Once, for example, talent with the spoken word took a back seat to appearance, the work of the actress would lose its primary association with demanding, respected skills in elocution. And if good looks were identified with freshness and immaturity, the ingénue would take on a decisive premium, and lifelong careers become elusive. An emphasis on youthful beauty would tend to create a constant turnover among actresses, a sort of human planned obsolescence.

In the 1830s the aural traditions of the stage remained strong, and the turn to the visual was still a crutch for thin scripts and incompetent performers, but the drive for profit by entrepreneurs like Hamblin promised that the remunerative potential of visual display soon would be more fully explored.

WOMEN AT HAMBLIN'S BOWERY

Hamblin readily exploited all means of profit, but he found women particularly useful. His wife, Elizabeth Blanchard Hamblin, had been his partner in founding the company. In the fall of 1831 she traveled to England to engage new talent for the Bowery. Mrs. Hamblin's authority to hire signaled that she held some share of the managerial responsibilities, but while she was gone, a young woman named Josephine Clifton (fig. 13) made her debut and became the first of Hamblin's "manufactured" stars.

Clifton was just eighteen at the time, statuesque and lovely, although quite inexperienced. Puffed as "native talent" and brought out in leading roles, she

Fig. 13 Josephine Clifton, of Hamblin's Bowery, became a star more because of her looks than her talent but before photography her beauty could not be pictured in inexpensive reproduction. Billy Rose Theatre Collection.

bypassed the theatrical tradition that called for beginning in small roles and working up. Clifton reaped few of the rewards of her emerging stardom, however, for she was bound to Hamblin by a three-year contract that provided expenses but no salary. When Hamblin sent her to Philadelphia for a star turn, one veteran theatre manager complained that Clifton had "no requisite for an actress except personal appearance." Nevertheless, as Hamblin had anticipated, some combination of newspaper puffery, patriotism, and prettiness sufficed to render Clifton a believable star.[20]

Soon, however, Clifton found herself eclipsed by another Hamblin pupil,

Naomi Vincent, who first appeared in Philadelphia in February 1832, and opened in New York in April of that year. Like Clifton, Vincent was only a teenager when she began her career with Hamblin. She was less beautiful but more talented: "Her features not remarkable for beauty yet bore the stamp of intellect, which, when lighted up by the enthusiasm of her assumed character, captivated the hearts of the audience." By the time Elizabeth Blanchard Hamblin returned in the spring of 1832, Hamblin had launched two attractive young protégées and gossip linked his name with both women. In June 1832 the Hamblins signed articles of separation whose terms clearly indicate that he was the party at fault.[21]

In the fall of 1832 Vincent and Clifton helped Thomas Hamblin meet the challenge of the Kembles, who were playing at the rival Park Theatre and taking New York by storm. Hamblin scheduled the two young women together in double bills and told audiences they had "the opportunity of comparing their NATIVE TALENT with that of the most distinguished artists Europe can produce." Hamblin's profits survived, with additional help from T. D. Rice, whose "Jim Crow" blackface song-and-dance numbers, then newly introduced, proved exceedingly popular.[22]

Soon Josephine Clifton began to appear less often, whether due to rumored ill health, to Vincent's greater talents, or to Vincent's having replaced her in Hamblin's affections. Whatever the case, Clifton left the country and went on to perform for two years in London and the English provinces. The London critics scorned her initial attempts to star, and she spent her second season in supporting roles. Nevertheless she gained some valuable experience, and she had learned enough of the arts of press manipulation by watching Hamblin to make sure that her homecoming in the fall of 1836 was attended by newspaper reports that claimed London triumphs. She appeared in August 1837 at the Park Theatre, the Bowery's higher-toned rival, in *Bianca Visconti*, a new play written especially for her by the journalist N. P. Willis. Philip Hone thought she "played well and looked *magnifique*." Josephine Clifton subsequently pursued her career without Hamblin's help. Although she never had a spotless reputation or a great deal of talent, Clifton had a modestly successful stage career into the 1840s.[23]

Clifton's escape from Hamblin's control left Naomi Vincent (fig. 14) his chief pupil. Vincent too was bound by a three-year contract that paid her expenses only. She reportedly told a sympathetic woman journalist that she detested Hamblin but had no money, no friends, and nowhere to go. By the summer of 1834, her qualms apparently overcome, Vincent was living with Hamblin. That same year Elizabeth Blanchard Hamblin won a divorce, under whose terms she was granted a handsome cash allowance. The court forbade Hamblin to remarry, but he began to call Vincent his wife, and he still had the management of her career. Hamblin was probably referring to Vincent when he wrote to a Philadelphia manager: "I do not let my wife leave her house unless a certain sum of money is paid her per night." Naomi Vincent was twenty-one when she died in childbirth in July 1835. After Vincent's death, Hamblin erected a sentimentally inscribed monument over her grave and promptly began a live-in relationship with Louisa Medina, whose scripts he had been producing since 1833.[24]

Louisa Medina arrived in New York City in the early 1830s, young and friendless and struggling to make a living. The daughter of a Spanish businessman, Medina was given a "masculine and metaphysical" education, including classical languages and mathematics. After her father's bankruptcy she had to support herself. Medina tried teaching French and Spanish and contributing poems and stories to the newspapers. She also submitted scripts to the theatres, and eventually her writing talents were discovered by Thomas Hamblin.[25]

Medina provided Hamblin with the great melodramatic hits that marked the Bowery of the middle 1830s. In 1835 her *Last Days of Pompeii* ran twenty-nine performances with only one interruption, apparently the longest run in New York theatrical history to that date. Her *Norman Leslie, Rienzi, Ernest Maltravers*, and *Nick of the Woods* also were durable popular attractions for Hamblin. Hamblin actually acknowledged her contributions in his will, written in November 1836, in which he left Medina an annuity "in consideration of the great advantages derived by me from [her] dramatic works." Working as an adaptor of popular novels, Louisa Medina had a fine sense of dramatic compression and deft control over the essential elements of melodramatic action. Her plays often feature stronger plot line and dialogue than the novels on which they were based. Supposedly she wrote thirty-four plays between 1833 and 1838, although only three appear to have survived. She was described by the actor John Lester Wallack as "one of the most brilliant women I ever met. . . . She was very plain, but a wonderfully bright woman, charming in every way."[26]

Hamblin's steady accumulation of wealth at the Bowery, which had been so much assisted by the talents of Clifton, Vincent, and Medina, came to an abrupt halt in September 1836, when the Bowery Theatre was destroyed by fire. Hamblin went to England and played starring roles at Covent Garden with little success. He returned to New York to star in July 1837, but after a crowded first night, the audiences dwindled away. It was a difficult time to recoup his fortunes, as the Panic of 1837 and the subsequent depression spread hard times in the theatre world. Hamblin performed occasionally at the National Theatre, managed by his friend J. W. Wallack, and laid plans. He devised a scheme to render his income as large as possible by combining both his earlier strategies — introducing a new melodrama *and* a ballyhooed new "debutante." Even though

Fig. 14 Naomi Vincent, another of Hamblin's protégées at the Bowery. Billy Rose Theatre Collection.

Hamblin would not garner a manager's share, he could expect to profit from the play he arranged to open at Wallack's theatre.[27]

Hamblin played his trump card in March 1838. The new play was Medina's *Ernest Maltravers*, an adaptation of a Bulwer-Lytton novel. It starred Wallack, Hamblin, and "a young candidate for public approbation" otherwise unidentified in the playbill. The play was a smashing success, and after public interest had been piqued by her anonymity and her very skillful performance, the much-praised female lead was finally identified as sixteen-year-old Louisa Missouri, a half-sister of Josephine Clifton and another special protégée of Hamblin's. She was a "nine days wonder and the talk of the town." But Missouri's ill health allowed the play to be offered only fitfully, and two months later she lay dead, a swirl of scandal revolving around her name. Clifton was said to have tried to block her sister's career out of jealousy. The older actress denied this, maintaining in a public statement that she had only tried to warn the girl of "the professional path and instruction which she should *avoid*"—namely, Thomas Hamblin's tutelage. This riposte, which implied that Clifton knew of Hamblin's evil ways through her own sad experience, was a sure-fire attention-getter, for it cast Hamblin as a destroyer of girls, "steeped to the lips in vice."[28]

A new wrinkle in the story then appeared, probably fed to the press by Hamblin in self-defense: the sisters' mother was revealed to be a wealthy and notorious brothelkeeper. This reportedly had been unknown to Missouri, who had been shielded from the truth at boardingschool, and the shock had contributed to the breakdown of her health. Clifton did not deny the story, but in a statement said simply that she and her sister were the "children of misfortune" required "by our own efforts [to] protect and maintain ourselves." The revelation about the mother served Hamblin well, for it tended to deflect attention away from the question of whether he seduced and exploited the young women to the issue of the mother's character. Hamblin's friends could even suggest that introducing Clifton and Missouri to the stage had been a meritorious act, "as it perhaps prevented them from becoming members of the Cyprian corps" and enabled them to earn an honest living![29]

There was much gossip about Missouri, "because of her decided ability, her beauty and her romantic story"; it was "more than insinuated that she was one of Hamblin's victims, and that Mrs. Hamblin [Louisa Medina], who had taken her out of the gutter, had written this part for her and helped create the great sensation for her, was fully aware of the fact." When Missouri died suddenly in the midst of her success, Hamblin was actually menaced by hostile crowds. The young woman's mother showed up, looking less like a prosperous madam than an ill-kempt member of the urban underclass, a "terrible old woman" with "long white witch-like hair flying about her face." She harangued a crowd of

"Bowery people" collected under Hamblin's window, charging that Hamblin had ruined her daughter and that Medina had administered poison to the girl out of jealousy. Apparently this story had enough credibility to prompt a postmortem. The doctors declared that Missouri died of an "inflammation of the brain," and Hamblin tried to treat this as a vindication. When, less than six months later, Medina herself died at the age of twenty-five, the old woman appeared again, this time to accuse Hamblin of murdering Medina in order to take up with someone else. It was, of course, comment enough on Hamblin that the charge had a degree of plausibility. According to one account, Hamblin's friend the popular actor-manager James Wallack hurried over to Hamblin's house at his urgent request and found Hamblin sitting there with Medina's corpse laid out and an angry crowd gathering outside. It took all of Wallack's personal popularity to quiet and disperse the crowd.[30]

After the scandal blew over, Hamblin reopened the Bowery in May 1839 but brought out no more fanfared young "pupils." Although his reputation had been damaged by the Missouri affair, Hamblin's business successes over the next decade tended to rinse his public memory of opprobrium. When he died in 1853 his obituaries praised him as a man who had always paid his business debts and had given generously to charity.[31]

Although the stories of Clifton, Vincent, Medina, and Missouri are all clouded in obscurity, the fragments that survive suggest that a theatre molded by the drive for profits was not favorable to women. The rise of powerful managers like Thomas Hamblin meant that hiring decisions were no longer mediated by traditional practices nor by the dispersion of power among the members of a theatre company. Now one man could hire an unknown for lead roles and, perhaps, make her a star; in the hands of a man like Hamblin, such power was an aid to seduction. With attention increasingly paid to profit, even managers with more scruples than Hamblin would find reason to hire players for as little as possible, and this was a calculus in which women, eligible for few other jobs that paid so well, stood to lose most. The shift to the visual compounded the problem for female performers, who were at greater risk to be apprehended as entertainment commodities, with their chief appeal good looks.

MELODRAMA AND WOMEN'S LIVES

Hamblin's Bowery played a different role as well; it was a pioneer in a new genre that appealed strongly to women—melodrama. Melodrama spoke to women because it personified, and thus gave gender to, virtue and vice. The villain was invariably a man, while virtue was represented wholly or partially by a heroine. The struggle to defeat the villain invited female audience members to identify with an embattled woman persecuted by an altogether hateful man, and to relish his downfall. The villain often combined material greed and sexual rapacity, and in his persecutions of the heroine lay some echo of the unfairness of life for women. His spectacular downfall let onlookers entertain the fantasy that cruel and powerful men in time would be punished. Of course the presence of the hero and the happily-ever-after ending forestalled any overt generalization from man to men: melodrama kept its hostilities well-sublimated and channeled them into socially acceptable plot resolutions. Nevertheless, melodrama was able to tap the deepest springs of unacknowledged anger that lay beneath the limited lives of women—the "madwoman in the attic" of every woman's brain, to use the phrase of the literary critics Sandra Gilbert and Susan Gubar.[32]

Clearly women in the audience enjoyed melodrama. The *New York Mirror* pointed out in praise of the work of Louisa Medina, "Her own sex enjoy in her popularity the triumph of a woman's genius, and go to witness it sure of never being shocked by grossness."[33] There was plenty of action and derring-do in melodrama, but it was "clean" action, and the wickedness of the villain was unfailingly punished. Women's taste for melodrama probably was linked also to the fact that its heroines often displayed extraordinary initiative, tenacity, and grit. Although melodrama frequently is described as featuring a passive heroine who must be rescued, it is easy to find numerous examples in the genre of active women. If not the heroine herself, the intrepid woman might be a secondary female character who helped and advised her. Given this actual tradition of assertive melodramatic heroines, it is not surprising that the first time the villain tied someone to the railroad tracks, in Augustin Daly's *Under the Gaslight* in 1867, it was a *man* who was tied down, and a *woman* who rushed out in the nick of time to cut him loose (fig. 15). Melodramatic perils seemed to license women to do unheard-of, astonishing things.[34]

Women were beginning to be counted as a large chunk of a mass audience, but the whole trick was to appeal to each part without offending any other. It was crucial to its broad audiences that melodrama offered itself for different "readings," and different veins of melodrama appealed to different subaudiences. Melodrama offered a special reading, for example, to working-class audiences, since it was full of aristocratic, greedy villains and praise for the simple laborer. Working-class audience members viewed the stories as a protest against the impositions of the rich and the cruelties of an acquisitive class society. But the settings in ancient history or never-never-land monarchies kept the message about class from becoming so insistent as to offend middle-class theatregoers.[35]

The technical innovations employed in melodrama facilitated simultaneous appeals to different audience interests. The original French term *mélodrame* meant literally a play with music. Musical chords could provide a sensation of

Fig. 15 Scene from *Under the Gaslight.* American Antiquarian Society.

danger, suspense, sadness, or surprise, so that thoroughly predictable scripts became entertaining. Melodrama also incorporated elements of the visual via the use of mime, tableaux, and stage spectacle and machinery. These combined media heightened emotional impact and facilitated the audience's suspension of disbelief, holding it interested in spite of undistinguished or hackneyed story-lines. And multiple media offered different things to attend to—music, scene, story, character—for different subaudiences. Thus the combination of formal or technical elements opened the way for the development of a repertoire of highly formulaic popular fictions. Entertainment was becoming a mass-consumption product, as entrepreneurs learned how to devise a large volume of imaginative "products" without relying excessively on unpredictable and expensive factors like genius or talent. They also learned how to appeal simultaneously to as many different subaudiences as possible. So, for instance, melodrama appealed to women, but men enjoyed it too.[36]

The popular melodramas of the day contained many active women who might have appealed to women in the audience, but also included patterns of multiple address, of "having it both ways," so that men would not be threatened or offended. Of the ten most popular melodramas of the 1830s and 1840s, for example, only four, *The Lady of Lyons, The Lady of the Lake, The Jewess,* and *Black-Eyed Susan,* contained truly passive heroines. *Rob Roy* featured the cool and adroit Diana Vernon, along with Helen Campbell, who led highland rebels in battle. *Thérèse* showed a much-wronged and long-suffering heroine, but the play turned when she decided to denounce the villain and he therefore tried to murder her; Thérèse appeared in the final scene menacing him with a knife. *The Ice Witch* took its audience into a fairy-tale realm where the power of Druda, the Ice Witch, could command anything except the love of a mortal, King Harold. *Guy Mannering* featured one of the most indelibly memorable women of nineteenth-century drama, the weird and prophetic gypsy queen Meg Merriles. Finally, the popular melodrama *Paul Jones* contained two young heroines, one of whom, Katharine, confounded their British captors by disguising herself as a man, slipping in and out of a secret passageway, and signaling a rescue ship with flags. At one point her companion exclaimed, "Kate, you have a soul formed for enterprise!" whereupon Kate replied, "There is no peril, however dangerous, that a woman of spirit and virtue should fear to encounter, to secure the heart of that brave and honorable man to whom she has previously given her own best affections." This line indicates how women of the melodrama so often equivocated concerning conventional gender roles. It was necessary that Kate's derring-do have an unimpeachably feminine goal—in this case, to be reunited with her lover, the hero. Yet her actions broke beyond their pretexts, just as this exchange first announced an unqualified testament to resolute female action and then tacked on a traditionally feminine rationale. Melodrama offered much to women, though it always qualified and contained its offerings.[37]

Medina converted the passive female characters of the original novels to active, central roles. In Robert Montgomery Bird's novel *Nick of the Woods*, for example, the Indian girl Tellie Doe cannot find her way through the woods, but in Medina's play of the same name Doe becomes a fearless pathfinder who at one point knocks the villain down and stands over him with a gun. Medina's *Last Days of Pompeii* featured an intrepid blind girl who successfully confronts the villain in a climactic final scene at the Coliseum. In Bulwer-Lytton's novel, the blind girl merely had provided information so that a powerful man could intervene; she herself had remained an unseen voice in the Coliseum crowd.[38]

There was considerable irony implicit in Louisa Medina's creations, for the melodramatic villain was nearly always a powerful man who was heartless toward others, obsessed by greed, marked by a subtly or explicitly predatory sexuality—a man, in short, just like Thomas Hamblin. The menacing crowds outside his door after Missouri's and Medina's deaths had no trouble recognizing the villain of this real-life "piece." And Medina once hinted that she recognized it herself. One of her poems, printed in the *Ladies Companion*, invoked a secret, hidden self that was both sad and furious:

Be silent! Be silent!—The heart will not brook
That the eye of the many on its secrets should look!

She pictured a calm sea under a midnight sky and warned,

> But if the wild wind should awaken the sea,
> 'Whelmed in foam and in fury then beauty would be.

And she pictured herself in the role of a Delphic priestess.

> The Priestess may smile in her uninspired hour,
> But when urged by the question to the Tripod of power;
> Wild, terrific and sad is the tone of those feelings
> Which burst from her lips as the Delphic revealings.[39]

It was formulaic doggerel. But Medina may have been talking about her own situation, indicating that, although she had accepted a life as Hamblin's mistress, she nevertheless understood and resented the injustice of a society that made him a wealthy businessman and her a pariah.

In poetry Medina might only hint at the fury that she felt, but in melodrama she could arrange for the villain to be named, blamed, and defeated in part through a woman's agency. Although her life followed a script appropriate to tragedy, wherein a heroine whose "virtue" was lost had to die, in melodrama the heroine was threatened but the villain was destroyed.

Neither Thomas Hamblin nor his women were influential in the way that Fanny Kemble was, but their stories illustrate emerging trends in the theatre business. Hamblin's willingness to harass and exploit—an old, old story—was less significant than the turn to the visual that he encouraged on the stage. The resulting emphasis on women's appearance, the declining significance of the craft of elocution, and the increased power of male management including "casting couch" decisions, meant that the skilled female performer was secondary to a beautiful face and figure. The commercial value of her looks might far outweigh any other options life offered their owner. None of Hamblin's women had Kemble's talent or good fortune. The commercializing theatre Hamblin pioneered employed them as commodities and then cast them aside. The form of melodrama provided women in the audience only partial compensation for this reorientation. Although the genre thematized men's sexual wrongdoing, patriarchal domination, and persistent inability to keep their implicit promise to protect women, melodrama's fantasized happy endings ultimately confused the issues. Women were achieving a certain kind of power as part of an emerging mass audience, but they were losing ground in other ways, both economically and culturally.

4 · Female Ambition: Charlotte Cushman Seizes the Stage

Charlotte Cushman sailed for England in the fall of 1844, determined to become a star. Cushman had been earning a living as an actress for eight years. She had just completed an engagement in Boston, appearing opposite the great English tragedian William Macready and enjoying applause that rivaled his. But Cushman's pay for two weeks totaled $100, while Macready pocketed a whopping $2,900. London success, she understood, made the difference. At twenty-eight Charlotte Cushman (fig. 16) was a tall, energetic woman with a plain, owl-like face, a powerful, throaty voice, and a fabulous talent. She hired a young African-American woman named Sallie Mercer to act as her maid and set off across the November North Atlantic.[1]

Cushman had made her way to this point wholly on her own. She had no family theatre connections. Her father, a Boston merchant of old Puritan stock, went bankrupt when Charlotte was thirteen. She had seen her mother forced to take in boarders, had stood by while the family furniture was seized to satisfy creditors. Charlotte went to work as a domestic and laid plans for more lucrative work. Her first idea was to make a living as a singer: this ended disastrously in 1835 when New Orleans audiences recoiled from her "squalling." She promptly switched to acting, began with modest parts and struggled to work her way up. In 1836 she landed a position in a theatre company at Albany and there found her first real success. She next served a grueling apprenticeship as "walking lady," or principal female support, at the Park Theatre in New York, playing all manner of roles night after night. She enlisted her sister, Susan, into the acting business and managed Susan's career too. By the early 1840s Cushman was playing leading female roles in Philadelphia and

Fig. 16 Charlotte Cushman. This portrait by Thomas Sully
shows Cushman early in her career. Library Company of
Philadelphia.

New York and plenty of breeches parts as well. In 1842–43 she tried managing
the Walnut Street Theatre in Philadelphia, but in the teeth of a depression she lost
money.[2]

Now, in 1844, Cushman was launched on the riskiest venture of her life. Her
mother and sister, who had come to rely on Charlotte as the family breadwinner,
felt it was selfish and irresponsible of her to take off this way, gambling on the
chance of achieving fame in London. Ignoring their complaints, Cushman stead-
ied her nerves while she was obliged, once in England, to wait several months
before the right offer appeared. The manager of the Princess' Theatre in London
initially turned her down, saying she was unknown and "not good-looking."[3] But
at last he relented and offered her one night starring on her own, to be followed by
an engagement supporting the American tragedian Edwin Forrest. The pay was
only £7 ($35) a night, but she had her chance.

On 13 February 1845 Cushman opened in *Fazio*, a favorite play of London audiences by the English clergyman Henry Milman. She played Bianca, Fazio's wronged wife, who, in a fit of jealous rage, turns her husband in for a secret crime. But when Bianca realizes Fazio is to be executed as punishment, she pours out her remorse and grief in a classically melodramatic star turn. The early scenes were quiet enough, but when Cushman played the climactic third act the audience was electrified: they stood and roared, frantically waving handkerchiefs and hurling hats in the air. Sallie Mercer surveyed the scene in the pit from behind the curtain and sailed into the dressing-room crying, "You got 'em, missus, you got 'em!"[4]

Charlotte Cushman became a star that night in London. On subsequent nights she thoroughly overshadowed Edwin Forrest, and Forrest hated her for it, but she was beyond having to care for his ill-will. Overnight she had found herself "the greatest creature in the greatest city in the civilized world," as her brother put it. Cushman became the most celebrated American actress of the nineteenth century, surpassing even Fanny Kemble. She made so much money that she soon went into semiretirement; she lived in style in London and Rome, supporting flocks of relatives and hangers-on. The penniless girl who went on to the stage to support herself and her family left an estate of half a million dollars at her death in 1876. Genteel public opinion embraced Cushman. Her obituary in Boston credited her with having shown "that a career upon the stage is not incompatible with the purest private life, the highest social standing, the most scrupulous self-respect."[5]

The growth of the female audience helps to explain Cushman's remarkable fame and influence. No other American woman inspired such worshipful attention from women, young and old alike. A working woman wrote to her:

> I have watched your career for many years, and being an unmarried lady have felt proud to direct other ladies who were struggling for bread, to take example from your noble career, and work out for themselves an independent and individual life. . . . I feel as a working woman I am under obligation to you for the footprints you leave on the sands of time.

A young woman who actually met Cushman described an even more extreme reaction: "Dearly as I loved my mother and my home, if Miss Cushman had asked me that day to go with her and be her slave, without even going back to say farewell to my friends, I should have consented." Julia Ward Howe told Cushman that because of her triumph, "I feel much better about womankind."[6]

Women embraced in Cushman a "female Richelieu," a woman powerful offstage and on. She made great amounts of money quite unassisted by men. She would not be reduced to the visual; she forced her audiences to acknowledge her excellence as an actress although she was "without one personal charm of face or figure." She played women's sufferings not as triviality, but as the stuff of greatness. She made herself into a commodity of her own design and sold that public persona triumphantly. She even played male parts so believably that her success raised questions about the extent to which gender itself is a matter of performance.[7]

AN EXPANDING THEATRE

Charlotte Cushman scrambled to the top of an expansive, competitive American theatre that appealed to a female audience more deliberately and effectively than ever. In the early 1840s the star system's corrosive effects on stock companies, the rise of entertainment competitors, and lingering economic depression combined to provoke premature announcements that the American theatre was dead. Soon, however, it was reviving—rebuilding and extending itself into new territories. Major cities built additional playhouses and theatre spread to smaller cities, towns, and rural areas, either by way of touring companies or through the construction of new playhouses. In 1839, just three years after the Alamo, there were already two theatres in the frontier settlement of Houston, Texas. In 1840 a Portland theatre company toured towns in Maine and New Hampshire playing to audiences of "river-drivers, slab-sawyers, spinning jennies, . . . bumpkins, . . . factory girls." By 1850 there were as many as fifty residential stock companies operating in American cities and apparently many more on the road.[8]

Having discovered that entertainment could be sold as a commodity, entrepreneurs soon began to see the merit of offering as separate pieces parts of the mixed fare that traditionally had constituted an evening at the playhouse. Groping toward the logic of what would come to be called market segmentation, managers began to offer music, dance, freaks, animal acts, and orations in different places and times, each with its own admission charge. Since many of the newly separated entertainments enjoyed lower overhead than drama, they were able to offer cheaper ticket prices. During the depression of the 1840s, with competition for entertainment dollars intense, the dramatic theatre found arrayed against it "ballet dancers, model artists, . . . Ethiopian serenaders . . . Italian and French opera." Lectures, concerts, equestrian troupes, and the newly organized minstrel shows seem to have been especially powerful opponents.[9]

The theatre accordingly tried to appeal more to the genteel middle classes who had long tended to regard it as morally suspect. As the historian Karen Halttunen has shown, a vogue for private theatricals swept the parlors of America beginning in the 1840s and 1850s. Having performed and applauded at home, the middle class found it easier to attend professional theatre. Private theatricals signaled a cultural shift: Americans were becoming reconciled to representation, to what would earlier have been condemned as insincerity or even lying.[10]

Seeking to expand the theatre audience, entrepreneurs noticed that women, the guardians of morality, were underrepresented. Thomas Hamblin seems to have been one of the first theatrical managers to realize that there was profit to be gained if more women could be persuaded to attend. Hamblin evidently instituted what he hoped would be a mutually profitable puffing arrangement with the editor of the *Ladies Companion* in 1836.[11]

Between the late 1830s and the early 1850s theatre managers took a number of steps to make theatre more attractive and less threatening to women. They barred prostitutes, and by the 1850s the naughty third tier had become a thing of the past. Theatre managers accomplished this feat by denying entrance to unescorted women and by hiring security officers who could recognize "women of the town." In this way the majority of "respectable" women were encouraged by the banishing of the nonrespectable minority, the occasional independent woman was lumped with the streetwalker, and reliance on a male escort, common among early female theatregoers, was made absolutely mandatory, at least for evening performances. These new measures laid bare the underlying economic and social power of men in the constitution of the theatre audience: women needed men for the price of the tickets and as escorts, but men did not need women. Many theatres also began to eliminate the sale of alcoholic beverages on their premises during this period. Although change was episodic and locally determined, these two alterations undercut the moralists' traditional case against theatregoing. An 1852 correspondent to the *Boston Daily Bee* corrected another writer's "antique notions": "We beg to inform our unposted friend that neither intoxicating drinks nor exceptionable women have been tolerated in our theatres for some years back."[12]

Theatres moved to accommodate more women by reorganizing their seating. Managers converted the pit into "parquette," replacing the old backless benches with more comfortable chairs and keeping the area cleaner in order to welcome ladies, who had seldom, if ever, ventured to sit in the pit. In 1837 a New York manager who was pulling in large crowds with a new melodrama tried the experiment of converting part of the pit into a parquette, precisely so as to attract more women: "I have made a parquette of the four front seats in the pit for Ladies—tomorrow night first experiment—don't know how it will succeed—I wish I had it before—hundreds of ladies have been turned away—no seats—they have even gone to 3 and 4 tier."[13]

During the 1840s and early 1850s managers also added to their weekly schedules one or two matinees. Because middle-class women were free to attend the theatre in the afternoons and could do so without male escorts, matinee audiences were predominately female. When Charlotte Cushman provided complimentary tickets to Mrs. Horace Mann in 1850, she apologized because the seats were rather high up but added that since it was a matinee, "There will be only nice people all over the house." Managers also encouraged women's attendance by offering a special price for couples, and it even began to dawn on some of them that plays without significant female roles had less appeal for women theatregoers.[14]

Attracting more middle-class women also meant cutting down on the most egregious forms of playhouse rowdyism. Managers began in the 1840s to employ police to keep order and to encourage members of the audience to police one another. The manager of the theatre in Mobile, Alabama, explained his new policy in 1841: "As no public establishment can succeed unless patronized by ladies, and as ladies cannot possibly countenance a place of public entertainment where the other sex are disorderly, it is the intention of the Manager to make every effort in his power to maintain that decorum in the theatre which is observed in the drawing room."[15]

Finally, the American theatre began to attract more women because managers sanitized the language and moral views of the plays, eliminating profanity and embarrassing double-entendre, and touting the uplifting effect of plays that exposed social ills and ended with virtue triumphant. As early as 1828 the playwright George Colman had told Charles Kemble he should feel free to drop "by Heaven," "in God's name," and "damn'd" in a production of one of Colman's plays. In the following decades theatre professionals often would comment on the increasing caution players had to observe with respect to language. Plays presented regularly in the 1790s would have been, they remarked, unacceptable to general audiences of the 1840s or 1850s.[16]

To reassure those hesitant to set foot in the theatre, managers touted the "moral drama" in the late 1830s; the great success of a temperance piece called *The Drunkard*, which opened in Boston in 1844 and played for more than one hundred nights, confirmed the wisdom of the policy. Since in melodrama the villain was always defeated, it was easy to call it moral drama, and by midcentury the term—which always had defined less a genre than a marketing strategy— became so widely used it was nearly meaningless.[17]

The advent of museum theatre, which combined a number of these innovations, demonstrated that sober, decorous audiences which included more women spelled profit. Museum theatres began when Moses Kimball's Boston Museum and Gallery of Fine Arts opened its doors on 14 June 1841. The street level held a collection of curios and on the second floor there was a spacious "music saloon"; the mixed programs, which at first emphasized concerts and recitals, gradually began to include more and more drama. Plays proved so popular that Kimball had to build a larger facility three years later. The *Boston Evening Transcript* explained that the museum's reputation for the maintenance of good order and for purity of language and morals "induce very many to visit there, who could not, with propriety, be seen at any other dramatic entertainment." The Boston Museum even offered free admission to ministers of the gospel and actively sought their attendance. Offering theatre under another name, the museum was patronized, according to one shrewd observer, by "a large class who do not frequent theatres, but who have a nice perception of the difference between twee-dle-*dum* and tweedle-*dee*."[18]

At P. T. Barnum's American Museum, which opened in New York in 1843, performances were delivered in an auditorium called a "lecture room" (fig. 17). Young Henry James, who went to Barnum's often with his family, clearly considered the exhibits of curios and freaks extraneous: he recalled "weary waiting, in the dusty halls of humbug" for the lecture room, "the true centre of the seat of joy" to open. Barnum scheduled performances every afternoon and evening six days a week, and on holidays, he boasted, the actors and actresses remained in their costumes from eleven in the morning until ten at night.[19]

Fig. 17 The Lecture Room at Barnum's Museum. The sheer size of theatres like this made it difficult to see the faces of the performers and encouraged broad, histrionic acting. Harvard Theatre Collection.

Like his predecessors in the museum theatre business, Barnum never had a third tier or a barroom. He also refused to issue pass checks, so that no one could slip out to a neighboring saloon for a quick drink and return without paying a second time. As at the Boston Museum, both the exhibits and the play were included in one uniform twenty-five-cent price of admission, and children were admitted at half-price. Barnum prided himself on the fact that parents and children could attend the dramatic performances at Barnum's "and not be shocked or offended by anything they might see or hear," and he claimed to have introduced the moral drama. In his shameless self-promotion and manipulation of newspapers, Barnum resembled Thomas Hamblin, but his good humor and ostentatious concern for respectability made it impossible to see him as quite such a villain. As P. T. understood, morality *was* the best policy, and his success accordingly overshadowed Hamblin's.[20]

Barnum recognized that the public he sought to cultivate was predominately female. In one version of his autobiography Barnum included an anecdote in which a "prim maiden lady from Portland" represented the new audience he was wooing. Speaking to Barnum in his office at the museum, she confessed that she had never before been to any place of amusement or public entertainment, for fear of wickedness. "But I have heard so much of your 'moral drama' and the great good you are doing for the rising generation that I thought I must come here and see for myself." At that moment the gong sounded to open the lecture room and as the crowd hastened in, she sprang to her feet and asked Barnum anxiously, "Are the services about to commence?" "Yes," he replied, "the congregation is now going up."[21]

Of course the same strategies that appealed to the timid lady from Portland also appealed to evangelical or moralistically minded middle-class men, but because women were so strongly identified with middle-class morality, their patronage constituted the best and highest form of endorsement. Charlotte Cushman never played at the museums once she had broken through to stardom, for the prices she demanded were too high. But her success owed much to the fact that the theatre was rapidly becoming a public realm where women's patronage was not just accepted but actively encouraged.

IN EVERY WAY RESPECTED

Charlotte Cushman, a contemporary noted, "loved society and fame and money." Her career was the product of an energetic campaign to get what she wanted. She carefully negotiated hazards that had ruined other women. Like Louisa Medina, Charlotte Cushman arrived in New York a talented but friendless young woman in the wake of her father's bankruptcy, and, like Clifton and Vincent, Cushman signed a three-year contract with Thomas Hamblin. Fortunately, however, the Bowery Theatre burned down shortly thereafter and she was released from her agreement. Cushman was lucky in the chance timing of the fire, but she was also smart and tough.[22]

She seems to have been fully equal to the manipulative ways of both managers and journalists and determined to use them before they had a chance to use her. While seeking her first break in New York she cultivated E. Burke Fisher of the *New Yorker*. Fisher published flattering notices in advance of her crucial New York debut in 1836, assuring audiences that Miss Cushman was possessed of both professional talent and "private virtues." When Cushman subsequently fell ill and then lost both her job and her wardrobe in the Bowery fire, Fisher wrote to a Philadelphia theatre manager and to the editor of *Godey's Lady's Book* to ask if they could supply her with work acting or writing.[23]

An encounter with another New York journalist revealed Cushman's steel nerves. In 1841 she and her sister, Susan, both had important parts in a new production. But the editor of the *New World*, Park Benjamin, demanded that the theatre manager substitute a favorite of his, a Miss Clarendon, for Susan. Fearing Benjamin's retaliation in the form of bad reviews, the manager agreed, but Miss Clarendon was not a success. James Gordon Bennett's *Herald* published particularly cutting remarks about her inadequacies, and Benjamin angrily charged that Charlotte Cushman herself had written the *Herald*'s censures. It was not an unreasonable conclusion: Bennett often let policy shape his theatre notices, and Cushman acted as protector of her younger sister. But Cushman coolly denied it, dared Benjamin to show proof, and shrugged off his threats: "With regard to being 'hissed from the stage' as your note threatens, that is a matter requiring some time and trouble, and when done no satisfaction would accrue to yourself, and I think you have business of more importance." She certainly had no illusions about the men she had to work with: when in 1841 the theatre of Hamblin's chief rival burned down, leaving Hamblin in a very advantageous position, Cushman seems to have hazarded the guess that Hamblin had hired an arsonist.[24]

She also began early in her career to cultivate the good opinions of the genteel middle class — especially middle-class women. In the fall of 1836, just weeks after she landed her first real job with a theatre company, Cushman wrote a short story, "Excerpts from My Journal: The Actress," and sent it off to *Godey's Lady's Book*. *Godey's* well-known editor, Sarah Josepha Hale, liked it and published it. Cushman's heroine, Leoline, is the daughter of a merchant whose death has revealed his bankruptcy. Her brother refuses to be of help, and Leoline goes on the stage to support herself and her mother. Her one fatal step is not before the footlights but to the altar: she marries, and retires from the stage, only to discover that her hus-

band is a drunken brute. To escape his outrages, Leoline is forced to return to acting and soon dies of a broken heart. Cushman's story in effect urged *Godey's* readers to see that an actress might be a worthy, cultivated woman. And the little tale
had some autobiographical touches, from the bankrupt father and the daughter's
support of her mother to its pointedly self-referential title. At the same time Cushman insured herself against the possibility of another failure onstage by testing an
alternative resource in her pen, she boosted her acting career by soliciting public
sympathy and securing the notice of journalists. Cushman found this sort of self-
promotional publishing so worthwhile she continued to produce poems and other
short pieces for a number of years, even after her acting career had proven stable
and remunerative.[25]

Cushman took other steps to cultivate genteel society. In Philadelphia she
encouraged Susan to join a "female organization" for the sake of social connections. Afterward she had to endure backstage taunts from an irreverent old comedian who made ludicrous inquiries about "the Female Sacred Buttonhole Society," or the "Organization for Promoting the Entrance of Actresses into the Upper
Ten Sphere." Cushman would shoot back a "very meaning look."[26]

During her time in Philadelphia in the early 1840s she met Fanny Kemble
and carefully encouraged the relationship. She offered Kemble sympathy as her
marriage fell apart and in return benefitted from Kemble's advice and, more
important, from her Anglo-American society connections. As a fellow actor
recalled, Cushman had "fine tact in the management of people whom she considered necessary to her personal interests or professional advancements." Eventually her friendship with Kemble cooled: it seems that Cushman offered to
gather proof of Pierce Butler's infidelities, and when Fanny at first authorized the
search and then called it off, Charlotte felt hurt. Nevertheless it seems likely that
when Cushman sailed for England in 1844 she carried letters of introduction
from Fanny Kemble. She went armed, she recorded, with no less than seventy
letters, and these letters carried her among some of the "wealthiest and most
delightful" people. Charlotte wrote to her mother triumphantly that they were
"the very right kind of people to make me in every way respected." Her letters
and connections helped her prevail upon the manager of the Princess' Theatre to
give her a chance.[27]

Impressing the "right kind of people" was very much on Cushman's mind
after she first won her London laurels. She found the resulting social whirl
fatiguing, "for my reputation is abroad as somewhat clever and it keeps me in a
constant excitement to keep that up."[28] From titled aristocrats to the Carlyles
and the Brownings and the banker-poet Samuel Rogers, Cushman made connections and friends; once back in the United States she similarly took pride in

the fine society that welcomed her. The Boston intelligentsia remembered her vaguely as a young woman who had sung in the choir in Emerson's Second Church: now she socialized with the Henry Wadsworth Longfellows and the James T. Fields.

Achieving not just box-office but social success required artful suppression of Cushman's tougher side. After all, she had been the sort of hardy young tomboy who, writing to a friend at sixteen, mischievously wondered, "Have you said Devill or Cus-Dame since you got home?" She had rubbed elbows professionally with men like Thomas Hamblin, and she confidently offered to find evidence against Pierce Butler. In her new position, she had to be careful. In 1845, for example, she was in an agony of fear lest her name be linked with a woman whom she had often defended but whose "base conduct" now seemed likely to reflect badly on her. Similarly in Edinburgh in 1846 she took great pains to squelch rumors that her sister, Susan, who had a young son, was not properly married. She boldly displayed the marriage license to stop the talk.[29]

Eventually her campaign for respectability paid off: by the 1860s she was respected, even revered, and she enjoyed financial rewards and social prestige in proportion. The last years of her life found her building "Villa Cushman" at Newport and accepting homage from the Boston School Committee, which voted to name a school after her. At the school's opening she declared, "Nothing in all my life has so pleased me as this." Upon her death one eulogist compared her public influence favorably with that of the Hartford theologian Horace Bushnell.[30]

Her stage success and her relentless social climbing presented Cushman with the option of leaving the public eye and her professional career altogether. Flushed with triumph in the spring of 1845, in London, she immediately began scheming to retire from the stage, calculating it would take five years to accumulate a sufficient sum of money.[31] In fact, it took her seven: after 1852 she owned a fine home in Portman Square, London, and spent her winters in villas in Rome, but periodically she felt compelled to return to her work. Like many another woman who would succeed at great cost in carving out a public career, Cushman found it both lonely and laborious, but she was not made for idleness either. In 1857–58 she performed in a "farewell tour" of the United States; she did so again in 1860, and then returned to the stage for the benefit of the Civil War Sanitary Commission in 1863 and reappeared in New York in 1871. Cushman's returns and retirements became something of a joke in midcentury theatre. They characterized a woman oscillating between the ideals of the cultivated classes of which she had become a member, which specified that ladies did not work, and the pleasurable exercise of her own restless talents.

A FEMALE RICHELIEU

In the course of her early career Cushman had played an astonishing variety of roles, but as a star she became identified with just a few parts, which she played over and over again. Her greatest roles were all strong women. As a supporting actress Cushman had been thought unsuited to ingénue roles and was often cast as an older woman, in character parts, or as a man. She played the Queen in *Hamlet*, Miss Squeers in *Nicholas Nickleby*, Patrick in *The Poor Soldier*, and John Rolfe in *Pocahontas*. The question was, how could she expect to move up to play female leads, which so often were romantic parts? Cushman answered that question through the magnitude of her talents: she was capable of enacting prettiness, making her audience believe what their eyes did not tell them. Once an actor scheduled to play opposite Cushman encountered a very plain woman at rehearsal and took her for the actress' mother. Discovering his mistake, he felt certain that this Miss Cushman would be a terrible failure as the romantic heroine, but at curtain time he beheld a lovely girlish vision who was so mesmerizing he nearly missed his cue. More often Cushman preferred to find or create roles that did not resolve into a romantic marriage plot with a happily-ever-after conclusion. Cushman made major parts out of minor ones through the power of her acting and channeled her talents into a few roles that permitted her to represent strong, independent women.[32]

Cushman's greatest role was Meg Merrilies in the stage adaptation of Sir Walter Scott's popular novel *Guy Mannering* (fig. 18). Charlotte first played Meg in 1837 and continued to play the part as long as she appeared on the stage. *Guy Mannering* is set in Scotland, and the key to the melodramatic plot lies in the fact that the hero, Bertram, does not know his real identity, having been kidnapped as a youngster. He is in truth heir to Ellangowan castle, but a scheming lawyer has arranged his disappearance in order to gain the property. Bertram, now a young man, comes back to the area by chance, and Meg, his old gypsy nursemaid, recognizes him. The whole action of the play turns on her recognition and knowledge.[33]

Meg "deals wi' the devil, they say," and as the queen of the gypsies, she can make the outlaw band do her bidding. In one swooping bound she comes from nowhere to the center of the stage and stands there, a wizened old crone clutching a staff, staring at young Bertram. Finally he asks, "My good woman, do you know me?" "Better than you know yourself," she replies in a hollow tone. Throughout the rest of the play Meg reappears at crucial moments, intervening to save Bertram and foil the villain's planned usurpation.

Meg represents female power. As a nursemaid she stands for the power of nurturing domesticity and motherly love before which men may in effect be reduced

Fig. 18 Charlotte Cushman as Meg Merrilies. Harvard Theatre Collection.

to the helpless infants they once were. But Meg also possesses the power of knowledge—in this case, the knowledge of the outsider or the downtrodden, for although she is a domestic servant, she alone has the knowledge that is required to set society right. Free from familial and social ties—even the gypsies fear her—Meg is privy to the most hidden, private realities in ways that are unexplained and even mystic. Indifferent to place or profit for herself, she uses her knowledge only for good. Her haggard, knowing figure is reminiscent, one critic writes, of "the Scandinavian Nornae or the Greek Fates," the sibyl, the mermaid, the Cassandra, and the witch. As much as any other character in nineteenth-century imaginative literature or drama, Meg personifies, in Nina Auerbach's phrase, the "divine-demonic womanhood" that so haunted writers and artists—and presumably their audiences—in that era.[34]

Meg speaks fewer than five hundred words. Her leaping entrance, her wild manner, and her agonizing death after she is shot by one of the villains make the part a model of melodramatic action. In the end Meg dies content, having returned Henry Bertram to his rightful place as heir to Ellangowan. Meg was Cushman's most popular role and, though she once lamented that "with an out-landish dress and a trick or two" she could bring more money to the theatre than in her "finest characters," she was probably not really unhappy about continuing to play this frightening, magnetic figure. Because of Meg Merrilies, Cushman was called the "greatest melodramatic actress in the world."[35]

Her other powerful role was as Nancy in the stage adaptation of Charles Dickens' *Oliver Twist*. When first assigned the part in 1839, Cushman reportedly disappeared for several days into the notorious Five Points slum in New York, reemerging fully prepared to play the whore who clings to—and dies for—her last decent impulse. In his novel Dickens employed carefully muted language to signal to the more knowing of his readers that Nancy was a prostitute; more innocent readers might merely associate Nancy with the thievery of Fagin's boys. But onstage no such ambiguity could survive. Cushman "shrank from nothing" in the part. She had been around the theatre and seen the notorious third tier: she knew what prostitutes looked and sounded like, how they walked and held their bodies. Cushman created a Nancy whose hardbitten manner and seamy sexuality could not quite conceal a note of care and tenderness for the innocent boy Oliver. Once again the despised, downtrodden woman, an outsider in every way, held the power to unravel mystery and forestall evil. Nancy's death scene gave Cushman license to pull out all the melodramatic stops. When Sykes dragged her off-stage, the audience heard a scream and a fall. Sykes reentered and Nancy crept back after him, struggling, dying. Begging Sykes to kiss and forgive her, Nancy sounded "as if she spoke through blood."[36]

Walt Whitman, no stranger to the stronger scenes of urban life, found Cushman's Nancy simply "appalling." Cushman's "portrait of female depravity" was praised by another observer in terms that suggested that she had actually gone too far in its realization: Nancy was "fearfully natural, dreadfully intense, horribly real . . . too true." Before Cushman left for London, the old tragedian Junius Brutus Booth took her aside and told her not to play Nancy there—"It will give you a vulgar dash you will never get over"—and she followed his advice. Fearing to be identified with a part she played too well, Cushman seldom played Nancy again. In roles that came out of the bitterest realities of female experience Cushman was incomparable; two of her greatest triumphs were a cast-off old crone and a fallen woman, and she made women's sufferings the stuff of greatness.[37]

Cushman once outlined her ideal part: "I long to play a woman of strong ambition, who is at the same time very wily and diplomatic, and who has an opportunity of a great outburst when her plans are successful—in short, a female Richelieu."[38] No playwright ever provided her with such a role, and in fact she played only a few parts as a mature star, seldom venturing into anything new. Limited by her close attention to the dollar, she hesitated to try new material for fear it would prove unprofitable. But she was also stymied by the difficulty of getting parts that fitted her ambitions.

Edwin Forrest, her male counterpart at the pinnacle of American theatrical stardom, ran play contests and so secured a set of prize plays written specifically for him. Forrest (fig. 19) knew exactly what he wanted, and in plays like *Spartacus* and *Jack Cade*, he played the same part over and over again—the champion of the common man, the noble commoner, the rebel against tyranny, the American democrat. Deeply involved in Democratic Party politics, Forrest wanted to personify the strength and virtue of male citizenry. He did so through his prize plays and by emphasizing his physical being. By means of a strenuous program of athleticism he had converted himself from a skinny youth to a Herculean specimen. Forrest would step onstage and strike a pose showing off his rippling muscularity, and the admiring men in his audiences would burst into cheers before he ever spoke a line.[39]

For Cushman, however, there was no established female public to which she could attach herself as champion. Nor could her body serve as a token of what women held in common: pretty or plain, the female body, when thus on view, aroused anxiety or envious distinctions rather than female solidarity, oriented as it usually was toward winning and pleasing men. In short, it was not easy to imagine what a strong woman might look like, nor what sort of action she might be involved in. The undistinguished playwrights of the era could turn out what Edwin Forrest wanted, but Cushman's hopes escaped them. The only Richelieu-like woman of strong ambition Cushman consistently played was herself.[40]

Fig. 19 Edwin Forrest. Harvard Theatre Collection.

Onstage she recurred to the safety of Shakespeare, while she neglected a bril-liant role like Nancy because it was too vividly lower class. She settled into two great roles, first Lady Macbeth and later Queen Katherine in *Henry VIII*. But even there, Cushman took inspiration from the rough, raw edge of life she had seen as a young woman. Her Lady Macbeth was strong and muscular, "a pan-theress let loose" (fig. 20). One actor who played opposite her complained that she was "too animal," that she "pitched into" Macbeth. But her ideas about the murderous pair were shaped by the toughs and rowdies and sharp operators who circulated through places like the Bowery. Cushman believed that Macbeth and Lady Macbeth were drinking wine during much of the play, and she accordingly assumed an air of reckless intoxication. Macbeth, she once declared, was the "grandfather of all the Bowery villains!"[41]

Queen Katherine was a part Charlotte Cushman began to play regularly after 1847. Of all her great roles, this one was most compatible with conventional, gen-teel notions of women's passivity and domesticity. In the "noble, pious, and long-suffering queen, who in a position of unmerited abasement, knew how to bear

Fig. 20 Charlotte Cushman as Lady Macbeth. The lithographer has attempted, in vain, to capture Cushman's terrifying intensity. Harvard Theatre Collection.

herself royally,"[42] there was a defense of the "true" woman. But there was also, in Cranmer's foretelling of Elizabeth I's greatness, an appealing reference to a strong woman who would be "a pattern to all princes." And, more significant, the play licenses a burst of righteous indignation against the ignominious doings of men, since Katherine's strength of character takes shape against Wolsey's scheming and Henry's callous discarding of his loyal wife.

Again, Cushman's own life enabled her to bring a certain intensity to the part, for she knew something of men's fickleness and selfishness. In fact she had never known a man who was reliable. Her father virtually disappeared after his bankruptcy, leaving his wife and children to make their own way. When Elkanah Cushman finally died in 1841, Charlotte does not seem to have bothered to attend his funeral. She claimed to have fallen in love with a man once, in Albany, but she had to break it off when she found that his intentions were "not honorable." Worse yet was the fate of her younger sister, Susan—the pretty sister, her mother's favorite. After her father's bankruptcy, a man named Nelson Merriman, a friend of her father's, offered to adopt fourteen-year-old Susan. The adoption was refused, but the girl was put in his care. Merriman fell ill, and on his deathbed he proposed to marry Susan so that she could inherit his property. The family agreed and the marriage took place. A miraculous recovery ensued. Soon Susan was pregnant. Merriman disappeared and a horde of creditors descended, revealing that there was no property, only debts. It was an episode worthy of the worst mustache-twirling melodramatic villain, the kind modern critics are apt to dismiss as unrealistic. Charlotte, already supporting herself and her mother, took in Susan and her child. Before long Cushman enlisted her sister in a stage career, and Susan performed sweet, ingénue roles competently enough. But the two sisters never got along. Among their many differences was their differing susceptibility to patriarchal power: in life and in art Charlotte Cushman never played the fool.[43]

BREECHES

When Cushman went to London in 1844, she carried with her a letter from the theatre manager William Burton attesting that she was "undoubtedly the best breeches figure in America." Her greatest male role was Romeo, which she first played in Albany as a novice in her teens. Her portrayal of Romeo in London opposite her sister, Susan, as Juliet became *the* feature of the 1845–46 London season and placed Cushman on the "highest pinnacle of fame" (figs. 21–24). Contemporary accounts make it clear that Charlotte Cushman's Romeo was one of the nineteenth century's greatest Romeos by *any* performer, male or female. From her fencing skills to her amorous manners—"of so erotic a character that no man would have dared indulge in them"—Cushman made an utterly compelling Romeo.[44]

The part initially was risky for her precisely because she was able to be so realistically, relentlessly masculine. The eroticism of her Romeo's wooing caused whispers when she first tried it out in Edinburgh; her host felt obliged to write to Fanny Kemble for reassurance about Charlotte's reputation and "private virtue." By way of insurance, then, Cushman made sure that the London opening of *Romeo and Juliet* was billed in advance as an effort to restore the original Shakespearean text in place of the popular Garrick version. If the play should fail it could be explained as an antiquarian exercise. But it was no failure. The playwright Sheridan Knowles, watching in the audience, attested to the sensation:

> You recollect, perhaps, Kean's third act of Othello. Did you ever expect to see anything like it again? I never did, and yet I saw as great a thing last Wednesday night in Romeo's scene with the Friar, after the sentence of banishment, quite as great! . . . It was a scene of topmost passion; not simulated passion,—no such thing; real, palpably real; the genuine heart-storm was on,—on in wildest fitfulness of fury; and I listened and gazed and held my breath, while my blood ran hot and cold.

Charlotte Cushman was justly proud of her Romeo, though she played it only occasionally after her initial "retirement" in 1852 and abandoned it altogether before 1860, probably because her increasingly matronly figure was making it difficult for her to sustain the illusion.[45]

The playing of breeches parts by actresses was not unusual in early and mid nineteenth-century theatre. Cushman herself appeared in thirty different male roles, and during the period when she appeared as Romeo, no fewer than sixteen other actresses attempted the same part. Actors were understandably unenthusiastic about the popularity of breeches parts since they were deprived of choice male roles, but audiences liked it. A breeches part was the sort of thing an actress would want to do for her benefit, counting on it to fill the house.[46]

Such performances were popular at a time when American society otherwise required men and women to dress quite differently. Appearing on the street in male garb could get a woman arrested. Yet female cross-dressing—proscribed in the rest of society—was not just tolerated but popular in the theatre. When, for example, a woman named Emma Snodgrass strolled the streets of Boston in 1852 wearing pants and a man's hat, she was arrested, but the *Daily Bee* remarked, "It is said she desires to appear on the stage. Cannot some of our managers negotiate with her?"[47]

The traditional explanation for this anomaly is that in breeches parts women could adopt the doublet and hose, show their legs, and titillate the predominately male audience. In this view, a woman playing the male role aimed only to call attention to her real sex and to focus attention on her anatomy. There is no doubt that some actresses were happy to exploit their looks and legs in this manner and

Fig. 21 Charlotte and Susan Cushman as Romeo and Juliet. The artist for the *Illustrated London News* chose to portray Cushman as she appeared to the audience—as a man. Harvard Theatre Collection.

that this is part of the reason that breeches parts were popular. The eighteenth-century actress Peg Woffington's Sir Harry Wildair was remembered for having "turned the heads of the beaux." And when Ellen Tree, a contemporary of Cushman's, appeared in a male role, she was praised as "not a whit masculine." But this explanation does not go far to explain Cushman's particular success, for she—one of the greatest breeches performers—was not noted for her sex appeal and had an extensive female following. And even before Cushman's star rose, the "most respectable female audiences" reportedly received an actress playing a breeches part "with much apparent satisfaction."[48]

Fig. 22 The Cushman sisters again. This artist tries to make the lithograph convey the gender ambiguity of a woman in a male role. Harvard Theatre Collection.

Fig. 23 A third version of the Cushman sisters as Romeo and Juliet, in which the artist chooses to give Charlotte's Romeo a notably feminine appearance. Harvard Theatre Collection.

Fig. 24 Staffordshire figurine of Charlotte and Susan
Cushman as Romeo and Juliet. This curio was part of the
considerable market in stage-related collectables and memo-
rabilia. The Art Collection of the Folger Shakespeare
Library.

A second explanation for the appeal of these parts might be found in the
romantic friendships that often flourished between women in the early and mid
nineteenth century. Intense same-sex relationships were not subject to the
heavy taboos and moral opprobrium that were later visited upon them. Dis-
plays of affection between women and lifelong relationships that approximated
marriage seemed pure and worthy to contemporaries. Only in the 1880s and
1890s would romantic unions between women begin to be labeled "congenital
inversion" or "perversion." Although such relationships between women were
seldom marked by cross-dressing, historians of sexuality have pointed out that
when a homosexual subculture first began to take shape in the years between
1880 and 1920, it often involved transvestism, as one of the simplest ways to
assert one's interest in the same sex was to dress like the opposite sex. In Char-

lotte Cushman's day, lesbianism was not yet defined nor was cross-dressing seen as its emblem, but some part of the theatre audience may have been inspired by just such interests, however inarticulate or unacknowledged they were.[49]

Cushman herself was powerfully attracted to women. Visiting Providence once, she met a woman at dinner: "The loveliest woman I ever looked upon. . . . What a lucky thing I am not of the other sex, for a heavy mortgage would have been made upon her from this hour. As it was, it almost deprived me of appetite for my dinner." Once successful, she entered into a series of relationships with women. She and Matilda Hays exchanged vows of "celibacy and eternal attachment to each other" in what Elizabeth Barrett Browning called a "Boston marriage." But as Hays's career faltered and she became more and more like a dependent Victorian wife, the relationship faded. Cushman then began an enduring twenty-year partnership with Emma Stebbins, a sculptor whose separate career seems to have helped to maintain a vital balance between them. Cushman sometimes affected male fashions offstage, including a man's collar, cravat, and boots— but not pants—and in Rome she surrounded herself with a group of young women that one acquaintance called her "harem (scarem)." Even though these friendships were not generally regarded with suspicion, Cushman felt obliged to be discreet, and most of her public audience probably knew little of this lifestyle. There was, however, nothing covert about a stage performance in male garb, and it seems quite possible that Cushman's own interest in women made it an attractive part for her to play, just as women who shared a preference for other women might have found her Romeo especially interesting.[50]

It seems clear that breeches parts had yet another valence, a third source of audience appeal even more powerful than the other two. Charlotte Cushman's uncannily accurate male impersonation raised important questions about gender and identity, and raised them in the only setting in which they could be both serious and nonthreatening. With her height and her husky voice, Cushman could look and sound like a man, and she knew how to move like one, too. An actor who appeared with her explained that when most women played breeches parts they were apt to "betray their female origin" by "quaint little movements" of the knees and legs. Not Cushman: her movements were bold, her limbs straight and "strident." One woman who saw Cushman in the part in 1858 noted that "a pair of handsome legs has oftener been the instigation to 'get up' in Romeo than any impression of intellectual capacity to do justice to the part," but Cushman was different: "in face, form and general make-up a most perfect specimen of the impetuous and yet loving Romeo." One British critic who saw her performance mused that Romeo might *best* be played by a woman, since "females together give us an image of the desire of the lovers of Verona, without suggesting a thought of vice."

The Victorian association of women with sexual purity was so strong that the woman playing a man actually was allowed to be more realistically erotic than a man in the same part—always assuming that the actress herself was believed to be pure. Cushman's carefully cultivated reputation was crucial to her success in this ambiguous role.[51]

The marginality of the stage licensed episodes that permitted women in the audience to identify with male talk and walk and gesture and motive—and yet escape male censure. Of another actress in a breeches part, Charles Dickens wrote in wonderment, "There is the strangest thing in it that ever I have seen on the stage. The boy, Pippo, by Miss Wilton . . . is so stupendously like a boy, and unlike a woman, that it is perfectly free from offense. . . . A thing that you *can not* imagine a woman's doing at all; and yet the manner, the appearance, the levity, impulse, and spirits of it, are so exactly like a boy, that you cannot think of anything like her sex in association with it." Nina Auerbach notes that, although Dickens was an archtraditionalist on women's roles and rights, "the trespass to which he responded savagely as both man and author moved him to awed admiration on the stage." Of course that same marginality licensed men to ogle women's legs. And neither possibility cancelled out the other.[52]

Charlotte Cushman in breeches took the central problematic of the theatre for women—its insistence on their bodies and its consequent tendency to reduce them to sexual beings—and turned it inside out, making gender identity itself subject to reflection. The stage was the one place in nineteenth-century culture where such identity was open to question or was at least "in play." Antebellum Americans believed in what modern critics call essentialism—the assumption that men are "essentially" one thing and women "essentially" something quite different. Essentialism went out the window when Cushman's Romeo trod the boards. Her Romeo undermined the assumption that gender was natural, inborn, undeniable, and suggested instead that it was something assumed, learned, performed. Ironically, she was able to do this only because her own (probably lesbian or bi-) sexuality was invisible to the society around her and, perhaps, to herself.

Of course an evening at the theatre is not a philosophical exercise. Something is lost when an idea is only demonstrated, and not set forth in language and argument, but something is gained as well in the direct simplicity of believable performance. The messages about gender of Cushman's Romeo were inarticulate, and they undoubtedly were muted by and submerged in other themes of the play. But the cross-dressing employed by Cushman and other actresses had a disturbing power precisely because they were playing serious roles in mainstream theatre. Later in the century, under the taboo of lesbianism, breeches parts would disappear from what was coming to be called the "legitimate" stage, and cross-dressing would be safely contained within entertainment forms like vaudeville, minstrelsy, and burlesque, whose comic tone and episodic structure assured the audience that they need not take this illusion of women-who-act-like-men too seriously. Cushman, in contrast, was always intensely in earnest, in her onstage roles and her public persona alike.[53]

Charlotte Cushman used the potential of the theatre to achieve independence and great economic rewards for herself and to communicate to her audience some sense of women's dignity, power, and self-transforming capacities. She took the liberating possibilities of the commercial stage to their limits, demonstrating that even if breeches parts had originated to titillate men and to present women's bodies as sexual objects, they might also be used by and for women to raise questions about the nature of gender itself. In playing Romeo, Cushman conquered the "body problem" by demonstratively disconnecting the sex of the body from the gender it might enact or assume. But her achievement took advantage of a particular historical moment before breeches were confined to humorous skits and their meaning largely (though never wholly) muted by silliness and marginality. Even before that, the dress reform efforts of the women's rights movement had made "wearing the pants" too much of a political statement to be tolerated by male audiences unless it was being lampooned. By the 1850s Bloomerism had already become a popular subject for theatrical spoofing.[54]

Cushman proved that a woman could survive the pitfalls of the commercializing stage and win success, but she paid a price. She was tough, manipulative, and more than a little selfish—none of which could be admitted in the public persona she crafted so carefully. She was resented. Jealous actors deplored her Romeo, calling it "epicene" and "painful." An unsympathetic press notice once declared that "in point of sex" she was "almost amphibious." An acquaintance recalled, "She liked to drive a close bargain and get the best of it, she liked to win and dominate and control." In short, she was a lot like the tough, successful men of her profession. The tragedian William Macready, himself a colossal egotist, wrote disapprovingly, "This woman is full of the idea of her own importance." Cushman's admirers praised her as a noble woman, but a detractor was probably closer to the truth when he called her "that most dangerous member of society, a strong-willed and large-brained woman." Through eloquence and power and sheer imaginative force, she made herself great. In her unromantic roles and her unattractive body, Cushman was everywoman—transformed and triumphant, making them all—detractors and worshipers, men and women alike—admire and cheer. No wonder women loved her.[55]

Yet there was a limit to what Charlotte Cushman could or would do with her success. Once able to support herself and her immediate family, she took on more dependents, in a kind of domestic empire-building. At the height of her career (fig. 25) she allowed financial considerations to curb her artistic reach and let respectability cramp her style as well; she spent much of her mature life in semi-retirement, demanding high ticket prices that cut her off from the working women who were formerly her peers. Cushman did not use her success to challenge the terms of the new commercial entertainment world or to make parts of it women's own. She founded no theatre, and she even seems to have discouraged other women from trying to emulate her achievements. Cushman's acknowledged genius, like that of Marie Curie among scientists, became the rationale for discouraging other women from making the attempt.[56]

Louisa May Alcott, who knew Charlotte Cushman and followed her career, used her fiction both to glorify Cushman's achievements and to discourage other women from theatrical careers. Alcott incorporated the proscription against acting into her novel *Work*, in which the heroine, Christie, is successful as an actress but feels she must leave the stage because of its moral costs. Alcott implied in the novel what Cushman said explicitly in a letter of 1861: it is "so hard for woman to get on as an artist . . . unless by giving up virtue." Yet in her later novel *Jo's Boys* Alcott presented a Cushman-figure, "Miss Cameron," who was pure and admirable in every way—and utterly exceptional. She gave Miss Cameron the task of advising a young woman with stage ambitions. The aging star told the younger woman, "I've had to do it for many like you, and most of them have never forgiven me, though my words have proved true, and they are what I advised them to be—good wives and happy mothers in quiet homes." Miss Cameron's message was simple: without *genius* a stage career ought not to be thought of.[57]

Perhaps Miss Cameron was right. In a theatre increasingly learning to commodify its offerings, Charlotte Cushman was able to function as a commodity of her own design, but women of lesser talents might find it difficult or impossible to do likewise, to resist being reduced to their looks and their bodies. In any case, to make the self into a commodity was to accept the limits of market demand in a marketplace where men had nearly all the money and power. Perhaps it did require genius to confound their desires and still succeed.

Throughout her career Cushman in effect acted out the most generous interpretation of the theatre's positive potential for women, and acted it before audiences where women were a larger presence than ever before. But no other woman performer could reproduce the particular combination of good timing, fierce determination, and boundless talent out of which Cushman forged her stardom. At the same time, stardom, which had revealed its positive aspects in Fanny Kemble, revealed its limitations in Charlotte Cushman. Starring was by definition not replicable by ordinary women, and, moreover, in enshrining a few talented

Fig. 25 Charlotte Cushman. This cabinet card photo probably dates from around 1870. Cushman once complained of "The libel which has been perpetrated upon me in the way of tyranny of photographs. . . . I am a plain woman but don't like to go down to posterity so much more ugly than my looking glass and some of the critics tell me I am" (Cushman to Miss Booth, 27 July 1874, Harvard Theatre Collection). Photograph is from the collection of the author.

individuals, it served to obscure the more ordinary course of commodification. Watching and listening to Charlotte Cushman, the female audience might gain inspiration, ambition, tools for thinking. But they might also learn to gauge the distance between the exceptional woman and the ordinary one, to see that gap as Cushman herself evidently saw it—as unbridgeable.

5.
Segmentation:
Many
Theatres

When Benjamin Baker, the prompter at the Olympic Theatre in New York, cobbled together a script for his benefit performance in February 1848, he used the well-worn plot device of a greenhorn's visit to the big city. The principal characters in Baker's *A Glance at New York* were the country rube and his sophisticated city friend, but Baker spiked the play with local color by adding a third male lead, a truculent New York City volunteer fireman named Mose. The working-class audience in the Olympic pit immediately recognized one of their own in Mose's costume, hair style, and up-to-the-minute street slang. At first they were silent, fearing that, as the Olympic was the home of burlesque, Mose was meant as a figure of fun. But when Mose spoke nobly about rescuing a child from a fire, they knew they could relax and cheer for this new working-class hero.[1]

Mose the Bowery B'hoy, played by Frank Chanfrau, resembled a street tough in his readiness for a "muss" or fight, but he also was a hard-working tradesman, full of contempt for those who sat idle, yet capable of waxing sentimental over an abandoned baby in a basket. Chanfrau's "astonishing accuracy" as Mose came easily to an actor who had grown up on the Bowery and had several brothers in volunteer fire companies. Mose may even have been modeled after a real fireman, a well-known brawler named Moses Humphrey. The play followed Mose enjoying the pleasures of working-class New York: Mose visits the Bowery Theatre; reads sensational novels; enjoys minstrel shows, restaurants, and saloons. *A Glance at New York* was an immediate hit, and over the next fifteen years thirty or more plays featuring Mose or his Philadelphia counterpart, Jakey, followed.[2]

After the play had run for a month, Baker revised it, adding several new scenes and new characters. Only at that point did Mose acquire his female opposite number, "Lize," played by Mary Taylor (fig. 26). "Our Mary" Taylor was a beloved favorite at the Olympic, perhaps as much for her "luscious" voice and charming manner as for acting talent. In the new version of the play, Lize and Mose shared a warm regard; in an aside to the audience Mose indicates his "strong suspicions I'll have to get slung to her one of these days." When Lize and Mose meet on the street in the morning on the way to work, they discuss the merits of a novel called *Matilda the Disconsolate*: Mose, having already finished it, recommends the part where "Lucinda stabs de Count." Later Lize sings songs she has heard at the minstrel shows, and when Mose treats her to a snack, she orders nine doughnuts with her coffee. She shares with Mose his most endearing trait — a hearty, matter-of-fact self-esteem. When Mose compliments her with "You're a gallus gal," she readily responds, "I ain't nothin' else."[3]

Like Mose, Lize reflected the social realities of the city; an increasing number of women, especially young unmarried women, worked for wages. But the "Bowery gal" was an afterthought, and later versions substantially altered the character or dropped her altogether. When Chanfrau went into management for himself, he presented *New York as It Is*, a Mose play in which Lize was replaced by Katy, a lady's maid betrothed to Mose. Another Mose play presented in the fall of 1848, *The Mysteries and Miseries of New York*, again featured Chanfrau but Lize had metamorphosed into "Big Lize," a prostitute and a thief, albeit one with a heart of gold. And another Mose play called *Linda the Cigar Girl* (1859) had a working-girl heroine named Linda, who fought off the persecutions of a lecherous villain and vowed "death before dishonor" as Mose arrived to save her. Just as women still remained a small presence in the workplace, Lize's character was not really essential to the Mose plays.[4]

Mose the Bowery B'hoy signaled the segmentation of American theatre audiences along class lines, first at the Olympic itself. Originally the Olympic had been attended by both the elite and the working class, and part of the charm of the first Mose play was the pit's delight "to see a congenial vulgarity thrust under the nostrils of a better class of people." Although working-class audience members found something that mirrored their lives and validated their ways, middle-class patrons, unable to identify with Mose and Lize in the same way, drifted away from the Olympic. The audience changed and "the boxes no longer shone with the elite of the city."[5]

As American theatre approached midcentury, it broke into segments along lines that registered increasing differences in American society itself. Some theatre, like the museum theatres or the Mose plays, directed itself toward one

MISS MARY TAYLOR & MR F. S. CHANFRAU

Fig. 26 Frank Chanfrau as Mose, the Bowery B'hoy, and Mary Taylor as Lize, the Bowery Gal. Given the poor quality of the lithography, it is fortunate that Mose can be readily identified by his hat, shirtsleeves, hair, and boots. Harvard Theatre Collection.

class. Some catered to Irish or German audiences. Given the working-class status of those groups, ethnicity stood as a rough proxy for class. And some entertainments like minstrelsy and burlesque originated in working-class precincts but derived their energy from the very fact that they could transcend class differences.

Audience segmentation also proceeded along gender lines in the 1840s. But it yielded no women's theatre, because women did not have the economic and social independence to constitute a separate audience. The split that emerged was not between women's theatre and men's, but rather between gender-integrated mainstream theatres and a new kind of sexually charged entertainment for men. In the "model artist" shows performance was for the first time based directly on the commercialized display of the female body designed to titillate male audiences. Only a minor presence in male-dominated working-class audiences, women were on center stage as sexual objects in these shows. The developing patterns of entertainment segmentation were not advantageous to women, nor were the new audience dynamics that accompanied them.

WORKING-CLASS THEATRE IN NEW YORK AND ELSEWHERE

By the mid—1840s the New York theatre audience began to fragment noticeably. In 1844 a critic in the *Spirit of the Times* wrote that the drama was reviving on a "division of labor" basis, because the tastes of the community were diversified: "The 'Corinthian' patronizes the opera, the literary, the legitimate, and the million go in for the national, the horrible, and the funny." As the historian Lawrence Levine has pointed out, the pattern of audience segmentation that was getting under way in the 1840s extended far beyond theatre and ultimately resolved itself into a great and enduring polarity between elite and popular culture—highbrow and lowbrow. This differentiation was partly the result of the middle-class drive for status through the "sacralization of culture" that Levine documents. Certainly the ostentatious respectability of the museum theatres reflected just such middle-class desires. But it was also the product of working-class audience preferences, as the story of the Mose plays suggests.[6]

More critical than any class self-consciousness, whether working-class or middle-class, was the increasingly routine calculus by which class differences in taste were preceived as profit opportunities. Entertainment entrepreneurs were coming to understand market segmentation—the process by which capitalist enterprise seeks to minimize fluctuations in demand by targeting specific segments of a larger market and catering to particularized demands. They were learning to match theatrical "products" with the markets constituted by divergent social groups.[7] Catering to specialized subaudiences was also motivated by heightened friction between social classes. The traditional function of the playhouse as a place where community politics were represented became problematic in the 1830s. Theatre riots began to take on a distinctly more menacing aspect as a general wave of violence associated with labor unrest, electioneering, and attacks on abolitionists spread through American cities. New York saw significant theatre riots in 1831, 1834, 1836, 1844, and 1846. In the Astor Place riot in 1849 more than twenty people were killed when the militia opened fire on a crowd of working-class partisans of Edwin Forrest protesting the appearance of his haughty rival, the English tragedian William Macready at the Astor Place Opera House, a theatre associated with what its opponents called a white-gloved aristocracy.[8]

The emergence of marked class differences rendered political confrontations within the playhouse, always rowdy, increasingly dangerous and even deadly. Since no calculating businessman—and managers increasingly fit that category—wanted riot in his playhouse, they sought an easy way to avoid it by catering to one class or the other but not both. Class divisions in the city were in effect making it harder to achieve a common culture, but the process was accelerated or exacerbated by the logic of market segmentation, according to which there was no incentive to achieve one entertainment for all.

Working-class theatre, which began at the Bowery Theatre (fig. 27), and flourished on New York's East Side at the Chatham, the New Bowery, and other less enduring playhouses, was gender-integrated, but women constituted a relatively small part of the audience for financial reasons. Since few women worked for wages, and fewer still earned a living wage, the price of theatre tickets normally had to come out of the earnings of husbands and fathers. The wages of a craftsman or a mechanic, although they might take him to the theatre readily, could only with difficulty stretch to cover his family, and the wages of unskilled laborers would be even less likely to accommodate a family outing. A journalist who sketched the typical patrons of the New Bowery Theatre presented a family group: A "sturdy mechanic, who has been shoeing horses all day, perhaps," brought his wife and three or four "sprouts." "The wife is a hearty-looking dame, neatly but plainly arrayed, yet showing in her care-worn features that life is no holiday pastime with her."[9] Unmarried working men, especially those from the skilled trades, seem to have been frequent attendees, not only because their wages stretched further but also because they lived in boarding houses whose cramped rooms offered little space for anything but sleeping and were probably unheated during the winter. As the historian Richard Stott has pointed out, antebellum working-class culture centered around the activities of young men with a few hours to kill after supper. Since saloons offered little opportunity to sit down, the more comfortable theatre was often the choice, even if the play was not a special favorite.[10]

Wherever industrialization created concentrations of young men living in boarding houses, the demand for theatre intensified. In 1852, for example, the city of Worcester was presented with a petition urging licensing of a new theatre. The population had doubled in the previous seven years, and the mechanics associated with new industry enthusiastically urged the approval of the theatre. Addressing some lingering puritanical opposition, one Worcester alderman explained his vote: "He would prefer to have no threatres, no bowling saloons, no oyster saloons, but in a population like ours, where there was so many young men without families who must and will have some place for evening resort, he, from what he had seen of the Museum [theatre in Lowell] in two visits, preferred that the young men should be there than at the other places mentioned."[11]

A young man attended the theatre alone or in the company of other men. In

Fig. 27 Interior of the Bowery Theatre, ca. 1856. Working-class theatre drew fewer women patrons than theatre aimed at the middle class. Harvard Theatre Collection.

A Glance at New York, for example, Mose proposes that a group of three young men go to the Bowery Theatre, but he does not take Lize there. A few young working women were beginning to live free of family surveillance and to "walk out" with men of their acquaintance as a kind of prelude to courting. Yet it was still compromising, risky, or taken as a sign of betrothal for an unmarried woman to go with a man to a place of public amusement; the phenomenon of the "date" would develop only after the Civil War, becoming established by the end of the century. Boys who could scrape up the money went to the theatre on their own; newsboys seem to have been especially faithful and voluble attendees. The *New*

Fig. 28 Mary Taylor, a favorite at Mitchell's Olympic Theatre. Early photographs of stage performers often reveal individuals of quite ordinary physical appearance. Probably the expansion of photography itself was the means by which the eye was "educated" to demand higher standards. Harvard Theatre Collection.

York Herald declared, "The theatre is almost the only amusement of the working man," and "to the working boy it is Elysium." No wonder that working-class theatres, with their disproportionately male audiences, were the last to retain the all-male pit.[12]

Constituting such a distinct minority, women in working-class theatre audiences could easily be overlooked. Walt Whitman wrote of the Bowery Theatre audience as if it were all male, although Charlotte Cushman noticed plenty of women in the same playhouse. A journalist referred to the crowd at the opening of the New Bowery Theatre in 1859 as "every man and boy of them." Another journalist spoke of "these broad-shouldered, lithe-limbed, steel-muscled men and boys of the East Side," yet he eventually noticed some women present and had to amend his assessment: "There are ladies here—true ladies, wives and mothers of whom worthy husbands and promising children are justly proud. Perhaps they slave in shops or in stores, or wear out the weary day in the home drudgery of large families." Even the mob outside the Astor Place Opera House on the night of the riot there contained women, although they are routinely overlooked in accounts of the action.[13]

Nevertheless, the predominance of men in the working-class audience prompted efforts to address specifically male tastes. Some actresses discovered that their most important skill was developing gestures laced with sexual overtones. At the Olympic in 1844, Sarah Timm became the darling of the "pittites" and drew approving "hi-hi's" from them by "a familiar glance or a well-timed wink," while Mary Taylor (fig. 28) was best loved by the "aristocrats of the dress circle," whom she rewarded with "the tenderest and archest side-long looks." After Mrs. Timm left, Mary Taylor and Constantia Clarke became involved in an intense rivalry for the affections of the b'hoys in the pit who had been Mrs. Timm's followers. No comparable rivalry addressed women's interests.[14]

ETHNICITY, RACE, AND CLASS

Having discovered that class-based theatre was profitable, theatrical entrepreneurs experimented with theatre organized around ethnicity and race. German-language theatre emerged from the amateur drama clubs and singing societies that flourished among German immigrants in New York. In 1840 there were the beginnings of irregular, semiprofessional performances in German staged in hired halls, and in 1854 German professional theatre settled into a permanent home at the Stadttheater on the Bowery. It was the largest theatre in New York at the time, and to the disgust of German intellectual emigrés it specialized in melodramas and farces. Other German-language theatres occasionally sprang up to offer competition, and a wide range of quasi-theatrical musical entertainments were offered in German beer gardens as well.[15]

Irish theatre was less segregated but still well-defined. A succession of touring Irish stars, beginning with Tyrone Power in the 1830s, won enduring popularity in plays like *Rory O'More* and *Born to Good Luck*. Power died in 1841, but he was succeeded by John Collins, John Brougham, Barney Williams, George Mossop, and John Drew. These "stage Irishmen" developed and passed down their own special style of comedy and always appeared in plays whose settings and themes were unambiguously Irish. While Power charmed all theatregoers, his successors became increasingly identified with low comedy and working-class audiences. Although the Irish comedians were only visiting stars rather than the nuclei of a separate Irish theatre, their repertoire and audience appeal were quite distinctive.[16]

With minstrelsy, entrepreneurs introduced race as the organizing principle for popular entertainment for white audiences. Blackface song-and-dance routines, as pioneered by T. D. Rice in the late 1820s, had long been popular entr'acte diversions; after the Virginia Minstrels opened an independent show in New York in February 1843, minstrelsy emerged as a separate entertainment form. Minstrel shows featured white men who corked their faces and performed songs and dances inspired by or borrowed directly from African-American folk music. The lively, toe-tapping music was the most potent source of minstrelsy's appeal, but the minstrels also offered humor, in the form of comic skits, parodies, and slapstick. By pretending to present the "real" African-American through characters who were foolish, incompetent, and ugly, minstrelsy reassured its white audience of their own superiority, regardless of class. Although minstrelsy had its complexities, and even incorporated moments that invited cross-racial identification, its prevailing racism operated to transcend social class among whites. Minstrels played to working-class audiences at the Chatham and to middle-class audiences at museums like Barnum's. They toured England and played for Queen Victoria. By 1848 New York supported five major minstrel companies and "heaven knows how many inferior bands tucked away in side-street or alley."[17]

Of course there was no comparable theatre developed to appeal to black audiences, although the players dispossessed from the African Grove Theatre in 1823 played occasionally in rented halls. African-Americans were not only too few in number and too impoverished to constitute an attractive market, but also were liable to violent reprisals for any public exercise of cultural self-assertion. Even attending white theatre was problematic, for although some New York theatres had separate "colored galleries," the rest seem to have barred African-Americans altogether. What might be accessible had little to do with the black audience's own tastes: there is some evidence, for example, that African-Americans attended minstrel shows. Thus, because audience segmentation was both market-driven and reflective of prevailing social distinctions, it recognized and catered to some social groups while rendering others culturally invisible.[18]

The theatrical genre of burlesque had its beginnings in the cheap "shilling" theatres of the early 1840s, especially the Olympic. At Mitchell's Olympic and its later imitators, burlesque spoofed anything that was popular and respected. Innocent of any connotation of sexual display, burlesques were brief comic pieces in rhymed couplets, studded with puns. Since irreverent laughter is a classic cultural weapon of the poor against the rich, burlesque might seem like a natural working-class entertainment form. In fact, however, it took its edge from the uneasy tension between high and low, elite and popular cultures then emerging, and it flourished by dissolving class tensions in laughter.[19]

Burlesque's strategy was to find a specific comic target, treat it with cool impudence, and keep the humor moving so rapidly that if one joke fell flat the next one could pick up the mood and restore the pace. It was crucial to select subjects everyone could feel comfortable laughing at. Burlesquing theatre itself, or high culture, was popular. Actors in *The Humpback* parodied Fanny Kemble's performance as Julia in *The Hunchback*. William Macready and P. T. Barnum were caricatured, as were Thomas Hamblin's Bowery and his puffing advertisements. *Lucia di Lammermoor* became *Lucy Did Sham a Moor*, while Byron was satirized in *Man-Fred*, and Dickens in *Boz, or, A Man Over-Bored*. The pretensions of white European civilization could serve as material, so long as they were tucked safely in the distant past. *Columbus et Filibustero* reduced the voyage of discovery to a crude scramble for gold. Most burlesques were never published and have been lost, but John Brougham's *Pocahontas* script, a comic send-up of Longfellow's "Hiawatha," gives some sense of what the fun was all about:

Now the natives knowing nothing
Of the benefits intended
By this foreign congregation
Who had come so far to show them
In what darkness they were dwelling,
And how much obliged they were to
These disinterested people
Who had journeyed to enlighten
Their unfortunate condition
Through those potent, triunited
Anglo-Saxon civilizers,
Rum, Gunpowder, and Religion.[20]

With the b'hoys in the pit and the elite in the boxes, the burlesque audience at the Olympic was an unsteady amalgamation that sometimes threatened to explode. Twice Mitchell produced satires that pulled his audience apart, once in 1840 with *Sparing With Specie*, too obviously a statement on the presidential contest between Van Buren and Harrison, and once in a burlesque about Wall Street speculators which the b'hoys liked so well their counterparts in the boxes took offense.[21]

Burlesque indeed seemed especially congenial to working-class tastes. The plays offered in 1852 at the Chatham Street Theatre, which catered to a working-class audience, were described as a mixture of "the horrible and the burlesque." Minstrelsy brought forth blackface burlesques of Hamlet and Othello. But the popularity of the burlesque sensibility across class lines can scarcely be overestimated. The historian Constance Rourke has written, "Through the 1840s and fifties ... the legitimate theatre came to a standstill, and many reasons were found for this condition. . . . The truth was that a vigorous burlesque had usurped the stage." Burlesque could flourish only among audiences who knew the solemn or sentimental originals it spoofed; it testified therefore to a moment in which theatrical segmentation was still partial and imperfect, when audiences could laugh at both their own tastes and those of others.[22]

WOMEN IN THE WORKING-CLASS THEATRE

The sectors of theatre linked directly or indirectly to the working class tended to present women as passive or insignificant when they were not indulging in humor at women's expense. Lize, though not central to the Mose plays, was at least spunky and admirable; other female figures seem to have been less well-served. The one play Mose refers to admiringly, *Don Cesar de Bazan*, had no strong female roles and focused on the exploits of a hero who was—of all things—the greatest swordsman of his day. The two hits of Frank Chanfrau's first managerial season after his breakthrough as Mose were another Mose play and *Rosina Meadows*, a melodrama whose heroine was seduced and abandoned, and then died. Chanfrau, playing her seducer, was strangled in the last scene by her vengeful father; the girl herself, an utterly passive symbol of innocence defiled, was reduced to an object of contest between the men.[23]

Even when women acted boldly, their actions were motivated by class or ethnic concerns. In *Ireland as It Is*, for example, an old woman named Judy O'Trot, about to lose her land to a mean and deceitful land agent, goes up to London to see the landlord in person. She bursts in on an elegant party, pleads her case, and returns home with a new lease at a nominal rent. "I'm an ancient and modern hero of a woman," Judy boasts, but her action is justified by the need to set old

Ireland right, a task that can only be completed in the play by two men, the hero, Dan O'Carolan, and the landlord himself, Lord Squander. The scene from sensational fiction that Mose recommends to Lize in which "Lucinda stabs de Count" similarly set a woman's bold actions within the confinement of class battles. Regular readers of sensational fiction would have understood the scene in this way: the provocation for the stabbing is that the count has made an attempt on Lucinda's "honor." And when the heroine acts in her own self-defense, she also represents her class in repelling the hateful impositions of the aristocracy. Although men could also act out of group loyalty, male characters tended to be more individuated and more central to the plot—like Mose, rather than Lize.[24]

In minstrelsy, performed by all-male casts, some women were represented by men in drag as demanding and ridiculously ugly black "wenches"; the minstrels also sang longingly of pretty "yaller gals." In either portrayal, the minstrels made women into dehumanized, interchangeable objects, as in the minstrel song Lize sings:

My wife dies—I'll get another
Pretty yaller gal—just like t'other.

As the literary critic Eric Lott has noted, the "emancipatory" moments of minstrelsy, where black and white men made common cause, were "conducted in the realm of male mastery—courtship plots at best, misogynist joking at worst—in other words, over the bodies of women." The historian Robert Toll concludes that "women, like Negroes, provided one of the few stable 'inferiors' that assured white men of their status."[25]

The malaprop-ridden "stump speeches" so integral to minstrel humor frequently focused on the subject of women's rights; it was, in fact, the only serious subject which the minstrels repeatedly lampooned in the ante-bellum period. In April 1848, for example, a comic piece by John Brougham entitled *Romance and Reality* featured a character named Barbary Manley, a maiden lady and member of the Social Reform Association who has been "carried away by that popular fallacy, 'the Rights of Woman.'" In a burlesque entitled *1940* the main character was transported one hundred years into the future via mesmeric trance to find that women had "assume[d] the prerogatives of men and the males are degraded into ridiculous specimens of effeminacy." The idea was appealing enough to be reworked five years later in a burlesque titled *The Mirror of Truth*. There was no parallel vein of stage humor burlesquing men. Indeed, one of the prejudices Anna Cora Mowatt had to surmount when she wrote her comic hit *Fashion* in 1845 was the idea that "it takes a *man* to write a comedy—No woman can!" Constance Rourke's argument that women "played no essential role in the long sequence of the comic spirit in America" is an overstatement but it does direct attention to women's disadvantaged position vis à vis stage humor, so much of which was developed for predominately male working-class audiences.[26]

MODEL ARTISTS

In 1847, at about the same time that middle-class theatres were banishing prostitutes and cleaning up double-entendre language, a new type of entertainment emerged that catered specifically to all-male audiences. In "model artist" shows women clad only in close-fitting tights or leotards stood motionless in imitation of classical statuary. Sometimes they were separated from the audience by a thin sheet of gauze; certainly the spectators were supposed to be able to entertain the illusion that the women on display were naked.[27]

"Tableaux vivants" were an old theatrical tradition and a popular parlor game as well. For a decade or more "living reproductions" of ancient sculpture or classical paintings had been offered occasionally at circuses or as entr'acte material at the minor theatres in New York; the models were usually men of athletic build. But when Hiram Powers' statue *The Greek Slave* was exhibited in more than a dozen American cities and viewed by more than 100,000 people in the mid-1840s, a few canny theatre managers saw new possibilities, for Powers' *Slave* was a naked woman. Bennett's *Herald*, which initially gave the model artists favorable press, attributed their popular acceptance to the influence of Powers' statue: "The mass of our community have no particular predilection for cold marble," said the *Herald*, but they found "the exhibition of living men and women" fascinating. In the fall of 1847 model artist exhibits began appearing in New York, employing a few male, but mostly female, models (fig. 29). The organizers sought to cloak themselves in the aura of high art by claiming connection to the royal academies of London and Paris, and by representing scenes from the Bible as well as from classical painting and sculpture.[28]

Perhaps the original shows were, as their newspaper puffs claimed, marked by such taste and propriety that they drew both men and women to the audience. If so, they swiftly degenerated, for by the winter of 1847–48, although men sometimes appeared in the shows, women's bodies were the really urgent source of audience appeal. This was demonstratively confirmed when one model artist manager advertised a "cotillion by the ladies of the company." A large crowd of men, many equipped with opera glasses or telescopes, jammed the theatre, but they were disappointed by the appearance of several dancing couples, the women having donned short skirts over their tights. The audience howled "Off with the rags!" and "To h——l with the men!"[29]

Model artist shows clearly appealed to men of all classes. By February 1848

Fig. 29 Playbill for a model artist show at the Franklin Museum, New York. The bill promises "Temptation," *Venus de Medici,* Powers' *Greek Slave,* and *The Three Graces.* Harvard Theatre Collection.

the *Herald* was fretting that "you can view them in almost every street and lane," for as little as three, four, or five cents, "thereby inviting newsboys, loafers and the veriest ragamuffins about town to see them." At the other extreme, some of these shows charged fifty cents admission and drew crowds composed of wealthy and respectable grey-haired men. Some accounts suggested that the wealthiest patrons demanded the most salacious shows—higher admission prices yielding a greater degree of undress—or that a higher-priced ticket produced a seat on the stage. In all venues the male audience seems to have reacted with abandon— whistling, yelling, and stomping. At one model artist show a near-riot occurred when a group of men charged the stage; perhaps they were outraged citizens, as the *Herald* suggested, but they may simply have been over-exuberant fans.[30]

It did not take long for the authorities to decide to make a show of suppressing the model artist business. In late March 1848, after a grand jury in New York City issued indictments naming seven establishments, most managers agreed to cease their exhibits and the cases were dropped. But in less than a month the model artists were back on the boards, probably after police payoffs, possibly assisted by a bit of self-censorship as well. Throughout the 1850s the police periodically were goaded by citizen complaints into raiding model artist shows, but their regard for the interests of the management was revealed by the fact that they arrested only the performers. To managers like George Lea, one of the most successful, the business seems to have been worth the cost of occasional disruption and regular payoffs.[31]

The problems with the model artist formula lay in its immobility and silence; managers tried to compensate by introducing revolving platforms on which the women would stand or recline. They also used music to warm up the crowd before the model artists were displayed. Women musicians were hired to play popular minstrel airs; they were dressed in short skirts with tights underneath and were called "female minstrels," though they did not black their faces. Throughout the 1850s model artists, often in combination with minstrel music, continued to be a regular feature of the New York entertainment world.[32]

In the continuing segmentation of theatre forms, a new type of entertainment had evolved. It addressed men. Its appeal was essentially sexual, its strategy almost wholly visual. Theatre managers had realized that women's bodily presence, always an element of theatre, could be made a separate commodity if the women were isolated in a semblance of nudity. This sexualized object for viewing was in many ways an ideal commodity: the demand for it was infinitely renewable, the experience pleasurable but never completely satisfying. Depending as they did on the low-salaried employment of anonymous women of little or no talent, the model artist shows combined low overhead with reliable demand. The women on display were reminiscent of the old third tier, but now the only sexuality offered for sale was visual titillation; from the point of view of public regulation and toleration—and hence profitability—such sexual titillation was a far more reliable and less dangerous product than the services promised by the prostitutes.[33]

THE CHANGING EXPERIENCE OF THEATREGOING

Segmentation spread outward from New York, the center of the commercializing theatre. In Philadelphia in February 1848, for example, the Arch Street Theatre and the Walnut Street Theatre offered the "legitimate," while Italian opera, the circus, Tom Thumb, and minstrelsy were available elsewhere. In Boston during the week of 6 April 1850, Boston's elite could attend Italian opera at the Howard Atheneum, while the working-class Irish population was lured by a play called *The Irish Farmer* at the National. Ranged in between were *The Enchanted Beauty* at the Museum, a comedy called *The Serious Family* at the Odeon, and a pantomime called *The Green Monster* at the Boston Theatre in Federal Street, as well as a full complement of minstrel shows. Boston actually was slow to develop a decidedly working-class theatre because a city ordinance long forbade theatre on Saturday evenings, for fear it would run over into Sunday morning. As the *Boston Daily Bee* noted, the greatest impact fell on "persons from the industrial classes of the community," who struggled with fatigue and the prospect of early rising on nights other than Saturday. In smaller cities where social subgroups were seldom large enough to constitute separate markets, the traditional divisions within the playhouse — pit, boxes, and gallery, or subsequent versions of cheap versus expensive seats — continued to represent and contain social distinctions. In 1860, for example, a comment on the one theatre in Memphis clearly assumed that the local mechanics were an important part of the audience but only a part.[34]

Yet New York's extreme version of segmentation by class soon had national significance, for as touring "combination" companies began to displace residential stock companies in the 1860s, New York became the theatrical proving ground for the entire country. Touring shows that originated in New York could project a distinct class, ethnic, or racial appeal in smaller cities and towns and draw different audiences to the same hall on different nights. Touring thus would open the way for further audience segmentation in smaller cities and towns: it was no longer necessary that an entertainment audience be large enough to sustain regular continuous offerings in one place.

Distinct theatrical styles and audience experiences evolved. The working-class theatres of New York's East Side featured exaggerated declamation long after middle-class audiences had begun to frown on such "ranting." Working-class audiences also continued to demand a lengthy mixed bill and to respond to it by means of old-fashioned selective inattention. "Wake me up when Kirby dies" was an oft-repeated tribute to the exaggerated death-throes of the favorite Bowery "heavy," J. Hudson Kirby, but it was also a statement about audience behavior. Even theatre language was segmented. At East Side theatres the players retained and perhaps even cultivated a working-class New York accent, which was quite marked by mid-century. When Kirby toured England in 1844, the London audience dissolved into helpless laughter when they thought they heard him bellow as Richard III, "A hearse! A hearse! My kingdom for a hearse!"[35]

Once segmentation was established, choosing a theatre involved choosing between very different audience dynamics (fig. 30), and it amounted to making a statement about one's identity. It was not that individuals never wandered from the entertainments predicated on their social position: on the contrary, since taking on an identity through theatregoing was temporary and revocable, it invited "passing" and slumming. The lines that set entertainments apart from one another were quite permeable, especially in a downward direction, where price presented no barrier, so that working-class theatre patrons accordingly were on guard against middle-class interlopers. "Anyone who looks hi-falutin will probably be hooted should they stick their face out of the boxes," said one account of the New Bowery in 1865. The youthful audience in the highest gallery was described as unwashed, ragged, and "repellent of encroachment, especially if it comes from Broadway."[36]

Choosing an entertainment could be a means to contemplate "others"—and thereby also make a statement about one's own identity. Henry James's family, for example, had seen *Uncle Tom's Cabin* at Barnum's but later went to see another production at the National, "deep down on the East side, whence echoes had come faintest to ears polite." James wrote, "The point exactly was that we attended this spectacle just in order *not* to be beguiled, just in order to enjoy with ironic detachment and, at the very most, to be amused ourselves at our sensibility should it prove to have been trapped and caught." For the shirt-sleeved crowd at the National that evening, *Uncle Tom's Cabin* probably involved uncomplicated self-affirmation in the company of their fellows, but young James was lost in complex, ironic possibilities, "wondering, among his companions, where the absurd, the absurd for *them*, ended and the fun, the real fun, which was the gravity, the tragedy, the drollery, the beauty, the thing in itself" began. Thus, for all sorts of theatregoers the initial choice, selecting from a range of socially differentiated theatres, had become *the* crucial act in theatrical reception.[37]

From a woman's point of view, the range of choice in the market for live entertainment was defective. There was no women's theatre, only a series of alternatives that were essentially men's theatre, even, to a greater or lesser degree, misogynistic. No women's theatre emerged because women lacked the money and the social independence to wield market power, although, by contrast, women were a significant factor in the market for fiction and literary work.[38] In a context in which social identity might be recognized by popular culture, the segmentation process that highlighted class differences tended to mute gender differences, or rather, to substitute for real differences the stylized and stereotypical differences that the male-dominated market was pleased to notice. Like black people in minstrel shows, women in theatre were counted out or reduced to "others."

Changing audience dynamics further silenced women in the audiences. The old, active tradition had granted everyone who attended a common public enter-

THE ACADEMY OF MUSIC AND THE OLD BOWERY THEATRE.

Fig. 30 The Academy of Music and the Old Bowery Theatre. Different styles of theatregoing were evidence of class differences. Harvard Theatre Collection.

tainment the right of demonstrative refusal. In the new situation, audience assertiveness increasingly was limited to the male-dominated working-class theatres or to genres that had originated in working-class theatre, like minstrelsy. Rowdiest of all were the all-male audiences of the model artist shows. Women were less likely to find themselves in situations where they could register public refusal or disapproval. In fact, the meaning of an audience member's vocal or active behavior was probably changing, since satisfaction could be obtained just as readily by going elsewhere as by correcting the performers. Noisy outcry was becoming less a dialogue with the performers than a matter of men establishing their class or gender bona fides—especially in the model artist shows, where the silent motionlessness of the medium literally forbade any response from the performers, but the howling was the loudest of all. Quiet audiences were assumed to have expressed themselves in the act of choosing among an array of entertainment alternatives. But the fact that men underwrote women's theatre attendance by providing admission fee and escort surely translated into considerable influence in making that choice, further muting women's voices in this last area of audience sovereignty.

The newly segmented theatre encouraged and cultivated a sense of male entitlement. Lize was a bold and confident female character, yet even she was simply irrelevant to one of the oddest episodes in Baker's *A Glance at New York*, a visit by Mose and his friends to a "ladies' bowling saloon," supposedly the latest craze among the first families of the city. Mose and his pals disguise themselves as women so as to have a look at this novel spectacle, but they are discovered almost immediately because Mose cannot resist trying to kiss one of the lady bowlers. The episode tapped male voyeuristic interests, along with a dose of contempt for upper-class pretension. However devoted Mose may be to his Lize, he wants to have a look around—and maybe more.

Segmentation of the theatre audience betokened not a true availability of the public realm for both genders but rather a disaggregation that rendered certain theatres safe for women only at the price of certifying others for male pleasures focused on the spectacle of women's bodies. Working-class theatres catered to male tastes by presenting passive women or misogynistic humor. Middle-class theatres were the safest choice for women theatregoers, offering the least chance of insult in the audience or onstage, the greatest chance of finding entertainment that spoke to their emotions and their interests.

6 ·
Managing: The Decline of Laura Keene

At the failure of her marriage in 1851, Mary Frances Moss Taylor of London was twenty-five, with two small daughters to support. Most young mothers would have thrown themselves on their relatives, but she buried all memory of her vagrant husband, a "loafer" and possibly a criminal, changed her name, and went on the stage under the name of Laura Keene. To hide her past marriage she even taught her children to call her Aunt Laura.

Laura Keene served a short apprenticeship with a London stage legend, the aging Madame Vestris, before sailing for New York in 1852. Vestris was the first female theatre manager of note, a worldly purveyor of breeches-parts sex appeal, and a pioneer in realistic production values. In New York, Keene joined the theatre company managed by Thomas Hamblin's old friend James W. Wallack, where she played leading roles in light comedy. The turn to the visual did her no harm, for Laura had finely chiseled features and striking auburn hair, as well as a clear melodious voice. She contracted with Wallack for a second year at a salary of $45 a week, but she took off in the midst of the season, heading for Baltimore with an unconvincing excuse about "family business." Keene had probably noticed that Wallack's profits for the previous season totaled $9000 and learned that there was a theatre for rent in Baltimore. A latecomer to the profession, Laura Keene was a woman in a hurry, and though she was proving herself a singularly talented actress, she had grander goals. Like her mentor, Vestris, Laura Keene wanted the power and the profits of theatre management.[1]

A great many actresses managed theatres in nineteenth-century America. Charlotte Cushman managed one in Philadelphia in 1842; Elizabeth Blanchard Hamblin used her divorce settlement money to go into theatre management, and even Josephine Clifton tried co-managing in Baltimore briefly. During the hard times of the 1840s so many women ventured into theatre management that more than one old-timer grumbled about "petticoat government." There were a number of women managers after mid-century, including Catharine Sinclair, who managed in San Francisco in 1853–56, Mrs. D. P. Bowers, who managed in Philadelphia in 1858–59, and Matilda Vining Wood, who took over Laura Keene's Theatre in New York after Keene left. One of the most distinguished was Louisa Lane Drew; she undertook the management of the Arch Street Theatre in Philadelphia in 1861 and was the founding matriarch of the Drew-Barrymore theatrical dynasty. An actress who worked for Laura Keene recalled the women managers of that day: "their name was legion."[2]

Laura Keene (fig. 31) was perhaps the most accomplished woman manager of all. From 1855 to 1863 she operated successfully in the intensely competitive New York City theatre market, which had emerged as *the* national center of American theatre. Laura Keene believed in complete, well-rounded theatre, rejecting the characteristic imbalances of the star system—the "one or two stars and nine or ten sticks" Fanny Kemble had complained of. Although her company

Fig. 31 Laura Keene. Harvard Theatre Collection.

often competed against stars like Cushman and Forrest at rival theatres, Keene herself refused to engage stars and instead assembled stock companies full of talented players. One of them was always herself, for Keene continued to act while she managed, and her skill as an actress was one key to her success as a manager. She won middle-class audiences with a superb orchestra, elaborate sets, gorgeous costumes and well-rehearsed ensemble playing—all offered in a clean, comfortable theatre. In 1863 Laura Keene left New York management and set off with a touring company. She entered the history books when her company played Ford's Theatre in Washington in April 1865 and Abraham Lincoln came to see her in *Our American Cousin.*

Managing meant handling large amounts of money and risking it all repeatedly; it meant assuming responsibility for play selection, casting, and production style. It meant recruiting and retaining temperamental performers, giving orders to scene-painters and stage carpenters and orchestra directors. Finally, managing in New York involved positioning oneself vis-à-vis the competition, for mere duplication of what was offered at other playhouses, however meritorious, might lead to ruin. The manager traditionally did everything but tell the actors and actresses how to play their parts, and Laura Keene tried to do that too, anticipating the modern director. For her pains she was thought a martinet and called "the Duchess." But she was a good-hearted person. "I never heard her speak ill of anybody but herself," one actor recalled, "and this she would sometimes do with a grim humor that was very entertaining."[3]

Keene saw that for her middle-class patrons new offerings were essential. The traditional favorites in which Kemble and Cushman had made their reputations were by Keene's day commonly dismissed as "stereotyped" or "completely played out." Although she periodically mounted lavish productions of Shakespeare, Keene was constantly on the lookout for new drama, especially comedy or melodrama, as tragedy had fallen out of favor. The difficulty still lay in the copyright laws, which discouraged talented authors, and so the new pieces she produced were mostly either terrible or just tolerable. Trying new plays and covering failures with old reliables, she often gave the appearance of having no settled "line of policy."[4]

Laura Keene's successful seasons in New York reveal the power of the female sector of the middle-class audience to encourage and reward dramatic material that spoke to women's point of view. But Keene's career also reveals the handicaps under which women labored to enter and remain in theatrical management—obtaining access to capital, engaging in legal battles, fighting for press coverage, competing with the unscrupulous men who dominated the business. As she supported her daughters and her mother as well as herself, she had to meet that competition if she wanted to continue in business. The light, fluffy "extravaganzas" that were coming to the fore in the 1860s held little interest for her, even though she was adept at making money from such fare. Ultimately, these shows bored and offended her and she left New York management to tour. Her last project, editing and publishing a magazine called *Fine Arts*, cost her thousands of dollars, but it gave her the chance to break the constraints of commercial theatre to say what she thought. Although too often in her career she had settled for doing what would sell, in her magazine Keene made it clear she believed theatre was an art, not a product. Caught in the emerging division between popular and high culture, Laura Keene did not have the capital resources or the purely instrumental values needed to compete in the mass markets of popular entertainment. But she could not find refuge in high culture, for there was no noncommercial theatre, and she lacked upper-class prestige, had dirtied her hands trading in popular fare, and had lived an unorthodox personal life. In the long run, Keene's career testifies to the limits of the power of either the female manager or the female audience to set the tone or control the content of public entertainments.

CAPITAL, COPYRIGHT, AND PRESS COVERAGE

Laura Keene managed the Baltimore theatre for only a few months before heading west to California in 1854. She starred and managed and even took ship to Australia for a brief tour, finally heading back to New York in 1855.[5] She leased the old Metropolitan Theatre, refurbished the huge and drafty hall, and renamed it "Laura Keene's Varieties" (fig. 32). Because the season had already begun, she made up her company by hiring players away from other theatres, sometimes luring them with higher salaries. She was trying to break into the all-male fraternity of theatre managers in the largest and toughest theatre market of all.

Theatre management took money. It was one thing for a woman to become a manager in the lean and hungry 1840s, when owners of theatre buildings were desperate to find anyone to take up a lease on any terms; it was another altogether to go into business as Laura Keene proposed, at a time and place when there was some real prospect of profit. Keene needed capital for rent, renovations, lights, salaries, and costumes—all before a penny came into the treasury. Keene had made some money in California, but she did not have much capital, and so she began her management in New York, as in Baltimore and on the West Coast, with the financial backing of a man named John Lutz. Lutz, whom she had met during her first year in the United States while playing at Wallack's, was a professional gambler. He came from a well-to-do Washington family, he possessed large sums of money, and he did not mind risking it. He seems to have brought some of his fellow gamblers in on theatre speculation.[6]

Fig. 32 Laura Keene's Varieties. Harvard Theatre Collection.

Theatrical overhead was soaring along with Manhattan rents, but theatrical entrepreneurship was too risky for banks to back, so a personal loan was the only answer for would-be managers without capital of their own. Those who had money to lend in 1855 were perforce almost all men. Why lend to a woman? What collateral could she offer? Laura Keene was in fact what the moralists had been warning against for years, a "woman with a past." Unlike Fanny Kemble, whose interest in the opposite sex seems to have been quenched by her failed marriage, or Charlotte Cushman, who could find her intimate companions among women, Laura Keene was a heterosexual woman who had already shown herself willing to ignore conventional pieties about marriage. John Lutz became not only her financial manager and backer, but also her longtime companion. They lived together, although somewhere he had a wife, as she had a husband. If Lutz was "not precisely a Grandison," as one biographer put it, he was sensible and kind and had a good head for the business end of the theatre. After their respective spouses had died, in 1860 Laura Keene and John Lutz married. In earlier years Keene strove to keep her relationship with Lutz a secret, just as she kept the fact of her first marriage hidden. But without Lutz's financial help all her talent and taste and hard work would have been unavailing.[7]

The existing corps of theatre managers did not welcome her enterprise. Last seen in New York absconding from Wallack's in mid-season, she returned to encourage other players to break their contracts and to threaten every "first class"—that is, middle-class—theatre with fresh competition. Still, the response she provoked was particularly nasty. In a bitter letter printed in the *New York Evening Express* on 22 December 1855, the author complained Keene was "bribing off at preposterous salaries the actors at other houses," and encouraging actors and actresses "in the scoundrelly business of breaking their engagements." He expressed concern that "worthy and experienced managers such as Burton and Wallack" might be "driven from our midst." This much was predictable, but he went further. He declared that Keene's management would bring the stage into "vilest disgrace and disrepute," urged the public to reject Laura Keene's "Amazonian onslaught," decried her "proposed extension of woman's rights in a female managerial experiment," and suggested that after renting to Keene the building's owner might want to "finish off the other portions of his premises for free love purposes." Two nights later, on Christmas Eve, Keene had to postpone her opening after vandals slipped into her theatre and slashed the sets. It was quite a welcome to New York.[8]

The complaints about hiring players in midseason, and perhaps even the vandalism, were to be expected in an unscrupulous business. But the letter revealed there were also certain kinds of mud available especially for tossing at a female competitor. She might be labeled indecent, by which readers would have understood she was sexually active outside of marriage. Male managers were not vulnerable to such an objection; Thomas Hamblin had demonstrated just how far a man had to go before he attracted any attention in that regard. Alternatively, she might be called a woman's rights crusader. She might even be associated with some combination of the two through the epithet "free love."

The social and cultural context of mid-century America gave Laura Keene's actions a resonance that had been lacking twenty or thirty years earlier. Now there was a full-fledged women's rights movement articulating women's ambitions and complaining of the injustices they suffered. In the 1850s women's rights conventions met regularly to discuss and publicize women's grievances, and itinerant speakers like Lucy Stone carried their message far and wide. A few radical advocates of free-love feminism like Mary Gove Nichols embarrassed more respectable feminists by broaching the subject of "self-ownership," or birth control. Women's position in the theatre had changed too, for enough women had undertaken theatre management to make Keene's efforts seem less an oddity than part of a trend. Under these circumstances some men felt threatened, personally or economically, and they found two weapons at hand—the old one of the double standard and the new one of a more explicit misogyny crystallizing in response to the emergence of the women's rights movement.[9]

Laura Keene responded with a "card" printed in the *New York Times* and the *New York Tribune*. She said she had read the *Express* article "with considerable pain and sorrow," not knowing why her efforts should call forth such "ungenerous and unjust allusions, malicious insinuations." She denied everything and appealed for chivalry, rather than equity:

> I seek no newspaper warfare. I am a woman and at your mercy. If you think you add to the value of your columns, the pleasure and instruction of your readers, or the character for manliness and generosity of yourselves as reporters, by cruelly wounding the feelings and mercilessly endeavoring to injure the prospects of one who, as an antagonist, is entirely helpless and who is unconscious of ever having merited such treatment at your hand, do so. I must submit to you as an individual, but to the people as a manageress. Let them judge between us.

There was, of course, another line of argument available, and at one point in her letter she touched on it: why, she asked, was she to refrain "from doing precisely what was done by the gentlemen" already in the business? But Keene did not pursue that approach. She probably thought she should hide her unorthodox personal life and deny any feminist implications in her work, and feared that being frank about the one or open to the other would scotch her management career before it had begun.[10]

Despite this stormy beginning, Laura Keene's first New York season proved such a success that by spring she intended to exercise her option to extend her lease for another four years. Her landlord at first agreed, but when a rival manager, William Burton of Burton's Theatre in Chambers Street, offered him an attractive deal for the outright sale of the property, the landlord discovered a technicality and told Keene she must vacate. Keene complained in an open letter, "I have invested many thousand dollars, and all I possess in the world, in his building, and all the profits of my arduous exertions through the past season are visible in the improvements, scenery and decorations." In a curtain speech delivered on the last night of the season, Keene joked with her audience about the "very clever" responses that her protest had evoked:

> It has been positively stated that I am a woman. [laughter] That I have no right to a managerial chair. That the theatre has not been profitable. That I have compromised with my artists for twenty-five cents on the dollar, and that unless I can meet the attack as a man I had best own myself conquered. I plead guilty to the charge of being a woman, and hope I have brought no discredit on my sex by my appearance as a man-

ageress. [laughter and applause] If the theatre has been so very unprofitable I suppose I ought to feel grateful to those who are willing to relieve me of a bad bargain. I am, however, contented with it. [cheers]

Keene's response seems mild enough, even good-humored, but the *New York Times* wrote disapprovingly that Keene's tone of "sardonic scorn . . . amply justifies the creed of Mrs. Lucy Stone Blackwell and strong ladies of that class."[11]

From start to finish her first season in New York demonstrated the difficulties she would find in securing nonprejudicial press coverage. The problem for Keene was that the major metropolitan press was just beginning to shake free of the system of paid puffery, and for the first time some journalists began to earn a salary by specializing in theatre news and drama reviews, basing their claim to a hearing on the fact that they were independent, expert, unbought. Journalists as a group, however, were far from incorruptible; it was still necessary to cultivate their favor with champagne baskets and oyster suppers. But now, one could not be so certain of the quid pro quo. In some ways a woman had been better off under the puffing system because buying good notices was an equal opportunity process. At least some of the new professional critics, men like E. G. P. Wilkins of the *Herald* and William Winter of the *Tribune*, were not only incorruptible but also incorruptibly misogynistic. All of the critics for the major papers (like virtually all the "bohemian" writers on theatre in the minor press) were men, and hostile press commentary about theatre women *as women* seems to have become more common in the 1850s. For example, one reviewer wrote, "Miss Keene is a brave, energetic manager, full of ambitious courage and love of adventurous enterprise, but she is also a woman and an actress; in other words, she is mentally unstable and professionally vain."[12]

Keene ultimately had to walk away from her first year's investment as Burton secured title to the building. But the theatre architect John Trimble offered to build her another playhouse, and with some financial backing from two hotel-keepers and an advance against rent from Keene herself, a new theatre went up on Broadway between Bleecker and Houston streets. Called simply "Laura Keene's Theatre," it opened in November 1856. It was well designed and tastefully decorated; it advertised that "every required convenience" was attached to the men's and ladies' "drawing rooms" in the dress-circle tier. Laura hired a distinguished acting company and a gifted orchestra leader and opened with *As You Like It*. To the opening night audience, which included more women than usual, Keene delivered a speech that promised, "No effort will be spared that industry can arouse—no results neglected that energy can achieve."[13]

It was a characteristic impulse. Keene wanted to do everything well, although such ambitions dictated a killing pace of work, and her health was always fragile. Keene knew that, like all theatre managers, she could not mount a commercially unsuccessful play for even a few nights without sustaining heavy losses. In fact, given her taste for lavish production and her dislike of cutting corners, her overhead was probably unusually high. Her ticket revenues were limited, as her theatre seated only about 2000; apparently she chose to make it smaller than most because she did not like the broad, histrionic style of acting that really large theatres demanded. Keene's financial margin for error therefore was narrow, and she sought to close the gap with the only resources she possessed in abundance — talent and energy. One contemporary recalled: "Laura Keene always had the best of everything in her theatres. . . . She worked herself to death, however, as it was a common thing for her to be at the theatre from nine in the morning until five in the afternoon, and then play at night."[14]

Like ready capital and news coverage, copyright was an area in which Laura Keene faced extra hurdles as a woman. Keene paid $1000 outright to the dramatist Tom Taylor for the rights to *Our American Cousin*. Thanks to brilliant casting and careful rehearsing it became the hit of the 1858 – 59 season, and its appeal grew week after week as two of Keene's most talented comedians, Joseph Jefferson and E. A. Sothern, constantly interpolated new gags and "business" as they went along. *Our American Cousin* became a fad and a phenomenon, its laugh lines part of the lingua franca of mid-century American life. The play also made Jefferson and Sothern into stars; it ran for 140 nights, a total then exceeded only by *Uncle Tom's Cabin*. Naturally, Keene's competitors were interested in producing it, but a new copyright law passed in 1856 seemed to promise that her investment in the play would be protected.[15]

Two Philadelphia managers, William Wheatley and John Sleeper Clarke, sought permission to stage the play early in its run, and in response to their query John Lutz mentioned the sum of $1000. Wheatley and Clarke took a simpler, cheaper expedient: they sent a secretary to Keene's Theatre to sit in the audience, copy down the dialogue, and take notes on the stage business. They opened *Our American Cousin* in Philadelphia and began profiting handsomely. Keene sued. The judge who heard the case required Wheatley and Clarke to pay the $1000 licensing fee that had been proposed, but he did not find the secretarial system of play acquisition unlawful. On the contrary, although the case became entangled in questions about other, earlier versions of the play and Jefferson's having passed information to the Philadelphia managers, the judge clearly stated that the performance of the play made it available thereafter to any and all who came to listen — to memorize, transcribe, and reuse if they liked. *Our American Cousin* was also pirated in Boston and New York, and Keene sued there, too, with mixed results, but *Keene v. Wheatley and Clarke* had proven that the new copyright law was fatally flawed. Had Keene been able to protect her property in the play, her financial future would have been secure.[16]

Laura might have appealed the judge's ruling, but Wheatley and Clarke, casting about for legal stratagems, found arguments to intimidate her, arguments that would not have served had their opponent been a man. Their lawyers alleged that Laura Keene was not competent to sue or to own property because she had a living husband. The existence of Henry Wellington Taylor had heretofore remained a deep secret; to the public she was Miss Keene, unmarried. The lawyers also cross-examined Lutz on his living arrangements and his relationship to Keene. Fearing to have these issues opened to the public in proceedings before a jury, Keene declined at that point to press the case further. The legal disabilities of married women and the double standard of sexual morality were influential in forcing Keene to abandon the struggle to protect what should have been a valuable copyright.[17]

WOMEN'S PLAYS

"I want a comedy!" Laura Keene urged Augustin Daly in 1863, praising his "rapidly growing reputation as an author."[18] Over and over again Laura Keene found herself in this position, searching for new plays, sometimes even writing them herself. Among her New York competitors, the Winter Garden brought in stars while Wallack's specialized in excellent stock company productions of classics. Laura was a graceful leading lady in Shakespeare (fig. 33) and might have wished to duplicate Wallack's approach, but she recognized her need for a market niche and hoped to find it in new drama. In her first New York season she selected a number of new plays that revealed the preoccupations and market power of the female audience in middle-class theatres like hers and incidentally helped to encourage a new vein of melodrama that spoke more directly than ever to women's issues.

From the start, Laura Keene's Theatre was identified to an unusual degree with the interests of the female audience. As her first season drew near its conclusion the critic for the *Albion* feared Keene was developing "a missionary complex" because of the number of plays she presented "of a highly edifying nature adapted to move the female mind, and to point the moral of life for spinster, wife and widow." Laura Keene's speech before the curtain on the last night of her first New York season thanked the ladies of the audience for their support, mentioning specifically how important it was to have their approval for "the interpretations of passion, the heart-struggling Camille, . . . the forsaken, despairing Clarissa."[19]

One of the most popular plays Laura Keene offered in her first New York season was *Camille*. Based on Dumas's *La Dame aux Camélias*, *Camille* is the story of a good-hearted courtesan who sacrifices herself for her lover Armand—the story

Fig. 33 Laura Keene as Portia. This engraving suggests Keene's love of the classics, which, however, she never found very remunerative. Harvard Theatre Collection.

Verdi immortalized in *La Traviata*. *Camille* had been introduced to American audiences in 1853, modified to meet straightlaced American tastes by casting its heroine as merely a coquette. Laura Keene's version of *Camille* retained the story intact but sought to avoid moralistic objections by having Camille awaken at the end to discover it had all been a bad dream. Ultimately a third, unexpurgated, version of the play became most popular, thanks to an actress named Matilda

Heron who saw the play in Paris, made her own translation, and rode it to stardom. When Heron opened in *Camille* in New York in January 1857 the play had been so popular for several years that one critic wrote off Heron's chances on the grounds that the city had seen "so many delineators of this role." Nevertheless Heron's Camille was both inspired and natural, and having won over New York audiences she went on to play Camille repeatedly for years, all over the nation. By the usual logic of popular culture, *Camille*'s popularity provoked a host of imitators.[20]

With *Camille*, the female audience had the opportunity to contemplate a woman who deliberately exchanged her beauty and her body for money, gifts, and admiration from men. Camille achieves economic independence and wields a kind of power. Ultimately, however, her good heart and true love for Armand render her subject to male domination when Armand's father pleads on behalf of family honor. Camille's story had vague but palpable connections to troubling cultural issues in a society where the links between sexuality on the one hand and marriage and procreation on the other no longer seemed indissoluble. In such a society, entertainments based on sexually charged spectacle were giving the prostitute's powers and dilemmas—her self-commodification—a wider resonance.[21]

Keene helped to launch an enduring hit and a new type of melodrama referred to variously as the "immoral drama," the "sensation" drama, the "hydraulic emotional school," or "problem plays." In such plays women who were guilty of sexual transgressions became central, sympathetic characters. Like the love of satire in an age reputed to be solemn, a taste for plays about "fallen women" and "wicked wives" may seem surprising in an age assumed to be sexually repressed and highly moralistic. But sex had always been one of the main motive forces in melodrama. The old "forced marriage" scenario eventually seemed limited, and mid-century melodrama began to consider the complexities of consent and responsibility. Of course, great reticence governed these productions, and nothing explicit, let alone graphic, could occur onstage. Yet in dealing with topics like seduction and prostitution, the plays acknowledged the disparity in power between men and women and sometimes edged close to a critique of the double standard. Certainly such drama questioned the definition of woman as sexual property whose virtue was either "intact" or "ruined."[22]

Issues of sexual morality seemed so current in 1856 that Laura Keene even tried to dramatize Samuel Richardson's *Clarissa* in her first New York season. *Clarissa* was not a success, but Keene's stage version of *Jane Eyre* won flattering critical attention. In 1856 Keene also introduced *The Marble Heart* to New York audiences. She played Mlle. Marco, who has been poor and now schemes to land a rich husband. Camille and Marco were bookends: between the good soul who broke all the sexual rules and the heartless coquette who was technically pure, these plays made a powerful case against the definition of female virtue in terms of adherence to conventional rules of sexual conduct. Marco subsequently became one of Keene's most famous roles.[23]

Plays focusing on women and sexual misconduct were popular throughout Keene's management years. In her second year, she introduced *Rachel the Reaper*, whose heroine was ruined by a counterfeit marriage. It became one of the mainstays of her repertory. The melodramatic hit of the 1860s, *East Lynne*, featured a wife who ran off with a seducer and then returned, disguised and repentant, to serve as her son's nurse. By 1863, when Laura Keene produced a new play called *Jessie McLane* in which a Pittsburgh miner's wife is seduced by the mine owner and runs off with him, one reviewer referred to the topic of wifely infidelity as "well-worn." Later in her career, after 1867, Keene repeatedly starred in *Hunted Down*, another in this genre.[24]

A special subset of such plays thematized the actress. During her first season Laura Keene played the eighteenth-century British actress Peg Woffington in *Masks and Faces*. Woffington is portrayed as gay, clever, good-hearted, and anything but naive. The heartless coxcomb Sir Charles Pomander wants her to become his mistress, but she is intrigued by an awkward, sincere country gentleman named Vane. Peg generously dispenses charity to starving artists, freely acknowledges her past as a poor "orange girl," and begins to fall for Vane. Just as Peg begins to know true love for the first time, Vane's wife, Mabel, appears in London. Mabel, a simple, artless woman, is devastated to realize that her husband loves another. When Peg understands the situation, she resolves to restore Vane's affections to his wife by means of her acting talent—she will *enact* the part of a heartless conniver. Mabel ultimately understands what Peg is doing for her, and they part as "sisters." Peg bids Mabel, "Think sometimes of poor Peg Woffington, and say, stage masks may cover honest faces, and hearts beat true beneath a tinselled robe." As if this were not pointed enough, Woffington then turns to the audience to say:

> Nor ours the sole gay masks that hide a face
> Where cares and tears have left their withering trace,
> On the world's stage, as in our mimic art,
> We oft confound the actor with the part.[25]

Peg suggested that women's roles were subject to revision while she neatly dispatched the body problem by depicting it as something women were free to ignore. In Peg Woffington the audience was presented with a sexually experienced woman who could not be reduced to a sexual object.

The character of Peg Woffington is not much concerned with the opinions of others, especially men. Her income enables her to live well, to help those in need, and to reject male advances if she chooses. She is denied a romantic "happily ever after" ending, but she has the power and the good will to arrange the happiness of others; she asks no pity and carries on cheerfully. Peg became one of Keene's most successful roles and *Masks and Faces* part of the standard drama of midcentury. It was, for example, selected by a group of socially prominent amateurs for a Sanitary Commission benefit in Chicago during the Civil War, with Miss Emilie Schaumberg playing Peg.[26]

The success of *Masks and Faces* inspired a host of less successful plays about actresses. Laura Keene played Nell Gwynn in *The King's Rival* in 1856 and she played the English actress Fanny Kelly in *World and Stage* in 1859. In *Nature and Art* in 1857 Keene presented the story of a young man who falls in love with an actress. At the solicitation of the boy's father, she attempts to end his infatuation by an assumed coarseness. The great French actress Rachel popularized Eugène Scribe's *Adrienne Lecouvreur*, also called *Adrienne the Actress*, on her American tour in 1855. It was the story of a great star of the Comédie Française who died the victim of poisoning by a jealous duchess. Mrs. John Wood played Anne Bracegirdle in *Actress by Daylight, or, The Woman and the Artiste* in 1863. Dion Boucicault, always a bellwether of popular taste, came up with a play called *Grimaldi; or, The Life of an Actress* in 1855.[27]

In each case a play's double masking—actresses playing actresses—was tied explicitly or implicitly to the genuine difficulties of representing oneself and knowing others. With the exception of Boucicault's *Grimaldi*, every work featured a "real-life" heroine. The plays offered a kind of special pleading against the sexual reputation traditionally accorded the actress: she is either misunderstood or, despite her missteps, a good woman. They also thematized the masking process, suggesting—since there was no comparable spate of plays about actors—that its powers and its dilemmas were particularly female. In these actress plays the main characters are often misread and mistreated by others, but they know and reveal themselves as matter-of-fact and good-hearted. They use their acting abilities to negotiate and manipulate the discrepancies between appearance and reality but do so only for benign purposes. They do not suggest danger, let alone demonic possibilities, but they do insist that self-definition is more important than the perceptions of others. Women in the audience may have been especially receptive to actress plays: a performance of *Adrienne the Actress* in Boston, for example, was reported to have "enraptured the ladies."[28]

Male sexual misconduct had always been an element of melodrama; one recent account, for example, describes melodrama as a genre in which "the threat of rape hung over hundreds of heroines." But dramas written after midcentury took a woman's point of view explicitly even when the issue was the less clear-cut one of seduction. Julia Ward Howe carried the genre to its limits in her play *Leonore; or, The World's Own*. Produced at Wallack's in New York in March 1857, *Leonore* seethes with anger at male sexual treachery and the double standard. Matilda Heron played Leonore, a trusting young woman who gives her heart to Lothair, a casual seducer who takes his pleasure and leaves. Devastated, Leonore follows him and, finding him married to another, vows revenge. She becomes the mistress of the Prince and uses her power to ruin Lothair, steal his child, and drive his wife mad. In the end Leonore commits suicide, but the real power of the play lies in the early scenes when Lothair coolly manipulates Leonore and boasts of his conquest to other men.[29]

Although *Leonore*'s first-night audience—packed with literary lions from Boston—seemed pleased, the play soon closed. The critics condemned *Leonore*'s structural flaws, but they also found its criticism of men too pointed, Howe's fantasies of female revenge too threatening. *Frank Leslie's Illustrated Newspaper* dismissed it as a "shameless production," full of "blasphemy, impiety, and barefaced wantonness." The critic of the *Albion* missed the point entirely, for he cited the play as an example of a spate of drama given over to "a crusade against the sins of women."[30]

Fanny Kemble had been, as usual, ahead of her time. Her play on the subject, *An English Tragedy*, was rejected in 1841 by William Macready, then manager of Covent Garden, as too painful and shocking. The play, which Kemble considered one of the best things she had ever written, was based on the true story of an English lord who was welcome in high society throughout a career of notorious sexual profligacy but suffered immediate and thorough ostracism when it was discovered that he cheated at cards. The turning of melodrama toward the woman's point of view after midcentury allowed for its rediscovery, and Kemble's *English Tragedy* was finally produced in New York in 1864.[31]

The "immoral" drama contained a muted echo by mainstream culture of the arguments about sexual morality being raised by elements of the women's rights movement. When a play delivered this message too explicitly, it was liable to be condemned in similar terms and tone as the movement—by misogyny either taken straight or cloaked in concern for public morality. One reviewer complained that the "morbid fictions" of a "herd" of female novelists had supplanted Shakespeare, Scott, and Dickens, and fairly spat with disgust at the idea that in contemporary plays husbands were "always forgiving to everyone, even the seducer of 'his dear darling pipsey-wipsey'. . . . Pah!" The *New York Herald*, which denounced the immoral drama, used similar rhetoric to blast a woman's rights speaker who claimed that every woman should be free to determine when and if she should become a mother. The *Herald* labeled such talk "gross indecency and immorality," "corrupting and sensual teachings."[32]

Thus Keene in her first season helped to open a vein of popular drama that dealt with women's themes and even began to consider whether women might have a special relationship to theatre. Some of these plays were very successful; others were derivative and found little public favor. But Keene's benefit in her second season drew an audience containing an unusual number of women. The female segment of the middle-class audience was never separate or independent, as it always depended upon men for escort service and ticket prices. But its power was palpable, and Laura Keene seems to have understood its interests.[33]

SPECTACLE AGAIN

The hit of the season in Keene's first New York year was not a woman's play but a spectacle called *Novelty*. Attributed to Benjamin Baker, the author of the original Mose play, *Novelty* clearly bore the marks of Keene's intervention as well. The play had "no pretensions to literary merit"; it was a type known as "burlesque spectacle"—plotless extravaganza packed with contemporary satire. Keene played herself, an actress-manager seeking pieces to please her audiences; she turned for help to three fairies, Fashion, Novelty, and Fortune. Their suggestions provoked a series of elaborate tableaux spoofing theatrical favorites, from Shakespeare and the French tragedian Rachel to Uncle Tom and Irish comedians. The only serious element in *Novelty* was its representation of theatre as an entertainment business, with the bewildered manager striving to anticipate the wants of a heterogeneous and unpredictable market.[34]

Keene discovered that she could recur to some version of burlesque spectacle when nothing else was at hand. Another such vehicle called *Young Bacchus* ran for three months beginning in January 1857. Later that year, in the "dark days" after the panic of 1857, Keene took on a scenic extravaganza called *Variety*. *Variety* began in the ruined Temple of the Drama, with the actress Kate Reignolds playing the "Spirit of the Drama." She dismissed her disciples "as no longer having the power to attract a house in legitimate business," whereupon a "fast young man" named Puff entered and revealed the different classes of entertainment that "the public of the present day admire and patronize" in a series of tableaux representing such genres as spectacle, melodrama, circus, and ballet. Again the play was packed with visual effects and satire on current affairs and organized around a self-deprecating comment on the state of contemporary theatre.[35]

Plays like *Novelty* and *Variety* revealed how much audience dynamics had changed in middle-class metropolitan theatres. In earlier times, their lively contemporary wit might have been expected to set off equally lively audience reactions. In fact, such behavior occurred only once, when in the secession winter of 1860–61 Southerners went to Laura Keene's to hiss or cheer during the political scenes in a spectacle called *Seven Sisters*. Hissing and rowdiness had all but vanished by the late 1850s and early 1860s in "legitimate" theatres, however, even in plays full of current affairs and contemporary "hits."[36]

Middle-class audience members were limited to a narrow range of positive demonstrations—applause, laughter, and, most significant, ticket purchase. They were partially compensated for this passivity by the fact that the management was closely watching for these signs of approval and, if they flagged or failed, would promptly alter or replace the piece. Since managers feared failure not just on their own demerits but also by being outdrawn, they learned to look horizontally as it were, to see what other threatres were doing. Indeed, the most important interaction determining what happened onstage was no longer that between player and audience, but rather the competition between rival managers, each continually checking to see what was drawing elsewhere. Individuals in the audience could not argue, express a divergent viewpoint, or noticeably reject a play's content. No wonder the dilemma of the manager seemed a subject for spoof, so abstract and yet so crucial had audience reactions become, as, no longer expressed actively and directly, they were refracted through the market.[37]

"Burlesque extravaganzas" like *Novelty* and *Variety* constituted the most popular theatrical genre between 1850 and 1870, and Keene knew how to make the formula work. She had the material resources to create scenic illusion; a fine orchestra to produce popular and even original music; skilled comedians, who could make lame materials sparkle. A bit of tinkering could keep such a play attractive long enough to make a nice profit. Thus, in the pursuit of new material, Laura Keene mined two veins—women's tastes and visual appeal. Although plays in the first genre might succeed, they might equally well fail, or even offend, but plays of the second type seemed to make money with great reliability. And Keene had to make money to stay in business.[38]

Like Keene, other women found ways to accommodate themselves to the new style of theatre. Keene's successor as leading lady at Wallack's, for example, was Josephine Shaw Hoey. Competent but unremarkable, Mrs. Hoey (as she was always called) married a rich man and was not compelled to live on her salary. With her gorgeous and expensive wardrobe, Mrs. Hoey became known as "the best-dressed actress in New York." She presided at Wallack's until her retirement in 1865 and set a new style for extravagant costuming among female performers, who were still, in those days, expected to provide their own clothing. This old tradition took on new significance with the shift toward the visual, undermining real wages and tempting women toward yet another variation of the self as spectacle.[39]

Laura Keene was more ambitious and less circumspect than Mrs. Hoey. She was a pretty leading lady at Wallack's (fig. 34) but was not content with that sta-

Fig. 34 Portrait of Laura Keene. Compare with the lithograph, figure 33, to understand how the technology of photography influenced theatrical stardom. It finally was possible to mass-produce inexpensive images that were more than simply crude aids to memory. Billy Rose Theatre Collection.

tus, and her very identity as "Laura Keene" involved an escape from the confines of an unfortunate marriage. Performing and managing yielded Keene fame, admiration, and financial rewards, but it is an open question whether such attainments made producing spectacle plays an entirely satisfactory compromise with society.

THE ARTS AND THE MARKETPLACE

Keene was, by one account, "the most cultured woman on the stage during her generation," a well-read, witty conversationalist who was apt to make mistakes in play selection because she had too high a regard for the literary qualities of scripts.

Her desire for a cultivated, refined theatre was reflected in the "Rules and Regulations" for Laura Keene's Varieties, which addressed the players as "ladies and gentlemen" and stipulated a decorous green room (backstage waiting area) where the men were not to wear their hats or talk "vociferously." Like other managers of her day she took care to prune "immoralities and improper language" from the plays she brought out.[40]

The theatre signaled Keene's intention to attract respectable, middle-class patronage in several ways: location on Broadway, no gallery of cheap seats, no third tier, and no bar. Ticket prices also indicated her position in the entertainment market: tickets at Wallacks cost twenty-five cents to one dollar, at Laura Keene's twenty-five to seventy-five cents, and at Barnum's twenty-five cents for all seats. But hers were not the stodgy family audiences to which Barnum's catered; her houses were crowded with "beauty, talent, fashion, position."[41]

Like Cushman, Laura Keene fell in with the middle-class enthusiasm for academically correct Shakespeare. She followed *Our American Cousin* with a strenuously authentic production of *Midsummer Night's Dream*, for which she consulted the Shakespearean scholar Richard Grant White, and perhaps also Fitz-Greene Halleck of Harvard. She cultivated the good opinion of genteel women by contributing $500, the proceeds of a benefit matinee, to the fund to preserve Mount Vernon. This project was being promoted by *Godey's Lady's Book*, through its editor Sarah Josepha Hale. She gave a benefit for the shirt sewer's union, and welcomed the Reverend Henry Bellows backstage when he was preparing a public address in defense of the stage.[42]

Yet if she wanted genteel respectability in the manner of Charlotte Cushman, Laura Keene was ultimately destined to disappointment. Her relationship with John Lutz could not remain a complete secret, especially after the commencement of legal wrangles with her own players. Because of inherent conflicts between stock company traditions and the problems of playing new pieces which could potentially become long runs, Laura Keene was peppered with suits from players: suits complaining of breach of contract when players were not awarded the parts they wanted; suits from players wanting to be paid for rehearsals of plays that never opened; suits from players protesting the new, authentic Shakespeare, which shrank some previously ample roles. Keene was even sued by a gambler's widow who alleged that her husband's contribution to the original capital Keene began with back in 1855, some $400, was never repaid. The lawyers cost her money, but more damaging still the suits revealed her relationship with John Lutz, since Lutz negotiated and signed all her contracts with performers. By 1858 the diarist and man-about-town George Templeton Strong would refer to Keene knowingly as "the fair and sinful Laura."[43]

Still her most pressing problem was the never-ending struggle to find the next new play, the next good draw. She tried more plays by *Our American Cousin's* author, Tom Taylor, but they failed. She tried plays written by E. G. P. Wilkins, the drama critic of the *Herald*, calculating that he and his journalistic compatriots would treat those productions kindly in print. But when she could not afford to pay Wilkins what he thought his plays were worth, they quarreled, and she made an enemy in the press.[44] She tried alternating new plays with revivals of previous successes, such as the melodrama *Sea of Ice* and the classic *School for Scandal*. Keene was a wonderful Lady Teazle, but there was a limited market for such fare; she had to have new plays.

In January 1860 she found an expedient—bringing the most popular play-wright of the era, Dion Boucicault, into co-management. Boucicault acted, as well as writing plays, and he presided over all details of the production of his pieces. He wrote two hits for Keene, *Jeanie Deans* and *The Colleen Bawn*. Taking Dion Boucicault into co-management, however, was surely medicine worse than the disease for which it was prescribed: he was one of the most accomplished scoundrels in modern theatre history. The possessor of a smooth brogue and the gift of gab, Boucicault "prided himself on never keeping his word unless he liked." He wrote successful plays in part because he was so ready to pirate from others, especially from the French, but he turned with fury on those who attempted in turn to steal from him. A manager who had dealings with Boucicault declared, "I don't believe he ever had a business transaction in his life, with man or woman, without terminating it in enmity." No record survives of fireworks between them, but Laura Keene did not renew the co-managing arrangements at the end of the season.[45]

So the fall of 1860 found Keene facing the same old problem, and in the per-ilous weeks after Lincoln's election when the secession crisis was disrupting busi-ness terribly, she turned to her familiar last resort, a spectacle she devised herself and called *The Seven Sisters*. Keene billed *The Seven Sisters* as "A Grand Operatic Spectacular, Diabolical, Musical, Terpsichorean, Farcical Burletta, in Three Acts," assuring the public that it was no drama at all but "merely a vehicle for conveyance of music, scenery, dresses, properties, appointments, fun, laughter." The heroine, Diavoline, is the daughter of Pluto, the lord of the underworld. She and her sisters visit New York, where she falls in love with a mortal who happens to be a playwright. The seven sisters of the underworld help him to get his play produced and become actresses in it. The scenic climax was the "birth of the but-terfly in the bower of ferns," but the play incorporated many elements from min-strelsy, including the popular tune "Dixie," as well as tableaux on political topics, including Columbia at the Tomb of Washington, and—after the attack on Ft. Sumter—"the good old ship Constitution in danger of being destroyed by the Fire-Eaters and Emancipators."[46]

Finally, *The Seven Sisters* incorporated one more visual feature — large numbers of pretty women. The corps de ballet was a traditional element of every first-class theatre company; Keene seems to have increased their number and emphasized their scenic qualities, judging from comments on the "short-petticoated ladies" who appeared in several production numbers, leaving the general impression of "a hundred miscellaneous legs in flesh-colored tights." *Seven Sisters* ran for more than two hundred performances, longer even than *Our American Cousin*, and kept Keene's theatre open into August 1861, long after all the other theatres in town had closed for the summer.[47]

Why did Keene turn to the leg business? Although one critic commented that "many a dull play has been saved by a judicious and liberal display of nether limbs," Keene's doing this, in such a big way, in a first-class theatre was new. Her innovation probably was provoked by the quickening competition of the "concert saloons" flourishing in New York in the early 1860s, in part because they were quite popular with soldiers passing through town. Men, including respectable middle-class men, paid a few cents' admission to see dance, comedy, songs, and acrobats, while enjoying a drink. Part of the attraction of the concert saloon was not the variety show onstage but the "pretty waiter girls" who served the patrons alcoholic beverages and sat down to drink with them, too. It seems to have been an open secret that at least some of the pretty waiter girls were prostitutes. There was a concert saloon right next door to Laura's theatre. In this environment, while legitimate theatres closed all around her, Laura Keene sketched out her *Seven Sisters* and added to the standard mélange an emphatic display of women's legs.[48]

The concert saloons, which had quickly put the last remaining model artist shows out of business, made viewing women's bodies an element of commercial entertainment in the most matter-of-fact way. For example, an advertisement for the Gaieties, a concert saloon, declared, "We are fully aware that the public would not care to listen to a woman singing if she were old or ugly, no matter how fine a talent she might be." Hence the Gaieties' policy "of engaging no lady artists without they possess the three requisites to please a New York audience — youth, beauty, and talent." On the other hand, the management assured the public, "Our male artists we engage on the score of ability alone."[49]

The audience and indeed the public were thus assumed to be male, and looking at pretty women was defined as their entitlement. If the existence of the female audience was a subtle fact, mediated by its immersion in mixed groups and its dependence on male incomes and male escorts, the existence and the desires of the male audience were not subtle at all. Free to cultivate their own tastes in all-male venues, requiring neither subsidy, approval, nor escort, men patronized a variety of entertainments, but entrepreneurs discovered two elements that combined low overhead and perennial attractiveness—alcohol and erotic titillation. Market segmentation revealed which kinds of audience tastes could yield the highest and/or most reliable profits. As entertainment dollars flowed into the concert saloons, theatre managers tried to lure men back with attention to these elements. Having eliminated prostitution and alcohol from their premises, they could offer only visual delights.[50]

In the fall of 1861 Keene opened the season with yet another burlesque spectacle, *The Seven Sons*. Once more making it clear that she had no illusions about the merit of a piece, she billed it as "an incomprehensible mass of dramatic nonsense." Still, it played until Christmas by offering "glorious scenery, pretty women, patriotic nonsense, hits at the war." One critic considered that she had in effect chosen a specialty: "In Europe there is in every country one Metropolitan Theatre, that is preeminent for its scenic and plastic effects. Miss Keene by her tact, good judgment and taste has secured this distinction for her handsome little place on Broadway." When *The Seven Sons* expired, Keene wrestled with the old problem of material, reviving *Our American Cousin* and even offering a melodrama she had written herself entitled *The Macarthy*.[51]

Keene opened the 1862–63 season as if she were giving up the struggle for new materials and determined to recapture her original goal of fine ensemble acting. She rotated plays like *She Stoops to Conquer, School for Scandal, Masks and Faces,* and *The Colleen Bawn*. The newspapers praised Keene's dedication to "the good old standard comedies," but Wallack's still held first claim to that segment of the market, and there was not enough demand to support two theatres. She made the effort until late November, then finally scheduled another frothy spectacle, this one called *Blondette*.[52]

At the same time she made plans to leave town and take some of her most talented players with her on a tour. She had once before taken a company to play in other cities, while she waited for her new theatre to be completed in 1856. Since then the expansion of the railroads had made such "combination" touring—that is, traveling with a whole company, costumes, sets, and all—even more feasible. Laura Keene recognized that if she took her company on tour there would be no need for new plays; instead, she could travel to new audiences. Impatient with the necessity of recurring to spectacle, Keene saw this plan as a way to solve all her problems.

Blondette opened in New York on 25 November, and Keene and her group arrived in Baltimore on 1 December. The New York theatre was under her nominal control, however, and she was held responsible for *Blondette* when Horace Greeley's *Tribune,* the city's most straightlaced paper, opened fire: "We do not believe that short dresses with chubby legs, however interesting in the concrete, will everlastingly be suffered to supply the utter absence of form and unity in any dramatic work. We do not believe that second rate stage tricks will forever disarm public reprobation of vulgar jests and unseemly situations." The *Tribune* critic backdated his outrage with a charge that *The Seven Sisters*, too, had appealed to "the prurient alone."[53]

Of course Keene never claimed any distinction for her spectacle plays, and she conveyed her opinion of *Blondette* and its ilk by her departure. She returned to New York only for a brief farewell engagement in the spring of 1863. Perhaps she agreed with the *Tribune* critic; certainly she found it impossible to maintain the kind of theatre she set out to create, impossible to fulfill her artistic ambitions. Having made some money and achieved a measure of financial security, she was ready to move on. Perhaps she knew that a brothel called "The Seven Sisters" had opened in New York; certainly she told her lawyer in 1865, "At this moment it is not very respectable to be a woman at the head of a theatre in New York."[54]

And so Laura Keene washed her hands of the New York theatre business and toured for a number of years. The type of play she had perfected—the frothy spectacle featuring lots of women's legs—would be revisited in the greatest success of postwar New York, *The Black Crook*. But by her own choice Laura Keene would not be there to reap the profits. Eventually wearying of the road, she repeatedly tried to settle down again by establishing another residential stock company. Always she lost money and had to resume touring. Dogged by illness, baffled by attempts to find some theatre business that was both commercially viable and artistically satisfying, Laura Keene finally left the theatre in search of another, better public. In 1872 she mortgaged her property and spent thousands to launch a glossy, elegant magazine called *Fine Arts*.

Every page of *Fine Arts* sent unmistakable signals about the class she sought to address: articles described the art treasures in Fifth Avenue drawing rooms, complained of the difficulty of recruiting good domestic servants, and detailed the opening of the new Metropolitan Museum of Art in New York. Keene complained about the ostracism of actors, but she did not defend them as a group: too many were ignorant and incompetent. Acting should be a learned profession, *Fine Arts* declared, just as "the theatre is a public school of virtue and refinement."[55]

Fine Arts reflected Keene's judgment that only the patronage of the upper classes could rescue the theatre from commercialism and place it where it belonged, among the ornaments of high culture. And within the elite *Fine Arts* directed a special appeal to women. It urged "the regeneration of Art" and stated flatly that "a far greater share of this worthy task lies within the power of woman, considered as a social and intellectual being, than she has hitherto been taught to believe." *Fine Arts* called for women to become enlightened amateurs and thereby elevate the arts. As an audience, they would not fritter their patronage away on "mere skillful technicalities . . . vapid sentimentalities, or on conventions of fashion."[56]

Despite these strong statements, Keene had little or no credibility as a spokesperson for high culture, having profited from just the sort of commercial ephemera she now condemned. Nor had she connections among the elite society she was addressing, and her magazine seems to have been ignored. Laura Keene saw theatre as a fine art and acting as a dignified aesthetic endeavor, but she also needed to make a living by her talents and, taught by experience, turned to thoroughly commercial, no-holds-barred business. Wandering between ideals and restrictions, she embraced first one possibility and then the other, and ended finally with neither. After a few months *Fine Arts* ceased publication, and a year later Laura Keene was dead of consumption at the age of forty-seven.

Laura Keene and the leg show she helped to devise stimulated a debate about who was to blame for the superficiality and the bad taste of popular culture. Was it the entrepreneur or the audience? Defending Keene, the critic "Bayard" (Franklin J. Ottarson) of the *Spirit of the Times* attacked the audience:

> When [Laura Keene] began in this city as a manager . . . her inclination for "legitimate drama" was liberally manifested in the selection of a company unrivaled even by Mr. Wallack, and the production of regular comedies in the most excellent style. But the public taste was rapidly setting in favor of Sensational play, and after struggling a long time, at the loss of much money, she gave up the fight and went over to the new style. It was too bad to see her ranting the wretched trash of the *Seven Sisters*, etc., she who is so true an artist in the very best characters of high comedy and pathetic drama. But she was not much to blame; the public would not have Legitimacy at any price; while they would trample each other in struggling through her doors to see some flimsy spectacle; and as that, and that only would pay, she made virtue of necessity.[57]

The influential critic William Winter (fig. 35) adopted the opposite position and blamed Laura herself. In a cold, dismissive obituary, Winter derided Keene for having presented audiences with "a miracle of rubbish." Winter claimed Keene wasted her talents and "seldom produced a symmetrical work of art." He declared that she would be forgotten: "Public life may be mutable, but solidity of character and talents well used do not fail to win for their possessors upon the stage a place of permanence, at least in the memory of the passing generation. Neither of these was possessed by Miss Keene, and hence it happens that her contemporaries will scarcely heed the sound of her passing bell."[58]

Over the years such arguments would become tedious with repetition; nonetheless, they missed the point about the systematic relationship between the entrepreneur and the audience. The market rewarded profitability, not artistic

Fig. 35 William Winter. The longtime drama critic of
the *New York Tribune,* Winter tried to give "highbrow"
status to the threatre, in part by deprecating the activities
of women like Laura Keene. Billy Rose Theatre
Collection.

quality: if entertainments of lesser quality could yield larger or steadier profits,
they would necessarily be preferred by all but the most self-consciously princi-
pled management. The audience, for its part, was reduced to relative passivity.
The only open course of action was to go elsewhere if it was dissatisfied, and it
soon learned to form standards of judgment within the range of what was available. Having ceased to dream of what used to be or what might be, audience
members were encouraged to adopt the pecuniary standard of merit—mass
appeal—as their own. Market forces were not apt to bring out the best in people
or to foster high standards or great art. Assigning blame to either side reduced the
problem to individual cupidity or to mass bad taste, both real enough, without
indicting the market system that made it difficult, if not impossible, for the parties
to avoid the characteristic failings with which they were charged.

Managing promised profits and power, but Laura Keene discovered that pursuing profits placed great constraints on her artistic choices and ensured that all her considerable powers would be directed toward besting her competitors. The search for profit resulted in her invention of the leg show, but she drew back in apparent disgust from what she had created. At first sensitive to the female audience, offering both playhouse and plays to please them, she ended her New York management career cooperating in the turn to the visual and catering much more to the male than the female audience. As she learned, the female audience did not have the market power of the male audience, not even in the middle-class theatre. Nor, for that matter, did the female manager enjoy the resources and latitude routinely granted her male counterparts. For just that reason, she had to play by the commercial rules more closely. Small differences yielded decisive cumulative advantages in the marketplace for entertainment, and women's powers—whether as audience members or managers—proved severely limited.

When Keene appealed to women again, in *Fine Arts*, she tried to step out of the marketplace and take a stand for noncommercial values. In the realms of high culture, it seemed to her, women might wield real, positive influence. But there was no noncommercial theatre in this country at that time. While other arts were beginning to discover ways to thrive under the protection of wealthy private patrons, theatre was more ephemeral and less tangible than the canvases and sculptures the nouveaux riches were hauling home from Europe. The emerging realm of the "highbrow" was one where middle-class males claimed control all the more insistently out of fear that, with female participation, art might be labeled effete. The first professor of dramatic literature at any American university, for example, Brander Matthews of Columbia, shared the hypermasculine anxieties of his friend Theodore Roosevelt. In all-male preserves like the Lambs Club and the Players Club, organized in the 1870s and 1880s, actors joined with socially prominent men both for fellowship and for the good of the theatre. When modernist theatre finally did arrive—when Ibsen's Nora slammed the door—it would return to some of the very themes that had been broached, however tentatively, in midcentury women's drama. By then Laura Keene would be thoroughly forgotten. And even then there would be more interest in the way the marketplace in entertainment distorted the arts than in the way it disadvantaged women.[59]

7.
The Rise
of the
Leg Show

In 1866 the managers Henry Jarrett and Harry Palmer imported a large ballet troupe and gorgeous scenery from Europe to play at the academy of Music in New York. The academy hall caught fire and burned down, leaving them threatened with a dead loss. Jarrett and Palmer then offered the troupe's services to William Wheatley, the manager of Niblo's Garden. Wheatley added the dancers and scenery to a production he already had in the works, a hackneyed melodrama spectacle based loosely on the Faust legend and entitled *The Black Crook*. To build up public interest, the partners trumpeted the large amounts they spent on properties, scenery, dresses, and stage alterations. The play opened in September 1866 and ran for an unprecedented fifteen months and 475 performances, generating huge profits. The story of *The Black Crook* is one of the best-known episodes in American theatre history; it is often cited as both the first Broadway musical and the original "girlie" or "leg" show.[1]

It was clear that *Crook*'s appeal was to the senses. As the critic William Winter of the *Tribune* put it, "the scenery is magnificent, the ballet is beautiful, the drama is—rubbish." Even the normally staid Winter, champion of the legitimate, had to gush about the visual feast:

All that gold and silver and gems and light and women's beauty can contribute to fascinate the eye and charm the senses is gathered up in this gorgeous spectacle. Its luster grows as we gaze, and deepens and widens, til the effect is almost painful. One by one curtains of mist ascend and drift away. Silver couches, on which the fairies lounge in negligent grace, ascend and descend amid a silver rain. Columns of living splendor whirl and dazzle as they whirl. From the clouds drop gilded chariots and the white forms of angels.[2]

The dancers were unusually accomplished and included several fully qualified "premieres danseuses," one of whom had been the lead dancer at La Scala (fig. 36). Another twenty "coryphées" were expert in pointe work. Their costumes consisted mostly of the customary ballet tutus worn at knee length with tights underneath; perhaps the skirts were shortened, the décolletage increased a bit (fig. 37). And one number, the "Demon Dance," was done in a pantaloon costume that omitted any skirt (fig. 38).[3]

When the classical ballet first appeared in 1827, in the person of Madame Hutin, American audiences had been shocked, but by the time Madame Celeste toured the United States in 1834 they were reconciled to seeing women dancing in the knee-length tutus which allowed for freedom of movement and permitted appreciation of their step execution. Although ballet highlighted the female dancer and called attention to the body, it was formal, its movements elegant rather than sensuous. And the romantic ballet which became popular in Europe in the 1830s presented the dancer as ethereal and otherworldly. The visit of the Austrian dancer Fanny Ellsler in 1840 confirmed ballet as a respectable popular art. Ellsler's performances incorporated strong narrative elements which distracted the audience from direct contemplation of the body. Her deft public relations — she danced in a benefit for the Bunker Hill monument — and her sparkling performance skills created a sensational two-year tour. The extent to which her ballet separated itself from connotations of sexuality was captured in a contemporary joke about the enthusiasm some of the most prominent transcendentalists felt for Ellsler. According to the story, Ralph Waldo Emerson and Margaret Fuller were gazing at Ellsler from the boxes. After some movement of unusual and particular grace, he turned to her and declared, "Margaret, this is poetry," whereupon she exclaimed, "Ralph, this is religion!"[4]

Thus *The Black Crook* drew upon the by-then established acceptability of ballet, but because the costumes were abbreviated and at least one of the dances overtly sensual, it reawakened worries about the display of the female body for purposes of entertainment. Attacks on the sensualism and the scanty dress of *The Black Crook* actually enhanced its run. James Gordon Bennett's *Herald* poured out a torrent of abuse, which may have been deliberately calculated to pique public curiosity and boost patronage. Bennett called it "one of the grossest immoral productions that was ever put on the stage," charging that it was just as "demoralizing" as Mormonism and that it converted the theatre into a "vestibule to other houses where vice seeks no veil to conceal its dangers." And if "bad" publicity could actually encourage attendance, the Reverend Charles Smyth also cooperated when he rented Cooper Institute and preached a sermon entitled "The Nuisances of New York, Particularly the Naked Truth." Smyth's attack on *The Black Crook* managed to detail its bewitching charms in such a way that cynics

Fig. 36 Sheet music cover from *The Black Crook.* The central figure is the ballerina Marie Bonfanti. Billy Rose Theatre Collection.

Fig. 37 Betty Rigl, one of the premiere danseuses of *The Black Crook*, in her tutu. Harvard Theatre Collection.

Fig. 38 Betty Rigl in her "Demon Dance" costume. Harvard Theatre Collection.

wondered if the Reverend Smyth were not in the pay of the managers. Another clergyman who meant to discourage attendance probably helped business when he denounced the "flesh-colored tights, imitating nature so well that the illusion is complete," and the "ladies dancing so as to make their undergarments spring up, exposing the figure beneath from waist to toe."[5]

Despite the controversy, *The Black Crook* reached a mass audience that included women as well as men. Remarking that "the scenery and the legs are everything," Mark Twain suggested that while the "beauties arrayed in dazzling half-costumes" drew in the men, the scenic effects attracted the women. Whether drawn by the excellence of the ballet, the charm of the music, or the gorgeous scenery, women certainly did attend. Gertrude Kellogg, a young middle-class woman from Brooklyn who saw *The Black Crook* three times, thought it "magnificent," "a splendid thing as far as scenery is concerned." George Templeton Strong's wife went to *The Black Crook* with some friends, although her reasons and reactions were not recorded. Stung by the suggestion that the play was not fit for ladies, Jarrett claimed to have counted the house on a certain night and found that 1345 of 2973 patrons were women. There were even children's matinee parties and toy theatres with all the main characters in cardboard cutouts. Just as certainly, however, *Crook* benefited from particularly intense masculine interest. The Union Club, a wealthy men's club, leased the lower-right-hand box at Niblo's for the entire run of the play. After the managers published a schedule of the dance numbers, crowds of "regulars" would show up at 9:30, just in time for the "Demon Dance." And a group of college men canoeing in Minnesota in 1869 were able to stay alert during a tedious leg of their journey because one of their number volunteered to recite the entire dialogue of *The Black Crook:* he had seen the play nearly a hundred times and memorized every line. It was another advantage of visual over aural entertainment that numerous different objects of interest could be offered simultaneously, thus appealing to different audience tastes. Women and men found different reasons to enjoy *The Black Crook:* visual complexity supplied the means.[6]

Although William Wheatley—the same Wheatley who earlier pirated *Our American Cousin* from Laura Keene—had to split his profits with Jarrett and Palmer, he accumulated $300,000 by the time *The Black Crook* finally closed in January 1868. By contrast, the play generated no new stars and only a few of the principal dancers became moderately well-known. The leading ballerina, Marie Bonfanti, was said to have been paid $150 a week, but only one or two in the company received such high pay; as a rule the salaries were small. In 1866 three *Crook* "ballet girls" who were being paid $15 a week wrote to the newspapers protesting that they had been promised more. Most of the dancers remained quite obscure; indeed, the cast changed in the course of the run with no appreciable effect.[7]

Although the story of *The Black Crook* is often told as though it were the product of happy accident, in fact the play was directly descended from Laura Keene's burlesque extravaganzas. Pursuing the logic of profit, theatre managers were discovering that sex paid. It was "the return of the repressed," as scholar Robert Allen has put it, for theatre managers had only recently expelled prostitutes from their premises. But this was sexual commerce with a difference: they were learning to sell a spectacle, an eroticized vision that offered suggestion and arousal rather than satisfaction. The trick was to find out how much sexual titillation could be interpolated into mainstream theatre without scaring away respectable — middle-class, female — audiences. Testing the limits of profit and public tolerance, theatre in the late 1860s raised questions about the commodification of the female body that remain troubling — and unanswered — even today.[8]

THE BIG TIME

In the 1860s theatre began to take on the contours of a big business; the scale of its capital requirements and profit opportunities changed, and managers began to act more and more like captains of industry. Like entrepreneurs in other fields, theatre managers tried to cut their risks as the size of their investment grew. In New York City they organized into a managers' association. Initially their goal was to resist the wage demands of their orchestra musicians, who were particularly prone to strike. But the group was also able to present a united front against the impositions of James Gordon Bennett, and later versions of the association in the 1870s tried to curb the salary demands of stars and curtail competition among theatres. The Manager's Association was a forerunner of the Syndicate, a group of six men who seized control of the entire American theatre business in the 1890s.[9]

With urban real estate and overhead costs running so high, it became less and less likely that an actor or actress inexperienced in financial matters could make a success in theatre management. Edwin Booth proved it: his new theatre, which opened in 1869, cost over half a million dollars to build, and despite many box-office hits he could never work his way out from under the mountain of debt he had assumed. A great player but a financial babe in the woods, Booth was taken advantage of by his business partners and ended in bankruptcy. Successful managers of the late 1860s brought capital and financial savvy with them, following the examples of Harry Palmer, a Wall Street speculator, or Augustin Daly, whose wealthy father-in-law backed him up.[10]

None of this increased capitalization or attention to business principles redounded much to the benefit of the players. On the contrary, there is some indication that the 1860s saw a decline in the salaries of the lowest-paid players and an increase in the prevalence of "job acting," that is, acting without the security of a season-long contract. The traditional benefit performance, in which a performer had some influence over her own compensation, was eliminated. Certainly ordinary players saw the occupation become notably less settled and more itinerant, with the increasing prevalence of the "combination" system, which involved an entire company going on tour. The residential stock companies were noticeably weakened by 1870, and the power of New York managers became more significant as New York became the theatrical proving grounds from which touring shows originated.[11]

Nothing symbolized the new era of big money in theatre more aptly than the arrival of the "robber baron" Jim Fisk on Broadway. Fisk (fig. 39) acquired control of three theatres in 1868 and 1869. He and Jay Gould paid $820,000 in December 1868 for the newly constructed Pike's Opera House on West 23rd

Fig. 39 Jim Fisk. Harvard Theatre Collection.

Street and 8th Avenue (actually, the Erie Railroad paid, though Fisk and Gould's names went on the deed). Fisk apparently regarded himself as the hard-headed entrepreneur who would shake up the old-fashioned theatre business to make it yield handsome new profits. He tried to hire William Winter as a paid puffer, but Winter indignantly refused. He did hire John Brougham, the veteran actor-manager and author of numerous burlesques, to be the manager of one of his theatres. Fisk's contract required Brougham to pay rent on the building and to meet all the expenses of management and production, but, unlike traditional managers, Brougham was to receive for all his troubles not the chance of profit but only a modest salary. The profits of production *and* the rent on the playhouse were both to go to Fisk. The arrangement lasted only a few weeks in early 1869, long enough for Fisk to bluster that he was not making his profit, while Brougham sustained a $20,000 loss. But Brougham had his revenge in his last production, a burlesque called "Much Ado about a Merchant of Venice," which placed Shylock on contemporary Wall Street to lampoon Fisk and his ilk. Although Fisk himself was soon distracted by the so-called "Erie wars"—a financial duel with Commodore Vanderbilt over control of the Erie Railroad—the influence and the lure of big money had become prominent influences in American theatre by 1870. There was no professional theatre that was not thoroughly attuned to the marketplace, and very little that did not aspire to do (and be) big business.[12]

"THE MENKEN"

Behind *The Black Crook* lay the earlier phenomenon of Adah Isaacs Menken. Menken's appearance, scantily clad, in a horse melodrama called *Mazeppa* earlier in the 1860s had created a sensation. Wearing pink silk tights and a short, light tunic, she played the hero, a Tartar chieftain who is captured by his wicked enemies, "stripped naked," and lashed to the back of a wild horse to die of exposure. (Of course he survives and returns to exact vengeance.) Menken was daring enough to disdain the customary use of a dummy and actually be strapped to a live animal onstage. But the source of the sensation lay in her costume (fig. 40), which combined with the pretense of the plot—the hero is supposedly stripped—to create unheard-of audience excitement. Menken never had much success in other roles, but *Mazeppa* played to enormous business in New York, San Francisco, London, and Paris. She became "the Menken," a show business phenomenon, fabulous and notorious. For a year or two in the 1860s Adah Isaacs Menken was probably the highest-paid actress in the world.[13]

Menken's unorthodox personal life encompassed a number of husbands and lovers, some of them famous. She wrote poetry that interested Dante Gabriel Rossetti and Charles Dickens and struck up friendships with a variety of more or

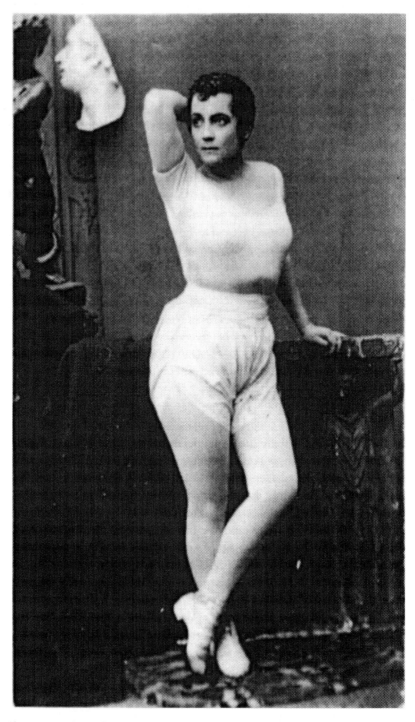

Fig. 40 Adah Isaacs Menken in the tights and tunic costume she wore to appear "naked" in the leading male role in *Mazeppa*. Harvard Theatre Collection.

less Bohemian writers on two continents. Menken was a self-dramatizing show-off, a willful, fascinating woman given to romantic posturing, but she was also gay, good-hearted, and generous to a fault. She recognized that her body was a realizable asset and freely proceeded to cash it in. She was indeed, as her first husband charged, an impudent, brazen "adventuress." She earned hundreds of thousands of dollars on the stage, but when she died in Paris in 1868 she was nearly penniless and virtually alone.

Menken set out to become an actress after her first husband, Alexander Menken, lost everything in the Panic of 1857. She had no patience for working her way up, and she fast-talked her way into leading roles for which she was unprepared. In Nashville in 1858, for example, she played Lady Macbeth opposite the tragedian James Murdock, and he had to prompt her constantly. She seems to have discovered that it was easier to charm newspapermen than to learn her lines properly. Certainly journalists' good notices helped her career immensely, though she found only modest success with audiences and became bitter about the "falsehood and duplicity of the managers."[14]

In 1859 she met and fell in love with a prizefighter named John Carmel Heenan. She and Alexander Menken had quarreled, and, believing he had obtained a divorce, she married Heenan, who promptly left for England for a title match. When popular interest in Heenan prompted newspaper speculation about the marriage, Menken came forward to denounce his wife as immoral, declaring there had been no divorce. Heenan refused to answer Adah Menken's letters and soon jilted her altogether. Menken, who said she felt disgusted with "exposing myself to the public," talked of supporting herself by writing or teaching school. But the only jobs she could obtain were back on the stage. She had to appear at a cheap Broadway music hall and even to bill herself as "Mrs. John C. Heenan" to attract audiences. Meanwhile Heenan's lawyers responded to a suit for nonpayment of a hotel bill by alleging that she was a prostitute. In the winter of 1860 Menken was out of work and so despondent that at one point she wrote a suicide note. But suicide was not her style.

Tough and adaptable, Menken decided that her notoriety could be made not a burden but an opportunity: persuading someone to stake her to a wardrobe, she want back onstage. Menken appeared in pieces like "Satan in Paris," emphasizing her looks and her legs and incorporating variety show turns. At one point her act included comic impersonations of both Charlotte Cushman and Edwin Forrest. She smoked cigarettes, cropped her hair, and cultivated her flair for the outrageous. Only after her career had gone flat and her good name was in tatters, did Menken turn to the *Mazeppa* role that made her a star.[15]

Playing the naked hero in *Mazeppa* was not her idea if we can believe the boast of a theatre manager. When Menken was playing in Albany in April 1861, John

B. Smith, the manager at a rival house, offered free beer to his patrons on Menken's benefit night. Having thus depleted Menken's audience and left her nearly penniless at the end of her engagement, Smith proposed that she play the lead in *Mazeppa* for him. After a flurry of suggestive publicity, including the parading of a set of horses billed as "the Menken stud," she opened to enthusiastic male audiences and played three record-breaking weeks.[16]

Menken seldom attempted a serious part again. She did try *Camille* in Pittsburgh, but the audience would not stand for it. So she cultivated the press, took *Mazeppa* to San Francisco and London, and returned to New York in the spring of 1866 to demand, and get, the fantastic sum of $500 a performance. At that point William Winter assessed her skills:

> She has not the faintest idea of what acting is. She moves about the stage with no motive, and therefore, in a kind of accidental manner; assumes attitudes that are sometimes fine, and sometimes ridiculous; speaks in a thin, weak voice, and with bad elocution; exclaims "death!" and "vengeance" very much as a mild and hungry female might order tea and toast; and in short invites critical attention, not to her emotional capabilities, her intellectual gifts, or her culture as an artist, but solely to her physical proportions.[17]

Her audiences seem to have been composed largely, if not entirely, of men. Winter's *Tribune* review described an all-male audience, and the *Spirit of the Times* estimated that not four in a hundred of those who attended her New York opening in 1866 were women. Of course this was an opening night, which women were traditionally less likely to attend, but the *Spirit* review can hardly have encouraged women to attend subsequent performances. It declared, "Every gambler, thief, pick-pocket, roué, old blasé man of the world, and would-be flash man of the city was there." Press notices of her performances in Sacramento and Baltimore, and later in New York, noted the presence of at least a few women. But there was little to draw them if Menken's acting skills were so scant; after all, *Mazeppa* was a well-worn entry in the melodramatic repertoire and everyone knew that the main character was to appear to be naked. Only in London and Paris, more tolerant about such issues, does Menken seem to have drawn any significant proportion of women to her audiences.[18]

Having decided to appeal to the visual, Menken saw no need to play multiple parts but realized there was always a demand for multiple images. The new technology of photography provided just what she needed: 1861, the year of her *Mazeppa*, was also a revolutionary year in the history of the image, as the mounted photographs called cartes de visite displaced various earlier technologies, such as daguerreotypes and ambrotypes. A market in celebrity photographs, and an underground market in "French postcards," quickly developed.

Fig. 41 Menken in the photographer's studio. Harvard Theatre Collection.

In such photos actresses could exploit—or be exploited by—close-ups, head shots, and full-body images. They were not limited to the views from a distance traditionally available to the live audience in a playhouse. Menken loved to be photographed, and as early as 1859 she had begun to advertise herself through this new medium. Hundreds and perhaps thousands of different cartes de visites of Menken were produced and sold by photographers in different cities (figs. 41–43). Boys also hawked these photographs outside theatre entrances. The photographers paid her no royalties, but she seems to have considered herself rewarded in publicity. One of her biographers argues that she became the most photographed woman in the world. The visual images of Menken—untitled, disconnected from narrative, perhaps sometimes even altered or faked (fig. 44)—fed her legend and whetted the appetites of the men who crowded her audiences.[19]

Although Menken exploited her looks and her body cheerfully and lucratively, she yearned for something more: she was a frustrated poet who wanted a voice. She claimed to have serious ideas and an individual point of view, although her protests often seemed to collapse into self-promotion. She wrote an article for the *Sunday Mercury* arguing that daughters should be trained to "higher and holier motives" than being fashionable and securing wealthy husbands, that there were other missions for woman than that of wife and mother. She complained that the coverage of her life in the New York *Illustrated News* in 1860 was too "light and flippant," "as of a woman who, with all her advantages, had lived on the surface of life." She was, Menken declared, "a thinking, earnest woman." She once

Figs. 42 and Fig. 43 Menken again. Notice the rich detail of costume, pose, and expression that the camera can capture, as opposed to the earlier lithographs. Harvard Theatre Collection.

wrote that it was her fate "to live within the marts of Pleasure and of Gain, yet be no willing worshipper at either shrine." But that poem was written before she hit the big time with *Mazeppa*, after which her poetic voice was stilled, and she seems to have thoroughly enjoyed her transactions with Pleasure and Gain. She who wanted to thrill the world with her poetic eloquence consented to enact her part mute when *Mazeppa* played in Paris.[20]

At thirty-three Menken succumbed to tuberculosis and its complications before she could see the complete ruin of her already dimming career. A great believer in her own romantic magnetism, Menken probably never feared the eager young imitators who constituted an "army of Mazeppas" coming up behind her, but perhaps she should have. As William Winter had pointed out in his review of her New York opening in 1866, "If artistic greatness is to be acquired by such means as Miss Menken has chosen for its pursuit, there would seem to be no good reason why the majority of females should not acquire it, if so

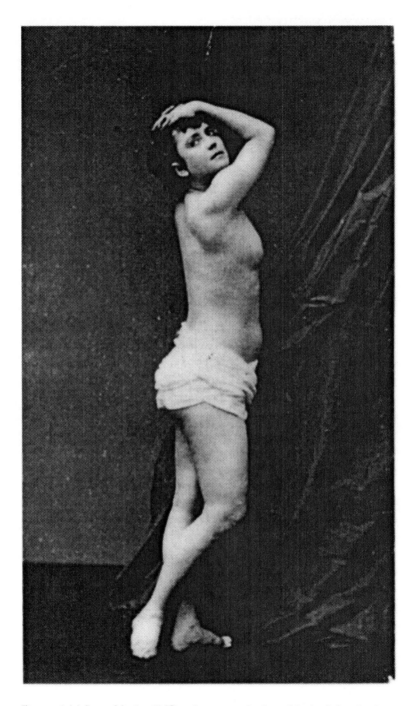

Fig. 44 Adah Isaacs Menken(?) This photo certainly shows Menken's face, but her head may have been superimposed on another woman's topless body. The power of the camera to claim surpassing realism and yet to lie may be captured here, fittingly, in the representation of a woman's body. Harvard Theatre Collection.

disposed." Menken had proved that displaying her body might be lucrative for a woman, but she also demonstrated that, given the realities of aging, the resulting career might be pathetically brief.[21]

Menken's career posed two questions to canny managers: Was it possible to convince American women in any numbers to attend such performances? And was it possible to profit from the display of the female body without empowering a star like Menken to demand a large share of those profits? *The Black Crook* appeared to answer both questions. Its success showed that when scanty clothing did not pretend to nakedness, and the script did not reinforce the illusion of nudity, abbreviated costumes might be tolerated by mixed, middle-class audiences. *Crook* also demonstrated that although one "naked" woman might become a star, a number of women half-dressed wielded no such power.[22]

LYDIA THOMPSON'S BURLESQUE "BLONDES"

A few months after *The Black Crook* finally closed on Broadway, the English actress Lydia Thompson and her troupe of "British Blondes" opened at Wood's Museum in New York and promptly renewed the leg craze. Thompson's play *Ixion; or, The Man at the Wheel* was a satire on the "fashionable weaknesses" of society and the foibles of contemporary politics. The music consisted of humorous verses set to popular tunes, and the dance was a mixture of high-kicking, jigging, and minstrel-like break-downs and walk-arounds performed to catchy up-tempo music. The dialogue bristled with puns, rhymed couplets, classical and literary allusions, and political jokes. Costumed in tights and short skirts or tunics that revealed the lower thigh, the Blondes were a great hit (fig. 45). Their burlesque changed forever the meaning of that word, as satire became associated with (and later eclipsed by) display of the female body. Historians agree that Thompson's *Ixion*, which opened in September 1868, marked the beginning of the modern burlesque show.[23]

At the end of the year *Ixion* moved to Niblo's Garden where it could be "got up" in more elaborate fashion and where the customary audiences were upscale, "first class" assemblies. The critics, tolerant while Thompson played at Wood's, began to worry and scold about the morality of such a production. But a little adverse publicity would not hurt, and might help, attendance, as Niblo's managers knew. Cartes de visites of Thompson and members of her troupe circulated freely, and in the winter and spring of 1868 – 69 the burlesque phenomenon spread, as imitators popped up in several New York theatres and in other cities as well. Burlesque played in five of seven Boston theatres that winter, prompting William Dean Howells to take notice of this new phenomenon in the pages of the *Atlantic Monthly*.[24]

Fig. 45 Lydia Thompson. The exaggeratedly golden
tresses were the signature of the "British Blondes." Billy
Rose Theatre Collection.

When Thompson's troupe took the stage, women dominated the action and
cross-dressing was the order of the day. All the parts in *Ixion* but one were played
by women, most of them in breeches roles. Their purpose in playing men was to
display their legs rather than attempt verisimilitude (see fig. 46). "Female face and
form carry all the honors," said the *New York Times* of Thompsonian burlesque,
remarking that "no ugly woman ever made a success" in it. Yet the cross-dressed
women also satirized men's manners and behavior, creating what the *Times* called
"an idiotic parody of masculinity." When Howells attended a burlesque show, he
was unnerved by the delight some of the young women seemed to take in male
impersonation.[25]

Fig. 46 Thompson in "male" garb designed to look charming, rather than masculine. Billy Rose Theatre Collection.

Like Menken and the *Crook* dancers, Thompson's brand of burlesque flaunted the female body. Her troupe's dancing was particularly "kinetic" and uninhibited. The moves came mostly from minstrelsy, but when performed by women they seemed to suggest worldly sensuality. One observer described "a frantic outburst of irrepressible animal spirits" in which the dancers appeared to have no control over their legs. The women in revealing costumes were not only showing their bodies but also moving them suggestively; their performance invited male sexual interest and hinted that women had their own desires and pleasures.[26]

The humor that was embedded in the various plays the Thompson troupe offered is hard to recover, but one skit featured Thompson as the "Girl of the Period." She carried a riding crop, smoked a cigarette, and wore a ridiculous hat crowned with a stuffed squirrel (fig. 47). The character declared that the "new" woman was very much aware of her "own awarishness." The skit was a take-off on a *Saturday Review* article by Eliza Lynn Linton that bitterly attacked modern women as vain, frivolous, materialistic, and manipulative. Linton's essay became enormously popular because it addressed male fears about independent women, and Thompson's burlesque seems to have done the same.[27]

Thompson also put women in charge of the critical wit traditionally offered at intervals when burlesque performers moved out of role and came downstage to address the audience directly. According to one observer, Thompson's actresses would trot down to the footlights, wink at the audience, and rattle off "some twaddling allusions to Sorosis or President Grant." In the show Howells saw,

Fig. 47 Thompson as the Girl of the Period. Photo is from the collection of the author.

women told jokes about Ben Butler, the *Alabama* claims, and Erie shares, canvassing the scandals and controversies of Reconstruction-era America. Delivering stand-up comedy, which makes others look ridiculous, involves a degree of power. But as the inclusion of a joke about Sorosis, a feminist club formed by New York professional women, indicates, their humor was at least sometimes based on a male point of view (fig. 48). Eventually burlesque performances seem to have made a special point of lampooning "strong-minded" women.[28]

Like *The Black Crook*, Lydia Thompson's burlesque troupe found a mainstream mass audience for a display of female bodies that had hitherto been con-

Fig. 48 Lydia Thompson as Robinson Crusoe. She makes
no effort to look like a man in this male role. On the contrary,
her costume insists on her woman's body, just as blackface is
employed to overstate race. Billy Rose Theatre Collection.

fined to male-only model artist or concert saloon shows. Audiences for Thompson's burlesque included a corps of male regulars, and yet there were women too, at least initially. In each case, mixed media probably helped to hold mixed audiences, for there were many attractions besides legs — dance and scenic illusion in *Crook*, puns and verbal humor in *Ixion*, music in both.[29]

But the female audience for burlesque did not last for long. In the summer of 1869 a wave of "anti-burlesque hysteria" in the New York press frightened away the middle-class audiences that had initially been drawn to *Ixion* and sent the Thompson troupe prematurely packing for a national tour. The press attack seems to have stemmed from a contretemps between Thompson's manager, Alexander Henderson, and the New York theatre managers and theatre press that occurred in May 1869 at a dinner party in a Manhattan hotel. Apparently Henderson gave a speech criticizing the state of American theatre, gloating over his own success, and upbraiding dramatic journalists for their criticisms of burlesque. It was the old story of British condescension, more irritating than ever since Henderson was raking in such profits and lacked the wit to see that a little press controversy about the morality of a piece could be helpful. He also took the occasion to attack a former member of the troupe — presumably Ada Harland — who had left to start her own company and thus enter into rivalry with him. He hinted that he had enjoyed a romantic liaison with her. As Laura Keene might have testified, such comments were to be expected as part of the mud-slinging used against women managers. But the journalists and managers, furious with Henderson, saw they could attack him on the flank he had so invitingly left open, the issue of managerial morality.[30]

The *Spirit of the Times* opened fire with an article dismissing Henderson as no better than a pimp, a "shovel-nosed shark" preying on nude female forms. The *Spirit* called him a "natural Mormon" with "multiple wives" among the performers whom he managed, and predicted that these press reports would "of course prohibit ladies and children" from venturing to see this "incarnation of Vice." The *New York Times*, disgusted that the success of burlesque had so crowded out legitimate theatre that even Wallack's was given over to the blonde invaders, warned darkly of "the inner vices and degradations of the Henderson rabble" and headlined an article "Exit British Burlesque."[31]

The New York press furor evidently had limited and local causes, but once unleashed it frightened the respectable and female audience away from the leg show. When the British Blondes' tour circled back through New York in 1870 and 1871 they drew a rougher crowd, containing few women and few "respectable" people. But Thompson and her manager discovered they did not need the women. By 1870 the audience for burlesque was all-male and rowdy, like the model artist shows and concert saloons, but the leg business remained profitable. According to Thompson's reminiscences, the "entire male citizenry" welcomed the Blondes' American tours of 1869 and 1872, and profits amounted to over $500,000. By late in the century, burlesque had settled into a durable formula that mixed humor delivered by male comics with a show of women's voiceless and scantily clad bodies.[32]

The future of the leg show lay primarily in "girlie" concoctions for male audiences, but, as Peter Buckley has pointed out, it was also "naturalized" into mainstream entertainments, especially in the form of the female chorus line that became part of musical comedy. If, as Robert Allen has argued, there was a "transgressive" stance that empowered women beneath burlesque's obvious appeal to male sexual interest, it was both short-lived and hard to detect, for mainstream playhouse audiences were not free to engage in demonstrative public responses. One spectator who tried to hiss "a *pas seul* of the indescribable" was hustled out by a policeman. By their very name the Blondes exemplified the reduction of woman to her physical appearance. They showed that placing female appearance on display could be lucrative in different ways, whether a manager chose to offer explicit undress to all-male audiences, or milder teasing to gender-integrated audiences.[33]

The influence of the new burlesque on women was greater than their brief appearance in its audience would seem to justify, since standards of female beauty shifted at about this time in the direction of the heftiness and blonde hair so characteristic of Thompson's troupe. But that shift probably owed more to the blizzard of photographs of Thompson and the Blondes that blanketed the nation than to the reactions of women in their live audiences (fig. 49). It is possible, for instance, that the new popularity of a sturdy form for women was in part due to the public's interpreting as truth the extra ten pounds bequeathed by the camera.[34]

Thompson was the logical successor to the women of *The Black Crook* and to Adah Menken because she matter-of-factly accepted both the commodification of women's bodies and the power of male management. She seems to have been a cheerful, uncomplicated hoofer. She joined a London theatre's corps de ballet at age sixteen and spent years charming audiences with her saucy stage manner and her flying feet. Widowed and left with a small daughter to support, Thompson was thirty-two when she opened in *Ixion* in New York in 1868, old enough to foresee the waning of her dance career. The Liverpool theatre manager Alexander Henderson, who traveled with her as the manager of the troupe for its American tour, was also her new husband, although the fact of their marriage does not seem to have been made public. Thompson always insisted that burlesque was harmless entertainment, and punctuated her own defense with simple economics: "I did not enter the profession as a source of amusement, but to enable me to earn a livelihood. I thus appear in the class of entertainment that is

Fig. 49 Lydia Thompson. Note the artful camera work in this publicity photo. Billy Rose Theatre Collection.

most remunerative." But what she took as a given, some women were prepared to recognize as a problem.[35]

A FEMINIST CRITIQUE OF THE LEG SHOW

About midway through the run of *The Black Crook* an actress and playwright named Olive Logan opened an attack on the "leg business" with a blistering article in the *Galaxy*. She renewed and expanded her complaint when the British Blondes arrived, in lectures, magazine articles, and even a book. Logan complained in her initial article that the "naked drama" was displacing respectable theatre, rewarding women who could not act, dance, sing, or mime. The leg business required a woman to do only one thing: to dress "in a way which is attractive to an indelicate mind." She clearly had Menken and her imitators in mind as much as the *Black Crook* dancers. Logan (fig. 50) reminded her readers that the stage

Fig. 50 Olive Logan. Billy Rose Theatre Collection.

had heretofore been "a channel for gifted and intelligent young women to gain a livelihood by honest exertion." The leg show threatened to change all that.[36]

She suggested that the new stars were cynically profiting while they drove other women from their livelihoods. Logan claimed that one of the "Mazeppas" had contacted her to ask for permission to use a play Logan had written. Since the play in question offered no occasion for undress, Logan expressed some surprise. She was told by an intermediary that the actress in question "hates the leg business as much as anybody," but, "bless you, nothing else pays now-a-days; so what can she do?"[37]

Finally, Logan charged that the leg business was built on fraud. She pictured the Mazeppas coolly peeling off roles of bills to buy flattering comments in the newspapers. Even the bodies they displayed were falsified, since the "art of padding" could be used to simulate a good figure. She quoted from what she said was a note written by a skilled "padder" in Philadelphia: "Mam—Them tites is finished your nees will be all OK when you get them on. Bad figgers is all plaid out now they will caust nine dollars."[38]

Logan spoke as one of the theatre's own. Her mother had been an actress, her father a well-known actor, playwright, and manager. Olive made her debut in her father's theatre at age four or five, and went on the stage full-time at fifteen, after her father died and left her mother to care for several young siblings. Her sister Eliza also became a professional actress. Olive Logan returned to the stage in 1864 after her first marriage failed. She toured as a star, playing opposite Frank Chanfrau in a long-running hit, *Sam*, in New York and on a subsequent national tour. She also wrote a couple of successful plays. Although she possessed neither great beauty nor powerful talent, Logan nevertheless knew the business well enough to do creditable work. By 1867 she had retired from the stage (in part because growing deafness made it difficult for her to hear her cues) and was making her living as a writer and a lecturer on the lyceum circuit. Logan's most popular talks dealt with the theatre, and she still identified with the stage and with the women who worked in it.[39]

Logan reopened her critique of the leg business in May 1869, as Thompson's British Blondes were concluding their highly successful New York season. The feminist pioneer Susan B. Anthony invited Logan to speak at the convention of the Equal Rights Association which was held in New York in May 1869. The Equal Rights Association was formed to press for the rights of blacks and women, and Logan shared the platform with such veteran reformers as Frederick Douglass, Lucretia Mott, and Henry Ward Beecher. Describing herself as a recent recruit to the cause of women's rights, Logan used her talk to emphasize the issue of economic opportunity and discrimination against women wage earners. She praised the stage as a place where "the equality of woman was fully recognized so far as the form of labor and the amount of reward for her labor are concerned." But she feared the leg show would change forever those favorable employment conditions: "I cannot advise any woman to go upon the stage with the demoralizing influence which seems there to prevail more everyday, when its greatest rewards are won by brazen-faced, stained, yellow-haired, padded-limbed creatures while actresses of the old school, well-trained, well-qualified, decent, cannot earn a living."[40]

After that speech, which was often interrupted by applause, Logan found there was a new demand for her lectures at women's meetings around the country, and she began to write occasionally for Stanton and Anthony's feminist newspaper, the *Revolution*. But she also wrote to the *New York Times* to clarify her position on the theatre. Logan argued that when a young woman applied to a theatre manager for work he would ask if her legs, arms, and bosom were symmetrically formed and if she were willing to expose them. He would go further: "Can you sing brassy songs and dance the can-can, and wink at men? . . . Are you willing to appear tonight and every night amid the glare of gas-lights, and before the gaze of thousands of men, in this pair of satin breeches, ten inches long, without a vestige of drapery on your person?"[41]

Logan repeated her argument against the leg shows in an article for *Packard's Monthly* and expanded on her position further in a book, *Apropos of Women and Theatres*. Logan distinguished burlesque from the ballet dancing of *The Black Crook*, which she thought less offensive because the *Crook* dancers appeared in character and remained silent. Logan indicated that she respected ballet as an art, but that the "nude woman of today," who appeared before audiences dancing the jig and cracking jokes, represented "nothing but herself." Logan detected the influences of both minstrelsy and the concert saloons in the style and content of burlesque. She emphasized the importance of the manipulation of public opinion through newspaper puffing and even charged that the *Crook* managers had used a claque to encourage applause at the first performance when the scanty costumes stunned the audience into silence. She understood the economics of what was happening only too well. By the time she published another book, *Before the Footlights*, in 1870, Logan was ready to point even more insistently to the responsibility of profit-minded management:

> Theatres—like newspapers, for the most part—are either immensely lucrative or very disastrous affairs, and the first part of this fact has induced numberless men—outsiders in every sense—to invest their money in theatrical stock as if it were live stock—hogs or cattle. It is these people who have been chiefly instrumental in bringing upon the stage that hideous disgrace known as the "nude drama" which took its rise with the flimsy absurdity called *The Black Crook* and who have continued it by importing "painted Jezebels" known as "English burlesque blondes."[42]

Logan went too far in blaming outsiders because her own family was involved. Her brother-in-law was the manager of Wood's Museum, where Adah Isaacs Menken had her sensational run in *Mazeppa* in 1866 and where Lydia Thompson and her troupe played in 1868. Wood had originally tried to book Thompson in the spring of 1866, to follow Menken, and he probably could tell himself that had he succeeded, the profits that flowed to *The Black Crook* might have been his instead. Even so, George Wood and Eliza Logan Wood profited handsomely from the leg business. The Logan sisters inherited a theatrical craft from their parents: they in effect disputed between themselves how a woman ought to regard the evolving theatrical business, in which the display of women's bodies was turning out to be so very profitable. Eliza's position was much like that of Lydia Thompson, allied by marriage with male management and profit, but Olive—divorced, self-supporting—identified with the independent and talented woman who needed a job.[43]

It was not easy for the organized women's movement to confront the issues

Logan raised. Logan's feminism was decidedly economic, recurring again and again to the fundamental facts of woman's need for self-support and the handicaps she faced in the marketplace. To activists nurtured in the non-market values of domesticity and evangelical obligation, Logan's concerns probably came across as selfish, worldly, and materialistic. Lucretia Mott, for example, deplored Logan's speech to the Equal Rights convention as "coarse." The self-seeking woman in the marketplace was especially disquieting in the context of an entertainment industry where she so often sold, explicitly or implicitly, some version of sexual appeal. Yet it was not a surprising sales pitch, since in a market where men controlled most of the money, women would be largely constrained to sell what men wanted to buy—which usually involved some aspect of child nurture, domestic services, or sexual pleasure. Seeking to establish women's dignity and autonomy, the early women's movement was loath to face such a humiliating calculus, and focused instead on issues like education or the ballot.[44]

WOMEN'S BODIES AS ENTERTAINMENT PRODUCTS

By the time of the leg show, lines of recruitment to theatrical work were more open than they had been fifty years earlier, so that theatrical traditions or craft scruples carried little weight against the demand for female performers willing to show their bodies. One aging actress remembered that costumes had been more modest when she was in the corps de ballet: "Ours was a regular profession, don't you see, and we knew that if a costume seemed unsuitable to us and we refused to wear it, there was no one else to be found who would." In the 1860s managers had no problem finding someone willing to wear any costume, however scanty it was.[45]

Visual entertainments that involved the display of women's bodies were cheap to produce: choosing young women for their beauty rather than skill kept wages low by enlarging the talent pool. But in an economy that taught every worker to regard herself as a commodity, theatre work was still easier and better-paid than most other women's work. Physical appearance, with or without a modicum of talent, became a kind of capital, and a simple calculation of comparative advantage might propel a young woman like Dreiser's Carrie Meeber onto the stage. Yet Howells, who wrote of "the hard-working sisterhood" of the burlesque troupe, "aiming, doubtless, at nothing but applause," doubted that simple economic motivations among the workers altered the character of the resulting entertainment product. A notorious woman like Jim Fisk's mistress Josie Mansfield, who never worked on the stage, felt free to call herself an "actress," as if in recognition of certain underlying similarities between what she and at least some of the women onstage were selling.[46]

"Devil take your legitimate drama!" one manager told Olive Logan, "I tell you if I can't draw the crowd otherwise, I'll put a woman on my stage without a rag on her." It would not take long for that threat to materialize, and Howells was prescient when he supposed that the future of such entertainments would become a matter for the statute books and the courts. The demand was there; as Logan had declared, "The paid money will indicate the made choice," and men controlled most of the money. Although burlesque moved out of the first-class theatres, leg or girlie shows became a permanent feature of American entertainment, varying over time only in the degree to which they have been underground versus "legitimate" business. The controversy would continue too. On the one side were the entertainment entrepreneurs who had discovered a most reliable and profitable market niche, and on the other stood vice crusaders like Anthony Comstock, who in 1873 asked, "Why is it that every public play must have a naked woman? It is disgusting, and pernicious to the young." It was a debate, however, in which women would figure more as objects than subjects.[47]

Visual entertainments displaying women's bodies to the male gaze flourished not only because of reliable demand and supply, but also because they were hard to police. The visual was difficult to specify, as the model artist shows revealed: why was the "Greek Slave" in tights objectionable, while Powers' statue, in marble, was not? If female nudity was acceptable in "high" art, how could you say what was wrong with the leg show? *The Black Crook* tapped the ambiguities of ballet, suspended between prestigious high culture and suggestions of the Paris demimonde. Edgar Degas's ballet dancers would capture exactly that ambiguity: his dancers are sometimes whores, sometimes angels, sometimes tired working women, sometimes all these at once. The difficulty of specifying the differences among visual representations made it appealing to entertainment entrepreneurs to test the limits of public or state tolerance for their products.[48]

The triumph of the visual, which was in the first instance at least as much a product of profit calculations as of the new technology that did so much to promote the value of appearances, infected the drama. The assumption that women had a special responsibility to be beautiful, and ought not to appear in public unless they were, flowed outward from the leg shows and concert saloons. Women who complained, like Olive Logan, could be dismissed with the taunt of "sour grapes." Women who cultivated the old skills had little hope of success unless they were also pretty. Gertrude Kellogg, for example, was a young woman who prepared for a dramatic career in the late 1860s and early 1870s; her voice and elocution were excellent, her looks nothing special. She was chosen by the aging Edwin Forrest to play opposite him on his last tour in 1872. Forrest still appreciated the merits of a fine voice, but his was a passing generation. William

Winter scornfully dismissed Kellogg on the grounds that she was not pretty enough. Winter, the self-conscious partisan of the legitimate and of theatre's claims to be high art, coolly applied the standards of the concert saloon when it came to female performers: "Miss Gertrude Kellogg . . . should be seriously invited to desist from attempting to embody ideals of loveliness."[49]

The only strategy that remained for female stage aspirants not blessed in face or form lay in fashionable dress. Augustin Daly routinely engaged middle-class women for walk-on parts with the requirement that they furnish their own clothes. These "Daly debutantes" were daughters of families willing to subsidize them while they accepted low pay that did not begin to cover the cost of their dresses. The gorgeous costumes of the women became one of the attractions of every Daly production. Here was yet another formula for having it both ways, since the fashionably clothed female body might interest both men and women.[50]

The same Augustin Daly wrote *Under the Gaslight*, the 1867 melodrama that featured a woman rescuing a man who had been tied to the railroad tracks. Daly's willingness to exploit women as objects but also appeal to them as subjects marked the methods that proved profitable: entertainment entrepreneurs could concentrate principally on their male audiences while retaining a submerged appeal to women's interests and muffling contradictions in rapid-fire action and spectacular visuals. Fancy dresses, debutantes, and daring heroines were a mix of entertainment products that permitted Daly to appeal to women and yet always make sure to give pleasure to men's eyes.

Even Olive Logan bowed to the new visual requirements when she went back on the stage in 1874. Fearing that deafness had vitiated her acting skills, she made her Paris wardrobe her chief attraction, posed for cartes de visite in her finest outfits, and billed herself as "The Best-Dressed Woman in the Country" (fig. 51). It was a sad come-down for the woman who had offered the first feminist critique of the theatre's commodification of women.[51]

THEATRE AND WOMEN

By 1870 American theatre had become a business that offered much less to women than it had in 1790. The early theatre had been male-dominated but also irregular and fly-by-night; the lack of regulation allowed women to find opportunities for financial independence and public expression. These were especially important in the decades before other means of self-support became available and before other public actions became thinkable or do-able. In the earliest moments of the women's rights movement, the theatre in general and Fanny Kemble in particular offered crucial proof that women could speak skillfully, act indepen-

Fig. 51 Logan as the Best-Dressed Woman in the Country. Harvard Theatre Collection.

dently, and support themselves respectably. Of course the early theatre was not a golden age for women: men routinely treated women as sexual objects, as Dunlap's *Memoirs of a Water-Drinker* or the men who criticized Fanny Kemble would serve to indicate. But they did so through unorganized, individual behavior rather than in the disciplined pursuit of profit.

With the rise of a theatre oriented toward profit-making, theatre managers gradually fell into regularized marketing strategies. Women were relegated to second-class status within general audiences, or commodified outright for all-male audiences. Since male economic power was preeminent, market-oriented theatre might sometimes please women but was invariably constrained to please men. Either way, the turn to the visual was useful. Spectacle could add one more element to the smorgasbord spread before general audiences, convey sexual pleasure to male audiences, and provide cost-effective fascination to both.

By 1870 the decline of residential stock companies and the increase in touring made it harder to combine an acting career with marriage and motherhood. The turn to the visual tended to require youth and beauty of acting women and thus made lifelong careers problematic. Ordinary players had less control over their working lives and were more dominated by management than they had been eighty or even thirty years earlier, and management was increasingly in the hands of men. Breaking into management — not uncommon for women in the 1840s and 1850s, when theatre was a small business — became an elusive goal as theatre grew into a big business from which women were excluded by lack of capital and credit. The emergence of a pronounced divide along highbrow/lowbrow lines did women of the theatre no favors either, for they lacked the raw economic power to compete for management control of lowbrow entertainments and, on the other hand, found the way to influence in the realms of highbrow drama blocked by middle-class men who feared that feminization would mean loss of status. The success achieved by female stars, inspiring at first, could not be replicated in the lives of ordinary actresses, and when a female star cooperated in her own sexual commodification, she set up other women for such commodification without her choice or her rewards. Finally, playwrights — male or female — never enjoyed much power in this period, a situation that would not change until new copyright protections came into effect.

Women in the audience were also less powerful by 1870. When going to the theatre meant one long evening of mixed entertainment, men and women might attend and enjoy different parts of the whole. But the segmentation of the entertainment market meant that different parts were offered in different places for separate prices; a woman's dependence on a man for the price of admission and for escort became thereby much more significant, since it routinely translated into having to defer to his choice. Women lost their ability to approve or disapprove, since all audience members at the legitimate theatre were by 1870 expected to maintain decorous quiet. The power of drama critics was increasing, but that all-male fraternity tended to undermine the individual's power of judgment or at least to frame any theatregoing experience within expectations shaped by a male eye and voice. Men could attend "men's theatre" at the concert saloons, where the female body was displayed for sexual titillation, but there was no analogous women's theatre catering to whatever women's tastes might have been. And men's appetite for sexually suggestive entertainment was even reinfecting gender-integrated mainstream theatre, as shown by *The Black Crook* and other such shows of the late sixties.

The rise of the leg shows revealed that many women were happy to profit from such commerce. In 1870 there were more women in the theatre than in medicine, including nursing; there were twenty times more actresses than newspaper women, four times more women in the theatre than in literary and scientific vocations combined, and about 140 times more actresses than women lawyers. The only profession that employed more women than the theatre in 1870 was teaching.[52]

But women's presence constituted no palliative, for when women sold not their acting skills but their looks, problems and confusions multiplied. First, only some women could, by the accident of their personal appearance, qualify for such work. Second, even pretty women would undergo the precipitous losses exacted by aging, enjoying brief moments of success before being displaced by younger women. Third, a performer's success as a visual, quasi-sexual commodity spread confusion in her audiences, encouraging men and women alike to adopt unrealistic standards of female appearance. Fourth, the performer probably experienced an attenuation of self, since, although humans are all inherently objects, we suffer to the extent that we are *only* objects. And finally, this welter of consequences was obscured by the undeniably practical but ultimately simpleminded assumption that whatever paid well needed no further justification. Today, for example, it is commonly asserted that, so long as the transaction is merely visual, women who market themselves as sexual commodities are acting as assertive, independent agents, profiting according to their own choices. But this argument is less than compelling as long as women have few lucrative alternatives in the labor market—which is precisely the context that prevailed in the nineteenth century and clearly lingers today.

The commercialized display of the female body was thus a result of the economic, legal, and social disadvantages under which American women lived when the entertainment business was first organized. These disadvantages seem to have created what is called a "system effect": women were handicapped in management, excluded from drama reviewing, denied influence as audience members, and so discriminated against in the labor market that they made themselves available for sexually suggestive work. Any one or two of these disadvantages would have been harmful, but the combination of all four proved overwhelming.

Conclusion ·
Looking
at Women

The central dynamic in nineteenth-century theatre was commercialization; there was no noncommercial professional theatre, and the increasingly systematic drive for profit reshaped everything. It is only a slight oversimplification to say that, since men had the money, that drive catered to them. Thus the problem of women's self-support in a market society was not just an economic fact, not just a slice of labor history: it was also, and crucially, the basis of *cultural* phenomena. By offering more and more of whatever sold, the entertainment business cultivated certain (male, and usually white male) fantasies and ignored others. We are now over one hundred years into that cultivation process. The result is sexual expression that only looks natural and cultural representation that only looks normal. As a matter of historical fact we do not know how sexually oriented entertainment would be arranged, or if it would exist at all, in a society in which women had as much money and power as men.

The entertainment industry that emerged in the nineteenth century incidentally created a new kind of public realm that was not concerned with politics or community interests, but that rather aimed at private profit and derived its publicness from the breadth of its marketing ambitions. This was another, parallel public realm that elbowed aside the older sense of the *polis*, a public realm where women were not excluded but were commodified. By marketing elements of the most intimate human relationships, and by making women's bodies the characteristic medium of such commerce, popular entertainments tended to paint the public sphere in crude, exploitative colors and then blame women for that crudity. Meanwhile, the emergence of popular entertainments catering to men's eyes tended to exacerbate the body problem for women who did not wish to sell their looks. Women who moved into the public realm to pursue higher education or equal rights or employment opportunities would find the territory already occupied by men inclined to treat them as sexual objects. While some part of that inclination was perhaps natural, another part had been flattered and enhanced by exposure to the entertainment marketplace. Sexuality is, in part, socially constructed, and popular culture has been busily engaged in construction work, building always to commercial (and hence largely masculine) specifications.

In conclusion, I would argue that the turn to the visual in modern popular culture paralleled, and subtly undermined, contemporaneous historical improvements in modern women's status and rights. Even as women gained access to higher education, politics, and the upper reaches of the labor market, they and the men around them were becoming more and more immersed in entertainment products that diminished women. Perhaps the turn to the visual exploited inherent differences between male and female sexuality. But as a historical matter, it is not at all clear whether male sexuality is inherently more susceptible to visual stimuli, or whether men have simply been able to claim and cultivate looking privileges as a result of possessing more social and economic power.

I would speculate further that the commercialized entertainments catering to male sexuality that grew up in mid-nineteenth-century America had other, more general effects on American culture. Although they did not address the spiritual crisis of the age, they probably helped to muffle it. Victorian men and women alike were profoundly worried by the loss of compelling Christian purpose in their lives and their society. The urgency of the sexual drives tapped by the new entertainments created a boundless marketability that made commercialized popular culture well suited to assist in secularization through sheer distraction from spiritual concerns. And the modern visual culture that began to emerge in that era has proved harmful not just to women; it also seems to erode the language skills and aural culture that are vital to the pursuit of higher learning, the crafting of public policy, and the practice of democracy. Although it is fashionable now to adopt deconstructionist scepticism about language's ability to fix or convey meaning, the culture of the image offers still less in the way of certitude. I suspect that the interests of women and the interests of humankind alike will have to be articulated in language—language that grasps either/or, language that comprehends contradiction and common ground, language that both empowers the speaker and waits for the listener's response.

The rise of the entertainment industry might be accurately termed a "mitigated disaster" for women—for its ill effects *were* mitigated. As a product that broke beyond marketplace utilities even as it enriched hardheaded entrepreneurs, commercialized entertainment always appealed to dreams and desires, always evoked unrealized human longings and the pure spirit of play. By selling the possibility, however brief, of flying beyond the realm of things-as-they-are, commercialized entertainment cloaked its connections to money and power beneath dazzling disguise. And just as the costume may transform the player, so theatre's disguises consistently made it more complicated than the simpleminded pursuit of profit that my analysis has labored to address. Women worked willingly in the theatre, and they paid gladly to watch and listen from beyond the footlights. All too often they did indeed parade as objects for men's eyes, or sit by during appeals to men's pleasures. But if they could live even occasionally within disguise or lose themselves temporarily in playfulness, the bargain was not entirely a bad one. In a grim and limited world, it might be better to be an object of play than to experience no play at all.[1] Thus even as the theatre was organized into an entertainment business heavily involved in the "traffic in women," it never quite lost its attractions for those who might wish to think or do "otherwise." Consumers of popular culture are never perfectly passive; audiences always have some leeway in their reception of entertainment products to find or make meanings that the producers do not intend. Since a female actor works through the possibility of self-transformation, her work is intrinsically akin to the actions of modern women who have learned to play new roles and thus have changed modern America. This essential promise—that because a role is a role, we may yet enact a different one—continues to throw surprising spice into the otherwise predictable commercial stews the entertainment industry cooks up.

And so I am left to wonder what the Victorian star Ellen Terry meant to my grandmother when she saw her in about 1890. I certainly cannot "prove" what that famous, gorgeous, accomplished actress meant to Sarah Haynes Dudden, any more than I can claim to have achieved "objectivity" in writing this history. The questions I asked surely emerged—as I suppose they do for all historians—out of my own life and time; the conclusions I drew must remain in some sense provisional. Perhaps Terry stood for pecuniary independence, authenticity, or the possibility of self-transformation; perhaps she was simply beautiful, famous, and desirable. Perhaps, indeed, she was both. Ellen Terry knew her Shakespeare, and she must have known the opening line from sonnet twenty-nine, which evokes a moment "when in disgrace with fortune and men's eyes." It is a line that always tempts me to read against Shakespeare, to wonder about the relation between a woman's lot in life and her standing "in men's eyes." Why should these two be conflated? How can they be separated? And what has acting to do with either one? I prefer to think that mine is not the first generation of women to have asked such questions—and to have been moved to ask by thinking about theatre.

Notes

1. See Agnew, *Worlds Apart*, for his influential argument about the relationship between the emergence of the market and English Renaissance theatre. His insight about how theatre can operate as a social metaphor has been crucial to my understanding of theatre and gender.

2. Molly Haskell, *From Reverence to Rape: The Treatment of Women in the Movies* (New York: Holt, Rinehart and Winston, 1973), 243. The Western philosophical tradition hostile to the theatre is traced in Barish, *Antitheatrical Prejudice*.

3. Jean-Jacques Rousseau, *Politics and the Arts: Letter to M. D'Alembert on the Theatre*, intro. and trans. Allan Bloom (Ithaca, N.Y.: Cornell University Press, 1968), 47. See also p. 49: "Look through most contemporary plays; it is always a woman who knows everything, who teaches everything to men."

4. On theatre's association with a side of woman that is hidden, powerful, and demonic, see Auerbach, *Woman and the Demon* and *Ellen Terry*. See also her *Private Theatricals*, especially p. 80, where she cites Cary Mazer to the effect that a woman acting could seem a dangerous thing "by the very transgressive act of becoming someone else, of finding within herself other selves to become." See also Richard Gilman, "The Actor as Celebrity," *Humanities in Review* 1 (1982): 115–16. Gilman argues that the actor presents us "with possible selves, or more accurately with the *idea* of possible selves," and that theatre is "a release from the unitary and ordinarily inescapable self and a reminder of the possibilities of transformation." Christopher Kent provides a related assessment of the Victorian stage: "It offered striking opportunities for independence, fame and fortune, and even for those outside it the stage incarnated fantasies, providing vicarious release in the notion that here was an area of special dispensation from the normal categories, moral and social, that defined woman's

place" (Kent, "Image and Reality," 94). I have profited from reading Ferris, *Acting Women*, especially her chapter 10. Theatre has some of the same subversive potential for all socially subordinate groups; hence the importance of masking in moments of social reversal like carnival. See James C. Scott, *Domination and the Arts of Resistance* (New Haven and London: Yale University Press, 1990).

5. There is a considerable body of scholarship that documents the association between the actress and the whore. It is the subject of passing notice, for example, in Michael Booth's survey, *Theatre in the Victorian Age*, 113. It has received more focused attention from women scholars. See, e.g., Johnson, "Enter the Harlot," in Chinoy and Jenkins, *Women in American Theater*, 66 – 74; or Johnson, *American Actress*. Perhaps the most thorough and nuanced exploration of this theme is found in Tracy Davis's work on nineteenth-century British theatre. See her "Actresses and Prostitutes," "Actress in Victorian Pornography," and *Actresses As Working Women*. I found Martha Roth, "Notes Toward a Feminist Performance Aesthetic," *Women and Performance* 1(1983): 5 – 14, helpful in suggesting that this persistent association derives from the fact that a woman who acts is on display, which makes her "sexually available to any man, in fantasy and often in fact." Compare Senelick, ed., *Gender in Performance*, xii: "To appear on stage is to display one's body to strangers: A commodity available to the gaze may, in given circumstances, be vendible in its entirety." I am also grateful to my colleague Ruth Stevenson for pointing out another connection: the acting that women do onstage may remind male audiences of the acting (i.e., dissembling) that prostitutes routinely engage in.

6. In thinking about gender and theatre, I profited greatly from excellent scholarship on the English theatre and drama, especially works by Jean E. Howard, Kristina Straub, Phyllis Rackin, and Karen Newman. My ideas about the nature of public and private spheres also benefited from Mary Ryan, *Women in Public: Between Banners and Ballots, 1825 – 1880* (Baltimore: Johns Hopkins University Press, 1990), although my interests and analysis differ from Ryan's.

7. Modern feminists have made the distinction between sex and gender one of the most basic of their tenets of analysis. There are a number of paths to the conclusion that gender exists only in performance or representation, but most of them wend their way across difficult theoretical terrain, including phenomenology, sociological research from the symbolic interaction school, and deconstructionist literary criticism. The best single introduction to this question is found in Laurence Senelick's introduction to Senelick, *Gender in Performance*. Senelick writes, "Like a Berkelian universe, gender exists only insofar as it is perceived" (ix). A good introduction to a phenomenological approach to theatre and identity is Bruce Wilshire, *Role Playing and Identity: The Limits of Theatre as Metaphor* (Bloomington, Ind.: Indiana University Press, 1982). On gender as performative, see Butler, "Performative Acts and Gender Constitution." I have benefited greatly from Garber, *Vested Interests*. I have also found useful David George, "On Ambiguity: Towards a Post-Modern Performance Theory," *Theatre Research International* 14 (Spring 1989): 71 – 85. Of course the best-known sociologist who has dealt with identity in terms of theatrical metaphor is Erving Goffman, in

works beginning with *The Presentation of Self in Everyday Life* (Garden City, N.Y.: Doubleday, 1959). For a specific interpretation of gender in terms derived from symbolic interaction, see Candace West and Don Zimmerman, "Doing Gender," *Gender and Society* 1 (1987): 125—51.

On theatrical transvestism, See Garber, *Vested Interests*. There is of course a limit to the extent to which any audience will "get it," and Garber is especially acute in noting the tendency of audiences to look "through" rather than at the cross-dressed performer, to focus on what he or she *really* is "underneath," or on the success with which he or she can "pass" for the other sex. Nevertheless, I argue, the stage is unique in presenting relatively simple access to what is otherwise a highly abstract concept, for society is deeply intolerant of individuals who reveal gender's constructedness in daily life—individuals who fail, that is, to make themselves unambiguously readable as either male or female to the casual glance of a stranger. Only on stage can we freely contemplate and even take pleasure in ambiguity and transvestism that would elsewhere be either invisible (successful "passing") or immediately censured. See Ferris, *Acting Women*, 147: "This practice of women dressing as men clearly gives the lie to the old maxim of 'we are what we look', at the same time it exposes gender as socially constructed and not innate, eternal or biologically 'natural.'" See also the very useful survey of a vast literature on cross-dressing in Vern L. Bullough and Bonnie Bullough, *Cross Dressing, Sex, and Gender* (Philadelphia: University of Pennsylvania Press, 1993).

8. John Berger, *Ways of Seeing* (New York: Viking Press, 1972), 47.

9. There is an effort now under way to refer to all performers—male and female—as actors, just as we refer to female writers of verse as poets, not poetesses, and have dropped other feminine suffixes. I approve of this move, but I have found such usage anachronistic for discussions of the nineteenth century.

   Given my focus on the decades before 1870, I will usually be discussing women and men who worked in or attended the theatre in cities on the East Coast. I believe, however, that the growth of touring and the development of an effectively national market in theatre by 1870 tends to make the implications of these biographies more national than local.

10. Prostitutes were normally present in playhouses' third tier seating area until the 1840s or 1850s. See Johnson, "That Guilty Third Tier," and my discussion of the campaign to banish prostitutes in chap. 4, n. 12.

11. Regarding the expansion of the public realm and the nineteenth-century obsession with "reading" strangers, see Sennett, *Fall of Public Man*. Sennett notes that the fictions of Dickens and Balzac reveal this obsession, as do the nineteenth-century "sciences" of phrenology and "ethology," which was the science of human character deduced from appearance.

1. POWER AND DANGER AT THE THEATRE

1. Biographical information on Susanna Rowson is found in Nason, *Memoir of Mrs. Susanna Rowson*; Weil, *In Defense of Women*; Kornfeld, "Women in Post-Revolu-

tionary American Culture;" Doreen Alvarez Saar, "Susanna Rowson: Feminist and Democrat," in Schofield and Macheski, *Curtain Calls,* 231–46; and *Notable American Women,* s.v. "Rowson, Susanna Haswell." Rowson's career reflects the fact that in the eighteenth and throughout much of the nineteenth century, American theatre was part of a larger Anglo-American theatrical universe in which players, plays, managers, and ways of doing business passed freely back and forth across the Atlantic. I will accordingly use sources on Victorian theatre both to support purely American evidence and to discuss the performers' experiences in England.

2. Susanna Rowson, *Slaves in Algiers* (Philadelphia: n.p., 1794); William Cobbett, *A Kick for a Bite; or, Review upon Review; with a Critical Essay on the Works of Mrs. Rowson,* 2nd ed. (Philadelphia: Thomas Bradford, 1796), 23–24. Like Cobbett, historians of American drama have classified Rowson as a feminist. Walter J. Meserve notes that "women characters dominate or direct the action" in Rowson's plays. See Meserve, *Emerging Entertainment,* 115. Arthur Hobson Quinn quotes her epilogue and refers to her "feminist activities" in his *History of the American Drama,* 122–23. See also Doreen Alvarez Saar, "Susanna Rowson: Feminist and Democrat," in Schofield and Macheski, *Curtain Calls,* 231–46.

3. William White to William Charles White, 20 December 1796, White Family Papers.

4. In making herself over into a schoolmistress, Rowson offered profound but silent testimony that the theatre could do just what its critics feared—enable women to represent, or reinvent, themselves as they pleased. The early work life of Susanna Rowson remained hidden: she had served as governess to the children of Georgiana Cavendish, fifth duchess of Devonshire, for five years. The duchess was given to gambling and drink, and after 1782 she was part of a *ménage à trois,* sharing the duke with Lady Elizabeth Foster, a fixture in the Devonshire household. Even though Rowson's was guilt by association only, to have been an upper servant in such a household was not the most correct early experience for a young woman, certainly not for a schoolteacher. See Phyllis Deutsch, "Dame Fortune's Decline: The Life and Death of the Duchess of Devonshire," paper presented at the Eighth Berkshire Conference on the History of Women, Rutgers, New Jersey, June 1990.

5. The "lost six or seven years" quote is attributed to Mordecai Noah by Dunlap, *History of the American Theatre* 2:321. On married couples see Blake, *Historical Account of the Providence Stage,* 12. Boston's only theatre company in 1797, for example, was listed as "Mr. and Mrs. Barrett, Mr. and Mrs. Marshall, Mrs. and Mrs. C. Powell, Mr. and Mrs. Graupner, M. and Madame Lege, M. and Madame Gardie, Messrs. Villiers, Kenny, Dickinson, and J. Jones, Mrs. Allen, and Miss Harrison" (Dunlap, *History of the American Theatre* 1:331). When John Bernard put together a small company in 1808, it was composed of three couples, plus two additional men and one additional woman (Bernard, *Retrospections of America,* 319–27). On Poe's parents, see Coad and Mims, *American Stage,* 66. The Hallams and Hodgkinsons are discussed extensively in Dunlap, *History of the American Theatre,* and Odell, *Annals of the New York Stage,*

vol. 1. The best brief introduction to their prominence is Billy J. Harbin, "The Role of Mrs. Hallam in the Hodgkinson-Hallam Controversy: 1794—1797," *Theatre Journal* 32 (1980): 213—22. When, in 1816, the actor and manager Noah Ludlow married a woman who knew nothing of the theatre, she gamely agreed to "try the experiment" of performing with an eye toward "continuing it as a profession" (Ludlow, *Dramatic Life as I Found It*, 108). The theatre manager Sol Smith got a laugh but illustrated the husband's control when he quoted a letter from a semiliterate actor seeking work for his wife: "I am informed u are in want of a woman. I can furnish you with my wife" (Smith, *Theatrical Journey-Work*, 139). Evidence that it was normal for a mother to return to her stage career is found in a comment in 1837 on a visibly pregnant actress: the reviewer suggested she withdraw for a month or two "until she is able to resume her professional labors" (*Spirit of the Times*, 28 Oct. 1837, 289).

6. Residential stock company practices and lines of business are described in Mammen, *Old Stock Company*, and Bost, *Monarchs of the Mimic World*. On feats and failures of memory, see Skinner and Skinner, *One Man in His Time*, 67, 102—03; Logan, *Before the Footlights*, 57; Gilbert, *Stage Reminiscences*, 30. The expression "winging it" denoted the desperate practice of studying the script in the wings just before stepping on to speak one's lines (Ritchie, *Mimic Life*, 323). One theatrical guide warned that beginners aspiring to first-rate roles would have to study—i.e., learn—500 lines per day (Rede, *Guide to the Stage*, 3). On early attempts to tour, see Ludlow, *Dramatic Life as I Found It*, and Smith, *Theatrical Management in the West*.

7. "Any lady" by Mrs. C. Durang, cited in Joseph N. Ireland, *Mrs. Duff* (Boston: James R. Osgood, 1882), 135. One Boston paper said in describing an actress, "She is known to be the kind, careful mother of a numerous family" (ibid., 45). See also Hughes, *History of the American Theatre*, 58. At Mrs. Sewell's benefit in New York in 1815, she reminded the public she was responsible for the education of her two children (Odell, *Annals of the New York Stage* 2:449).

The standard source on American theatrical dynasties is Montrose J. Moses, *Famous Actor-Families in America* (1906; reprint, New York and London: Benjamin Blom, 1968), which discusses the Booths, Jeffersons, Sotherns, Boucicaults, Hacketts, Wallacks, Davenports, Hollands, Powers, and the Drew-Barrymore clan. Charles Dickens, who knew the theatre well, wrote the familial character of early nineteenth-century theatre into *Nicholas Nickleby* (1839) with the Crummles family troupe.

On women managers, see Gresdna Ann Doty, *The Career of Mrs. Anne Brunton Merry in the American Theatre* (Baton Rouge: Louisiana State University Press, 1971). Other early women managers included Mrs. Henry Placide in Charleston in 1812, Mrs. Elizabeth Powell in Boston in the early 1820s, and a Mrs. Baldwin in New York at about the same time. See Hughes, *History of the American Theatre*, 121; Odell, *Annals of the New York Stage* 2:598; Blake, *Historical Account of the Providence Stage*, 155.

8. Hughes, *History of the American Theatre*, 63; Oral Sumner Coad, *William Dunlap*

(New York: Dunlap Society, 1917), 40. (Note, however, that Bost, *Monarchs of the Mimic World*, is able to make a case for the authority of the manager even in the eighteenth century.) See Mammen, *Old Stock Company*, 10—11, and the memoirs of two managers: Wood, *Personal Recollections of the Stage*; and Dunlap, *History of the American Theatre*. Managers typically leased the theatre building from a group of stockholders, who also collected rents from the concessionaires who sold refreshments in the lobbies. While the stockholders might demand free passes as a privilege of ownership, they were not involved in day-to-day matters. The first "professional manager," one who had never acted and was concerned only with the finances of the company, was Stephen Price. In 1808 he became co-manager of the Park Street Theatre in New York, sharing managerial duties with Thomas Abthorpe Cooper, the eminent tragedian, who was thus freed to concentrate on matters related to the actual performance of the plays (Barnard Hewitt, "Stephen Price," in Donahue, *Theatrical Manager*, 87—144), William Dunlap, discussed below, was also a manager and not a player, but his elevation to management did not result from concern with rational business practices.

9. See Bernard, *Retrospections of America*, 263, for one-third figure. The *New York Post* (June 14, 1806) explained: "Receiving for the most part salaries barely sufficient for immediate maintenance they must either depend upon a successful benefit night or have to struggle with poverty from the time their engagements cease until nearly the commencement of winter" (cited in Odell, *Annals of the New York Stage* 2:257).

10. Bernard, *Retrospections of America*, 263. On Merry, Gilfert, and Wheatley, see Gresdna Doty, "Anne Brunton Merry: First Star," in Chinoy and Jenkins, *Women in American Theater*, 62; Brown, *History of the New York Stage* 1:13, 36; "Mrs. Sarah Wheatley," *Ladies Companion*, November 1837, 8—9. This point about actresses' compensation is made persuasively in Johnson, *American Actress*, 54—57. Ludlow told of actresses who had acquired "handsome sums of money that with their talents would make them independent, pecuniarily, for life" and fretted that they too often fell prey to fortune-hunting suitors (Ludlow, *Dramatic Life as I Found It*, 451—52). Fending off fortune hunters was certainly no problem for other wage-earning women in this era. Performers more often complained about regularity and reliability of pay than rate. Managers who suffered a losing season might abscond without meeting the payroll at all. And because theatre seasons ran from fall to spring, the summer layoff could be a time of penny-pinching.

11. "Seamstresses" from Ludlow, *Dramatic Life as I Found It*, 65. Adam Smith, *An Inquiry Into the Nature and Causes of the Wealth of Nations* (New York: P. F. Collier and Sons, 1909), 108—09.

12. "Retentive memory" from Wood, *Personal Recollections of the Stage*, 26; "thrillingly expressive" from Wilson, *History of American Acting*, 46; "When she spoke" from ibid., 66; Anne Brunton Merry's voice from Odell, *Annals of the New York Stage* 2:135, quoting the *New York Evening Post* of 20 April 1802; Mrs. Barnes from Blake, *Historical Account of the Providence Stage*, 163; Mrs. Whitlock from Willard, *History of the Providence Stage*, 74; Mrs. Melmoth from Dunlap, *History of the American The-*

atre 1:202; Clara Fisher from Maeder, *Autobiography*, 88. The unprepossessing appearance of early actresses is remarked in Whitehead, "Fancy's Show Box," 94–96.

13. Webster crowd figures are from Maurice G. Baxter, *One and Inseparable: Daniel Webster and the Union* (Cambridge, Mass.: Belknap Press of Harvard University Press, 1984), 431, 503. Cooke description from Willard, *History of the Providence Stage*, 65. "As elegant speaking" from Alexander Sutor, *An Essay on the Stage* (Aberdeen: D. Chalmers, 1820), 166. Sutor contested this notion, but he had to grant its currency.

14. Rourke, *American Humor*, 64; "little Miss McBride" in Odell, *Annals of the New York Stage* 2: 512–13.

15. Stone, *Personal Recollections of the Drama*, 127. Constance Rourke comments, "A deep relish for talk had grown up throughout the country, on solitary farms, in the starved emptiness of the backwoods" (Rourke, *American Humor*, 30).

16. James, *Small Boy*, 323. Mayor Philip Hone quote is cited in Shank, "The Bowery Theatre, 1826–1836," 13–14. On the characteristically bare stage of the early theatre, see Grimsted, *Melodrama Unveiled*, 83–84; Wilson, *History of American Acting*, 4, 12, 26; and Stone, *Personal Recollections of the Drama*, 9.

17. Dickens, *Great Expectations*, chap. 27. "It was Roaring Ralph" from Stone, *Personal Recollections of the Drama*, 173; "one would suppose" from Smith, *Theatrical Management in the West*, 175–76. For examples of ties between acting and law, politics, or the ministry, see White Family Papers; Ludlow, *Dramatic Life as I Found It*, 176–77; Dunlap, *History of the American Theatre* 1:295; *Notable American Women*, s.v., "Claxton, Kate."

18. Mrs. Melmoth's school is mentioned in Joseph N. Ireland to Mr. Toedtberg, 23 Feb. 1871, Dramatic Museum Collection, Columbia University Library; Rowson's teaching methods are from Kornfeld, "Susanna Haswell Rowson's American Career." For other examples of actresses who moved into schoolteaching, see Hughes, *History of the American Theatre*, 58; Mary Julia Curtis, "Women Open Augusta's First Theatre," in Chinoy and Jenkins, *Women in American Theatre*, 197. According to the historian Mary Kelley, who is currently working on a book on the emergence of an intellectual elite among women in the early republic, elocution was a standard element in the curricula of female academies in the early republic. See also Joy Rouse, "Rhetorics of Citizenship in Nineteenth-Century America" (Ph.D. diss., Miami University, 1991), chap. 2.

19. Kenneth Silverman, *A Cultural History of the American Revolution* (New York: Thomas Y. Crowell, 1976), 292–95, 350, 364. As early as 1774 the First Continental Congress resolved to "discountenance and discourage every species of extravagance and dissipation, especially all horse-racing, and all kinds of gaming, cock-fighting, exhibitions of shews, plays and other expensive diversions and entertainments" (cited in ibid., 271).

20. "Nightly the scene" from Arthur Hobson Quinn, "The Theatre and the Drama in Old Philadelphia," *Transactions of the American Philosophical Society* 43 (1953): 316;

"genius" and "tissue" quoted in Meserve, *Emerging Entertainment*, 139—40; disapproving Federalists in Dunlap, *History of the American Theatre* 1:209, and Odell, *Annals of the New York Stage* 1:348. Political rivalries in the Boston theatre are discussed by Clapp, *Record of the Boston Stage*, 50—51, and Blake, *Historical Account of the Providence Stage*, 58—59. Another example of politics at the theatre occurred on the tenth anniversary of the British evacuation of New York. A celebration broke out spontaneously at the Park Theatre when American and French military men in the audience led the call for patriotic songs and the audience stood and sang the Marseillaise (Dunlap, *History of the American Theatre* 1: 204—205). Yet another example was the performance of *The Siege of Tripoli* at the Park Theatre in New York on May 24, 1820 to an audience crowded with "Tammany men and Buck tail renegadoes" (*Letters from John Pintard to His Daughter Eliza Noel Pintard Davidson, 1816—1835*, 4 vols. [New York: New-York Historical Society, 1940], 1:293).

21. Quote from Frances Trollope, *Domestic Manners of the Americans*, ed. Richard Mullen (1832; reprint, New York: Oxford University Press, 1984), 111. Universal manhood suffrage was not achieved in New York State until the 1820s; see Dixon Ryan Fox, *The Decline of Aristocracy in the Politics of New York* (New York: Columbia University Press, 1919); and Lee Benson, *The Concept of Jacksonian Democracy: New York as a Test Case* (Princeton, N.J.: Princeton University Press, 1961), chap. 1.

22. Quoted in Odell, *Annals of the New York Stage* 1:347.

23. Rowson, *Slaves in Algiers; or, A Struggle for Freedom* (Philadelphia: Wrigley and Berriman, 1794), 3.

24. Another political play was Sarah Pogson's *The Female Enthusiast* (1807), which featured Charlotte Corday as its heroine (Meserve, *Emerging Entertainment*, 199—200). For Warren, See Jean B. Kern, "Mercy Otis Warren: Dramatist of the American Revolution," in Schofield and Macheski, *Curtain Calls*, 247—59; and Alice McDonnell Robinson, "Mercy Warren, Satirist of the Revolution," in Chinoy and Jenkins, *Women in the American Theater*, 131—37.

25. Linda Kerber, *Women of the Republic: Intellect and Ideology in Revolutionary America* (Chapel Hill, N.C.: University of North Carolina Press, 1980), 271.

26. Quotes from *The Traveller Returned* (Boston, n.p., 1798), act 4, sc. 4; and *The Medium, or, Virtue Triumphant* (Boston, n.p., 1798), act 1, sc. 3. On Judith Sargent Murray as playwright, see Mary Anne Schofield, "'Quitting the Loom and Distaff': Eighteenth-Century American Women Dramatists," in Schofield and Macheski, *Curtain Calls*, 260—73.

27. Quinn, *History of the American Drama*, 194; Wood, *Personal Recollections of the Stage*, 234; Celia Morris Eckhardt, *Fanny Wright: Rebel in America* (Cambridge, Mass.: Harvard University Press, 1984), 27—33, 39, 189.

28. It is not easy to assess the relative popularity of any play from this era, since the last thing a playwright wanted to do was to publish his or her work. Without copyright protections, it would be pirated immediately. The bias against publication meant that many plays were lost; we know of others by name only, and those that were published

usually went to press only after several years in circulation. Shifting our attention to performances does not clear up the picture: as custom called for a nightly change of bill, even very popular plays would run only a handful of nights before being alternated with other pieces. Only an extended day-by-day tabulation based on the daily press enables us to say for sure which pieces were most popular. Such tabulations have been made for some cities and some decades, but they are far from complete. See the very useful appendices in Grimsted, *Melodrama Unveiled*, for a summary. These tabulations make it possible for us to know which ten or twenty plays were most popular, and to assess the relative mix of different genres, but they are no help in distinguishing the second-rate piece from the truly obscure.

The problem of crafting a native American drama is treated in Quinn, *History of the American Drama*, and Meserve, *Emerging Entertainment*. The quoted conclusion ("The passive sentimental heroine") is from Daniel F. Havens, *The Columbian Muse of Comedy* (Carbondale, Ill.: Southern Illinois University Press, 1973), 112. His findings are not unlike those of Margaret Dalzeil, who argued that American popular novels and magazine fiction of the mid-nineteenth century featured tougher, more energetic and resourceful heroines than British productions from the same period (Dalzeil, *Popular Fiction 100 Years Ago: An Unexplored Tract of Literary History* [London: Cohen and West, 1957], 87, 90). On the European tradition of cross-dressing stories, see Rudolf Dekker and Lotte Van de Pol, *The Tradition of Female Cross-Dressing in Early Modern Europe* (London: Macmillan, 1988).

29. On the African Company see: Brockett, *History of the Theatre*, 481; James V. Hatch, "Here Comes Everybody: Scholarship and Black Theatre History," in Postlewait and McConachie, *Interpreting the Theatrical Past*, 157—58; Errol Hill, *Shakespeare in Sable: A History of Black Shakespearean Actors* (Amherst: University of Massachusetts Press, 1984), 11—14; Herbert Marshall and Mildred Stock, *Ira Aldridge: The Negro Tragedian* (Carbondale: Southern Illinois University Press, 1968), chap. 4; Yvonne Shafer, "Black Actors in the Nineteenth Century American Theatre," *CLA Journal* 20 (1977): 387—400. Denied a chance to participate or create in theatre, to find paying jobs and public voices onstage, African-Americans by the 1830s found their songs and dances appropriated by white men who corked their faces to create the minstrel show (see Toll, *Blacking Up*).

30. Dunlap was a playwright of some note, and he was part or sole manager of the Park Theatre in New York between 1796 and 1805; he was a partisan and an apologist for the stage at a time when it was still an embattled institution. The form his apology takes in his 1836 novel is to project the stage's moral ambiguities onto an actress and then to dispose of her as a guilty suicide. Biographical information on Dunlap is available in Coad, *William Dunlap*; and Robert H. Canary, *William Dunlap* (New York: Twayne, 1970). All references to the novel below will refer to Dunlap, *Memoirs of a Water Drinker*. The first edition carried a slightly different title: *Thirty Years Ago; or, The Memoirs of a Water-Drinker*, 2 vols. (New York: Bancroft and Holley, 1836).

31. *Memoirs of a Water-Drinker* 1:7, 11. Spiffard supposedly was modeled on the comedian

William Twaits. The real Mrs. Twaits had also been married before. Elizabeth Westray Villiers was the young widow of Mr. Villiers, a low comedian, when she met and married Twaits. Her misconduct, if any, has not entered the historical record. Ireland writes: "In 1805 she returned to New York, a girlish widow, and her youth and misfortune naturally exciting the interest and sympathy of the public, she soon became one of the main attractions of the theatre. Though greatly admired by the gallants of the day, she again bestowed her hand on a genuine son of Momus—Twaits—with whom she was content to share the vicissitudes of an actor's life" (Ireland, *Records of the New York Stage* 1:200).

Memoirs of a Water-Drinker is often described as a temperance novel, and Dunlap may have tried to catch temperance readers with his title change in the second edition, but alcoholism is not especially central to the plot. It is possible, however, that the character of Mrs. Trowbridge owes something to Dunlap's own contact with Mrs. Hallam, whose episodes of on-stage intoxication caused him trouble in the middle nineties. See Harbin, "Role of Mrs. Hallam in the Hodgkinson-Hallam Controversy," 213—22.

32. One of Dunlap's characters explains that respectable society excludes Mrs. Spiffard because she is exposed to a theatre audience's "*mingled* character, in which so much of the baser material predominates" (1:166, emphasis added).

33. Primary sources offer abundant evidence of the rowdiness, conviviality, and social heterogeneity of early audiences; these are effectively summarized in Grimsted, *Melodrama Unveiled*, chap. 3; Levine, *Highbrow, Lowbrow*, chap. 1; and Bost, *Monarchs of the Mimic World*, 74—89. Tickets cost $1, 50 cents, and 25 cents. Such substantial prices meant that the well-do-do were a significant element of the audience, but anecdotal evidence shows that many people of modest means were also present. Impecunious would-be theatregoers found it relatively easy to wait outside the theatre door, secure pass checks from departing patrons, and thereby enter for free. On the recycling of pass checks, see, e.g., Leman, *Memories of an Old Actor*, 11.

34. Washington Irving, *Letters of Jonathan Oldstyle, Gent.*, ed. Bruce I. Granger and Martha Hartzog (Boston: Twayne, 1977), 12. James D. Hart, *The Popular Book: A History of America's Literary Taste* (New York: Oxford University Press, 1950), 29: In the eighteenth century, "plays were even more widely known in print than on the stage." Sol Smith, son of a Cortland County, New York, farmer, and Anna Cora Mowatt, daughter of a New York City merchant, for example, both knew Shakespeare's plays before they saw them onstage. Mowatt said she had read the whole of Shakespeare's plays "many times over" by the age of ten, although she learned in Sunday School that theatres were "abodes of wickedness," and had no wish to attend (Ritchie, *Autobiography of an Actress*, 31, 37—39). See Dickens, *Great Expectations*, chapter 31, for witticisms during Wopsle's performance. The cheerful disorder of an American theatre audience in the 1830s—the men spitting and the women nursing babies—was noted by the censorious Mrs. Frances Trollope. See Trollope, *Domestic Manners of the Americans*, 108—11, 230, 300.

35. Quote from Mark Anthony DeWolfe Howe, ed., *The Articulate Sisters: Passages from*

the Journals and Letters of the Daughters of President Josiah Quincy of Harvard University (Cambridge, Mass.: Harvard University Press, 1946), 218. Details about audiences are from Morgan, *A Season in New York*, 39, 57, 59, 153, 172–73; *The Letters of Margaret Fuller*, ed. Robert N. Hudspeth (Ithaca, N.Y.: Cornell University Press, 1983), 1:115; Dunlap, *History of the American Theatre* 2:300–301; Dewey, *Life and Letters of Catharine Maria Sedgwick*, 74, 118, 210, 263–64; *Letters from John Pintard*, 1:178.

36. On women turning their backs, see Médéric L. E. Moreau de Saint-Méry, *Moreau de Saint-Méry's American Journey*, ed. and trans. Kenneth Roberts and Anna M. Roberts (Garden City, N.Y.: Doubleday, 1947), 347; and *Dramatic Mirror* (Boston), 16 Sept. 1829, cited in Swift, *Belles and Beaux on Their Toes*, 49. On ladies staying away on opening night, see Leman, *Memories of an Old Actor*, 45; and the *Thespian Monitor and Dramatick Miscellany*, 25 Nov. 1809, cited in Pritner, "Theater and Its Audience," 75. On women's flight, or absence, in instances of rowdyism, see Wood, *Personal Recollections of the Stage*, 146, 321; Brown, *History of the New York Stage*, 1:27; and Vandenhoff, *Leaves from an Actor's Notebook*, 215, speaking of a performance when there was "not a bonnet to be seen," which "looked ominous."

37. On men's attendance in the company of other men, see Morgan, *Season in New York*, 42; and N. Beekley Diary. Tracy Davis argues that men who attended the theatre in Victorian London were prepared to "read" actresses salaciously because of their prior exposure to pornography. See her "Sexual Language in Victorian Society and Theatre."

38. Eliza Southgate Bowne, *A Girl's Life Eighty Years Ago* (New York: Charles Scribner's Sons, 1887), 64. Although we lack good diary evidence, it seems likely that working-class women would have been just as ready to venture into public space without fear of sexual contamination, and might have been much more accustomed to the process of sifting and ignoring described here. Casual prostitution as a way of getting by in hard times was not uncommon among the working poor, and prostitutes were, accordingly, much less shocking and exotic to working-class women. See Christine Stansell, *City of Women: Sex and Class in New York, 1789–1860* (New York: Alfred A. Knopf, 1986). Class differences in the theatregoing experience are dealt with below, in Chapter five.

39. Kemble, *Journal* 1:190. Reaction to gallery noises is mentioned in the *New York Mirror* of 5 May 1827, cited in Shank, "Bowery Theatre," 112.

2. STARRING: FANNY KEMBLE AND THE ACTRESS AS HEROINE

1. Hone in Nevins, *Diary of Philip Hone*, 77; "audacious girl" in "Editor's Easy Chair," *Harper's Magazine*, February 1865, 394–95. Historians have granted Fanny Kemble passing notice as the author of some acute observations on slavery in her *Journal of a Residence on a Georgian Plantation, 1838–39*. Her career has attracted numerous biographers; the best treatments are Furnas, *Fanny Kemble*; Bobbé, *Fanny Kemble*; and Constance Wright, *Fanny Kemble and the Lovely Land* (New York: Dodd, Mead, 1972). Dated but still valuable are Leota S. Driver, *Fanny Kemble* (Chapel Hill: Uni-

versity of North Carolina Press, 1933); and Margaret Armstrong, *Fanny Kemble: A Passionate Victorian* (New York: Macmillan, 1939). Useful primary materials are found in Wister, *Fanny, the American Kemble*; and Ransome, *The Terrific Kemble.* Kemble's own publications offer considerable insight into her life, especially her *Journal, Records of a Girlhood, Records of a Later Life*, and *Further Records.*

2. Nevins, *Diary of Philip Hone*, 77; "realization of their ideal" in Kemble, *Records of a Girlhood*, 149.

3. Catharine M. Sedgwick to Mrs. Frank Channing, New York, 12 Feb. 1833, in Dewey, *Life and Letters of Catharine Maria Sedgwick*, 230.

4. "We could annihilate time" is from Wood, *Personal Recollections of the Stage*, 391. Wood comments on what historians call the "transportation revolution," brought about by the use of steamboats, turnpikes, canals, and railroads. On Cooke's tour, see Barnard Hewitt, "'King Stephen' of the Park and Drury Lane," in Donahue, *Theatrical Manager*, 92–94.

5. Cooke's seventeen nights at the Park on his first tour, for example, yielded him about $4000, and the managers three times as much (Hewitt, "King Stephen," 93, 107–08). But stars learned to stipulate a percentage of gross receipts, to avoid being swindled by managers who overestimated costs in computing net receipts, and to negotiate guaranteed fees, thus transferring to the management the risks associated with bad weather or a good draw at a rival house (Calvin L. Pritner, "William Wood's Financial Arrangements with Travelling Stars," *Theatre Survey* 6 [Nov. 1965]: 87–88). On the ill effects star visits had on the members of a stock company, see Wood, *Personal Recollections of the Stage*, 447.

6. Willard, *History of the Providence Stage*, 143; Kemble, *Journal* 1:140. An observer commented in 1841: "So long as they could furnish one name in large letters, all others were selected with reference to low salaries" (*Spirit of the Times*, 14 Aug. 1841, 288). See also Henry W. Bellows, *The Relation of Public Amusements to Public Morality* (New York: C. S. Francis and Co., 1857), 48, referring to the theatre as "overpaid in its favorites and underpaid in all who are not;" Ford, *Peep Behind the Curtain*, 65, 83, on how the star system brought "beggary" to ordinary actors; Wood, *Personal Recollections of the Stage*, 298; Hewitt, "King Stephen," 119, 130. On similar trends in British theatre, see Booth, *Theatre in the Victorian Age*, 117, and Davis, *Actresses as Working Women*, 29–35. An English actress booking passage in 1827 spoke of herself as headed for "America, that El Dorado" (Drew, *Autobiographical Sketch*, 17).

7. The biographical narrative conveyed here and below is based on the Kemble biographies cited in note 1. No hint of sexual irregularities ever touched Siddons' name, nor that of the Kembles. On the dimensions of Fanny's London success, see Bobbé, *Fanny Kemble*, 44.

8. For reception of Kemble's writing, see "Memoir of the Dramatic Life of Miss Fanny Kemble," by S.D.L., in Frances Anne Kemble, *Francis the First*, 6th American ed. (New York: Peabody and Co., 1833), 2, and (citing the *Quarterly Review*) 15. On the significance of women writers at this time, see Mary Kelley, *Private Woman, Public Stage:*

Literary Domesticity in Nineteenth-Century America (New York: Oxford University Press, 1984); and Nina Baym, *Women's Fiction: A Guide to Novels by and about Women in America, 1820–1870* (Ithaca, N.Y.: Cornell University Press, 1978).

9. In an April 1828 letter to Harriet St. Leger, Fanny refers to the "idea of exercising and developing the literary talent which I think I possess" as "meat, drink, and sleep to me, my world, in which I live and have my happiness" (cited in Wister, *Fanny, the American Kemble*, 32).

10. "Sacred motive" and "*sacrificed* unto fame" are from "Memoir of the Dramatic Life" in *Francis the First*, 14, 2. "Painful notoriety" is from the London *Times*, cited in Bobbé, *Fanny Kemble*, 38–39. T. Noon Talfourd described Fanny's debut as an occasion in which "the interest was almost too complicated to be borne with pleasure" (cited in Furnas, *Fanny Kemble*, 51). For the new women novelists, see Kelley, *Private Woman, Public Stage*, chaps. 6–7; and Baym, *Women's Fiction*.

11. "How I do loathe" is from Kemble, *Journal* 2:26. "Duty and conformity" is from Kemble, *Records of a Girlhood*, 191. Compare p. 220: "And so my life was determined, and I devoted myself to an avocation which I never liked or honored." She did at one point admit that she enjoyed "giving vivid expression to vivid emotion, realizing in my own person noble and beautiful imaginary beings" and, above all, "*uttering the poetry of Shakespeare*" but maintained that the theatre included too much else that was "odious" (letter of 22 April 1842, reproduced in Kemble, *Records of a Later Life*, 319).

12. Sheridan Knowles, *The Hunchback* (New York: Peabody and Co., 1832), act 5, sc. 3. The play's popularity is reflected in a *Godey's Lady's Book* reference to "*The Hunchback*, which is succeeding now and forever," with an accompanying engraving of Knowles (Nov. 1834, 204). On Fanny Kemble as the original Julia, see "Mrs. Frances Anne Kemble" by James Parton, in James Parton, Horace Greeley et al., *Eminent Women of the Age* (Hartford, Conn.: S. M. Betts, 1872), 105.

13. This melodramatic trope is discussed in Grimsted, *Melodrama Unveiled*, 182–83; Booth, *English Melodrama*, 126; and idem, *Theatre in the Victorian Age*, 155–56. Brooks in *Melodramatic Imagination* (31 and 35) refers to melodrama as "a drama of pure psychic signs—called Father, Daughter, Protector, Persecutor, Judge, Duty, Obedience, Justice." See also Martha Vicinus, "'Helpless and Unfriended': Nineteenth-Century Domestic Melodrama," in Fisher and Watt, *When They Weren't Doing Shakespeare*, 175–76; and Gabrielle Hyslop, "Deviant and Dangerous Behavior: Women in Melodrama," *Journal of Popular Culture* 19 (Winter 1985): 69.

14. The best explanation for this focus on a man of magnetic personal powers is Halttunen, *Confidence Men and Painted Women*, 23–24. See also Fred Somkin, *Unquiet Eagle: Memory and Desire in the History of American Freedom, 1815–1860* (Ithaca, N.Y.: Cornell University Press, 1967); and Marvin Meyers, *The Jacksonian Persuasion: Politics and Belief* (Stanford, Calif.: Stanford University Press, 1957). Of course these historians were influenced by the original observer of the anxieties of a boundary-less society, Alexis de Tocqueville, who, in *Democracy in America* (1835 and 1840) also noticed that great care was taken to trace two distinct lines of action for the two sexes.

On Jackson, see Robert V. Remini, *Andrew Jackson and the Course of American Empire, 1767–1821* (New York: Harper and Row, 1977); idem, *Andrew Jackson and the Course of American Freedom, 1822–1832* (New York: Harper and Row, 1981), and *Andrew Jackson and the Course of American Democracy, 1833–1845* (New York: Harper and Row, 1984); as well as John William Ward, *Andrew Jackson: Symbol for an Age* (New York: Oxford University Press, 1953). The connection between Jacksonian-era hero worship and theatrical stardom was first suggested by Bruce McConachie in "Pacifying American Theatrical Audiences, 1820–1900," in Butsch, *For Fun and Profit*, 54.

15. Ralph Waldo Emerson, *Representative Men*, in *Collected Works* (11 vols, 1903; reprint, New York: AMS Press, 1960) 4:8,5. See also Thomas Carlyle, *On Heroes, Hero-Worship and the Heroic in History* (London: Oxford University Press, 1957; first publ. 1841).

16. This explanation of nineteenth-century domesticity as both a reaction to the marketplace and a female claim to power was first elaborated in Kathryn Kish Sklar's landmark biography *Catharine Beecher: A Study in American Domesticity* (New Haven, Conn.: Yale University Press, 1973).

17. Quotes from F. H. F. Berkeley to Pierce Butler, 8 Oct. 1832, Wister Family Papers; Henry Lee, "Fanny Kemble," *Atlantic Monthly*, May 1893, 663–64; Whitman cited in Bobbé, *Fanny Kemble*, 72–73. The accumulation of love letters is mentioned in Kemble, *Journal* 2:16.

18. Meeting with President Jackson recorded in Kemble, *Journal* 2:131. Fanny, with her complexion muddied by smallpox, was not beautiful; indeed she was "next door to homely" offstage according to a young cadet at West Point, Robert E. Lee (Lee to John Mackay, cited in Furnas, *Fanny Kemble*, 91). The interpretation of Jackson's remark as a reference to the Peggy Eaton affair is suggested by James Parton, *Life of Andrew Jackson* (3 vols., New York: Mason Bros., 1861) 3:599.

19. *Life and Letters of Joseph Story*, ed. William W. Story, 2 vols. (Boston: Little, Brown, 1851), 2:116–17.

20. The Adams anecdote is found in Bobbé, *Fanny Kemble*, 83. "I don't try to" comes from M. A. DeWolfe Howe, "Young Fanny Kemble," *Atlantic Monthly*, December 1944, 98. Howe gives no source for the anecdote. To search for the mention of other women's names in the memoirs of men prominent in the ante-bellum period is to understand how unusual was Kemble's repute.

21. Kemble, *Records of a Later Life*, 409; "affecting phrases" in Henry Wikoff, *The Reminiscences of an Idler* (New York: Fords, Howard and Hulbert, 1880), 37. Hutton notes that the language of *The Hunchback* "became as familiar as household words ... quoted in pulpits, on the platform, and in leading articles of leading journals, ... in the albums of the young ladies" (*Plays and Players*, 146–48).

22. Autobiographical fragment, 1875, Charlotte Cushman Papers. This line is stricken, as if, upon reflection, Cushman thought it better not to give so much credit to a predecessor. Ritchie [Mowatt], *Autobiography of an Actress*, 37–39.

23. "A wild desire ..." in Kemble, *Records of a Girlhood* 1:202–03. Ellen Moers discusses the tradition of heroinism in *Literary Women* (Garden City, N.Y.: Doubleday, 1976).

24. *Memoirs of Margaret Fuller Ossoli*, ed. R. W. Emerson, W. H. Channing, and J. F. Clarke, 2 vols. (1884; reprint, New York: Burt Franklin, 1972), 1:187–88. Loose editing makes it seem that this passage dates from later in the 1830s, after Fuller had moved to Providence, but Fanny Kemble was not performing at that time.

25. The Mariana story is found in *Memoirs of Margaret Fuller Ossoli* 1:42–52, and in its original version in Sarah Margaret Fuller, *Summer on the Lakes in 1843* (Boston: Charles C. Little and James Brown; New York: Charles Francis, 1844), 81–102.

26. For biographers' treatments of the Mariana story, see Paula Blanchard, *Margaret Fuller: From Transcendentalism to Revolution* (New York: Delacorte, 1978), 44–46; and Mason Wade, *Margaret Fuller: Whetstone of Genius* (New York: Viking, 1940), 11–13.

27. Horace Greeley from *Memoirs of Margaret Fuller Ossoli* 2:160; "paid Corinne," and "so materialistic" from ibid., 1:332, 250. Fuller's sending the book is noted in Kemble, *Further Records*, 105–06; Fuller's meeting with George Sand is described in *Memoirs of Margaret Fuller Ossoli* 2:195. William Henry Channing also compared Fuller to Corinne; see Bell Gale Chevigny, *The Woman and the Myth: Margaret Fuller's Life and Writings* (Old Westbury, N.Y.: Feminist Press, 1976), 88. Fuller feared the "display," the visual, embodied aspect of the theatre, but she understood the glance of recognition between herself and Sand as empowering. Fanny Kemble probably would not have endorsed Fuller's philosophy; she wrote that she was glad she had not met Fuller, "as I am afraid I should have incurred her contempt for my small sympathy with her views respecting the emancipation of women." Kemble thought that the speeches and writings of the women's rights movement were beside the point; the thing to do was to prevent young women "from becoming desperately in love with, and desperately afraid of, very contemptible men." Kemble's own experience, as we shall see, had taught her such a lesson. Nor did Kemble approve of George Sand, though she admired her literary genius (see Kemble, *Further Records* 1:106, 315).

28. Fuller, *Woman in the Nineteenth Century* (1845; reprint, New York: W. W. Norton, 1971), 35, 174 (emphasis added).

29. See "Declaration of Sentiments and Resolutions, Seneca Falls," in Miriam Schneir, ed., *Feminism: The Essential Historical Writings* (New York: Random House, Vintage Books, 1972), 81; Elizabeth Cady Stanton to Martha C. Wright, 22 April 1863, Stanton Papers; and Stanton, Speech before the Young Men's Suffrage Association, Plympton Hall, 1870, Stanton Papers.

30. *Records of a Girlhood*, 224; *Records of a Later Life*, 194–95.

31. Quotes from Kemble, *Journal* 1:114; Kemble, *Records of a Girlhood*, 223. Leigh Hunt recalled that theatrical journalism in those days was "an interchange of amenities over the dinner table; a flattery of power on one side, and puns on the other; and what the public took for a criticism on a play was a draft upon the box-office, or reminiscences of last Thursday's salmon and lobster-sauce" (Hunt, *Autobiography*, as cited in Herschel Baker, *John Philip Kemble: The Actor in His Time* [New York: Greenwood, 1942], 280).

32. Kemble, *Journal* 1:191. See Frank Luther Mott, *American Journalism: A History of Newspapers in the United States through 250 Years, 1690 to 1940* (New York: Macmillan, 1942), chaps. 12—13; Michael Schudson, *Discovering the News: A Social History of American Newspapers* (New York: Basic, 1978), chap. 1; Gerald J. Baldasty, *The Commercialization of News in the Nineteenth Century* (Madison, Wisc.: University of Wisconsin Press, 1992), chap. 2; Reynolds, *Beneath the American Renaissance,* 171—81.

33. Kemble, *Journal* 1:122, 123, 308, 138, 149. It is not clear whether Charles Kemble went to call on Clifton or merely to see her perform.

34. Kemble, *Journal* 2:131—45, 148. Later Fanny was told that the person responsible for the handbills was in fact an Englishman; the effort to arouse American nationalism had been wholly cynical. The actor-manager Thomas Hamblin had been injured by competition from the Kembles in New York and Philadelphia, and had responded in each case with a bald appeal to patriotism. In New York he trumpeted his "native talent" and renamed the Bowery Theatre the American Theatre. In Philadelphia, where he and Miss Vincent appeared opposite the Kembles in March and April 1833, he had adopted the motto "Vox Populi" and the American eagle insignia for his Walnut Street Theatre. (See Shank, "Bowery Theatre," 304; and Walnut Street playbills in the collection of the Library Company of Philadelphia.) Since only someone with a real interest in destroying the Kembles' stage success would have bothered to print up and distribute handbills, the British-born Hamblin must be the chief suspect. Hamblin is discussed at greater length below, in Chapter 3.

35. Quotes from Kemble to Harriet St. Leger, Philadelphia, 22 Oct. 1832, in *Records of a Girlhood*, 552; and Frances Kemble Butler to Pierce Butler, fall 1838, in Butler, *Mr. Butler's Statement*, 28. In *Francis the First* a scheming monk, really a Spanish nobleman in disguise, stalks a member of the French court to avenge his sister, whom the courtier seduced and abandoned. Meanwhile the aging queen has conceived a great passion for a young army commander, and she threatens him with death and dishonor should he spurn her advances. Her son, the idle young king, exacts sexual favors from a young woman when her brother is imprisoned. In this *Measure for Measure* turn, no "bed trick" intervenes: to free her brother the girl surrenders her virtue and, in the last scene, commits suicide.

36. Newspaper quotes from *Commercial Advertiser*, 3 Jan. 1835, cited in Furnas, *Fanny Kemble*, 150. I rely on Furnas' treatment of this episode, pp. 150—53. He points out the apt line from Dickens on p. 153. The best single account of the publication is Clifford Ashby, "Fanny Kemble's 'Vulgar' Journal," *Pennsylvania Magazine of History and Biography* 98 (1974): 58—66.

37. See Furnas, *Fanny Kemble*, 127, for this version of the story with the blanks filled in. The Brander Matthews Collection in Columbia University Library includes a copy of the *Journal* originally given by Fanny to Charles B. Sedgwick of Syracuse, in which she has written most of the names, but problems of legibility still leave room for some confusion about the identity of the people under discussion. Confusions are reproduced rather than dispelled by a new edition of the *Journal* from Columbia University

Press, edited by Monica Gough. Fanny supplied the specifics of Adams' complaint in her *Journal of a Residence on a Georgian Plantation* (1863). See p. 121 of the 1984 John A. Scott edition.

38. Edgar Allan Poe, "*Journal*—By Frances Anne Butler," *Southern Literary Messenger* 1 (May 1835): 524—31.

39. "Mrs. Butler's Journal," *North American Review* 41 (July 1835): 110, 144.

40. See "Fanny Kemble's Journal," *Niles' Register*, 1 Aug. 1835, 379; "Female Impertinence" came from the *Literary Gazette*. Poe quote is from Poe, "*Journal*," 530. A contemporary satire on Fanny's *Journal* indicates just what was considered vulgar. It focuses on her slang, her frank talk of eating and even of drinking, and her good opinion of herself. See *My Conscience! Fanny Thimble Cutler's Journal of a Residence in America Whilst performing a Profitable Theatrical Engagement: Beating the Nonsensical Fanny Kemble Journal All Hollow!!!* (Philadelphia: Alexander Turnbull, 1835).

41. *The Girlhood of Queen Victoria*, ed. Viscount Esher, 2 vols. (London: John Murray, 1912), 1:128; Alicia Hopton Middleton Travel Diary, 11 May 1835, South Carolinian Library, University of South Carolina. Henry James cited in Wister, *Fanny, the American Kemble*, 14.

42. Poe, "*Journal*," 525; Lucy Markoe Kenney, *Description of a Visit to Washington* (Washington, 1835), 4; Catharine Sedgwick to her niece Kate Minot, Massachusetts Historical Society, as cited in Furnas, *Fanny Kemble*, 162.

43. See Wister, *Fanny, the American Kemble*, 32—33, 53, 71; and Furnas, *Fanny Kemble*, 145.

44. Fanny Kemble to Sarah Perkins, in Wister, *Fanny, the American Kemble*, 151—52.

45. Fanny Kemble Butler to Pierce Butler, fall 1838, in *Mr. Butler's Statement*, 28. Later Harriet St. Leger asked Fanny whether she preferred earning her living or being supported as a wife. She replied that "the feeling of independence and power consequent upon earning large sums of money has very much destroyed my admiration for any other mode of support" (Fanny Kemble to Harriet St. Leger, 14 May 1842, in Kemble, *Records of Later Life*, 330). When her sister, Adelaide, retired from a successful operatic career in order to marry, Fanny was alive with worries. She spoke of Adelaide's talent about to be "folded in a napkin," and thought it "amazing to abdicate a secure fortune and such a power . . . for that fearful risk" (Fanny Kemble to Lady Dacre, 30 Sept. 1842, in Kemble, *Records of a Later Life*, 357—58).

46. Kemble, *Journal of a Residence on a Georgian Plantation*, 114, 161.

47. On the sums of money paid for her publications, see J. Murray to Miss Cobbe, 8 March 1893, Fanny Kemble Papers; and G. M. Dallas to F. Fisher, 31 Oct. 1849, Fanny Kemble Papers. On the milliner's bill, see Kemble, *Records of Later Life*, 336—37, 344—45.

48. Charles Greville, 8 Dec. 1842, *The Greville Diary*, ed. Philip Whitwell Wilson (New York: Doubleday, Page, 1927) 2:547.

49. See Philadelphia County Court of Common Pleas, *Pierce Butler vs. Frances Anne Butler: Libel for Divorce, with Answer and Exhibits* (Philadelphia, 1848), 5; Butler, *Mr. Butler's Statement*, 117; *A Statement by James Schott, Jr.* (Philadelphia?: n.p.,

1844?). All three sources can be found in the collection of the Library Company of Philadelphia.

50. "Fanny Kemble Butler Divorce Case," *New York Herald*, 28 and 29 Nov. 1848. Fanny's claim of Pierce's adultery was contained in her reply to Pierce's divorce petition, reprinted in the *Herald*. Or see the full legal document in *Butler vs. Butler: Pleadings in Suit for Divorce, with Mrs. Butler's Answer*, Kemble Papers.

51. *Philadelphia Ledger and Transcript*, 28 Nov. and 4 Dec. 1848. The Philadelphia paper, at first reticent, declared on 4 December that it might as well publish full documentation since the *New York Post* had already done so. See also "Libel for Divorce," *Home Journal* (New York), 16 Dec. 1848, 1—3. The *Home Journal's* editor, N. P. Willis, took Pierce's side. In an editorial he expressed amazement that Mr. Butler's counsel used "no one of the numerous class of circumstances usually admitted in his defense, or urged in his justification, by those who have discussed the matter for the last two or three years in society." As such arguments, presumably detailing Fanny's want of proper wifely submission, would be "most effective" with a jury, Willis could only attribute their omission to "severe gentlemanly delicacy" on Pierce's part. As Willis implied, private word of their troubles had long circulated. For example, in January 1838, the young princess Victoria, aged seventeen, was told by Lord Melbourne of actresses marrying "out of their sphere" and "its often not answering," with a list of examples that included "Mrs. Butler" (see *Girlhood of Queen Victoria*, 1:256). For Kemble's friends' clippings, see Bobbé, *Fanny Kemble*, 241; for the parties' various motives for settling, see Frances Anne Kemble to Eliza Middleton Fisher, Lenox, ca. 1848, and G. M. Dallas to J. Cadwallader, 21 Feb. 1849, in the Cadwallader Family Papers.

52. The best coverage of her readings is found in Gerald Kahan, "Fanny Kemble Reads Shakespeare: Her First American Tour, 1849—1850," *Theatre Survey* 24 (May and Nov. 1983): 77—98. Fanny actually gave her first few readings in England but was obliged to cancel her remaining engagements and leave for America when Pierce filed for divorce. Quotes are from Fanny Appleton Longfellow, *Mrs. Longfellow: Selected Letters and Journals of Fanny Appleton Longfellow, 1817—1861*, ed. Edward Wagenknecht (New York: Longmans Green, 1956), 148—49; *Letters and Journals of Thomas Wentworth Higginson*, ed. Mary Thacher Higginson (Boston and New York: Houghton Mifflin, 1921), 35; anonymous critic from *Spirit of the Times*, 3 Feb. 1849, 600. George Templeton Strong heard Kemble read *The Tempest* in 1859 and wrote "Very admirable performance. Vocal resources wonderful. She has half a dozen voices in her" (Nevins and Thomas, *Diary of George Templeton Strong* 2: 432—33).

53. For Kemble as the standard of excellence against which other women speakers were measured, see reference to a Gertrude Kellogg reading in the *Buffalo Express*, 7 March 1870, in the Gertrude Kellogg materials, Kellogg Family Papers. In 1849 Philip Hone estimated that Kemble was making $2000—$3000 a week for her readings in New York City (Nevins, *Diary of Philip Hone*, 863). Though this figure is almost certainly too high, she did well enough. In October 1849 Sidney George Fisher heard that she had already invested $20,000 from her earnings, and he supposed that she could go

on making $10,000 or $20,000 a year for some time to come (Sidney George Fisher, *A Philadelphia Perspective: The Diary of Sidney George Fisher Covering the Years 1834–1871*, ed. Nicholas B. Wainwright [Philadelphia: Historical Society of Pennsylvania, 1967], 226).

54. Hale complained that in the three years since the book had been conceived some dozen or more biographical compendia devoted to prominent women had appeared. Feeling the embrace of female publicity might be overdone, Hale felt compelled to add a word in favor of those women who adhered to domesticity and private life: "I am far from considering this outward semblance her [woman's] best or loveliest praise. Millions of the sex whose names were never known beyond the circle of their own home influences, have been as worthy of commendation as those here commemorated" (Sarah Josepha Hale, ed., *Woman's Record; or, Sketches of All Distinguished Women from "the Beginning" til A.D. 1850* [New York: Harper and Bros., 1853], 712–13, vii, ix).

55. There is reason to think that her female audience paid particular attention to this question. Ellen Moers has argued that literature by women from this period shows an explicit concern with money and that, given the difficulty for women of supporting themselves, it constituted a particularly urgent kind of "female realism" (Moers, *Literary Women: The Great Writers* [New York: Doubleday, 1976], chap. 4).

56. *Galaxy* 6 (Dec. 1868):801.

57. Fisher, 28 Feb. 1844, *Philadelphia Perspective*, 153; *Memoirs and Letters of Charles Sumner*, ed. Edward L. Pierce, 2 vols. (Boston: Robert Bros., 1877), 2:319: "She seems a noble woman—peculiar, bold, masculine, and unaccommodating, but with a burning sympathy for all that is high, true, humane."

58. *The Letters of Herman Melville*, ed. Merrell R. Davis and William H. Gilman (New Haven, Conn.: Yale University Press, 1960), 77–78. It has been suggested that the character of Goneril in *The Confidence Man* was based on Fanny Kemble (See Egbert S. Oliver, "Melville's Goneril and Fanny Kemble," *New England Quarterly* 18 [Dec. 1945]: 489–500). If so, this savagely hostile portrait of Goneril would be another case of Fanny's story providing the means for thinking about what women might become, here accomplished in wholly negative terms.

59. "Mrs. Butler," *Home Journal*, 22 Sept. 1849, 3; "Mrs. Butler's Pantaloons," *Home Journal*, 15 Sept. 1849, 2. The passage quoted is from an article that carries the byline "Fanny Ferret," but it seems likely that Willis himself was the author.

60. Butler, *Mr. Butler's Statement*, 48.

61. Kemble, *Records of Later Life*, 574.

3. SPECTACLES: THOMAS HAMBLIN AND HIS WOMEN

1. There is no biography of Hamblin. Useful information is found in Ireland, *Records of the New York Stage* 1:154,460; and Bruce McConachie, *Melodramatic Formations*, chap. 6, which Professor McConachie generously shared with me in draft. See also Shank, "Bowery Theatre."

2. On the importance of travelers to the theatre audience, see Cowell, *Thirty Years Passed*, 62; *New York Mirror*, 23 Jan. 1830 and 3 Oct. 1835, as cited in Shank, "Bowery Theatre," 223; Kemble, *Journal* 1:140. On the increasing number of performances per week, see Wood, *Personal Recollections of the Stage*, 212; Odell, *Annals of the New York Stage* 2:464; Mammen, *Old Stock Company*, 14. On the increasing length of the theatre season and the boom in theatre construction in the 1820s, see Quinn, *History of the American Drama*, 162, 199. According to Peter Buckley, there was a six-fold increase in the number of theatre seats in New York between 1825 and 1850, due in part to the construction of more theatres, in part to their increased size (Buckley, "To the Opera House," 142). On the strength of this increased capacity, New York City seized theatrical leadership decisively from Philadelphia. On the competition and uncertainty that accompanied expansion, see Wood, *Personal Recollections of the Stage*, 267; Hughes, *History of the American Theatre*, 155. On ticket prices see Odell, *Annals of the New York Stage* 2:291; Brown, *History of the New York Stage* 1:12. This generalization about prices necessarily conceals local variations and fluctuations over time. In the 1820s theatre managers began to cut prices to compete with rival houses. But only the severe depression of the late 1830s and 1840s caused them to accept a general round of deep price cuts. On 1820s price-cutting, see *Boston Daily Advertiser*, 26 May 1823; Wood, *Personal Recollections of the Stage*, 299; Phelps, *Players of a Century*, 143; Hughes, *History of the American Theatre*, 152. On price cuts in the 1840s, see Buckley, "To the Opera House," 145—46; Phelps, *Players of a Century*, 244; Ludlow, *Dramatic Life as I Found It*, 530, 544—45, 617; Clapp, *Record of the Boston Stage*, 378; Whitman, *Prose Works* 2:595.

3. The best explanation of capitalist development's impact on workers at this time is found in Sean Wilentz, *Chants Democratic: New York City and the Rise of the American Working Class, 1788—1850* (New York: Oxford University Press, 1984).

4. "Ill usage and persecution" from Odell, *Annals of the New York Stage* 2:419; quotes from the *Theatrical and Literary Journal*, May 1830, 6, 12, 27, 19, 18, at the Historical Society of Pennsylvania; "unprincipled speculators" in Wood, *Personal Recollections of the Stage*, 458. See also reference to actors who refused to perform when matinees were first introduced in Ludlow, *Dramatic Life as I Found It*, 605. On Wood's old-fashioned ways, see also Bruce A. McConachie, "William B. Wood at the 'Pathos of Paternalism,'" *Theatre Survey* 28 (May 1987): 1—14. A comment on similar changes in the methods of managers in the English theatre is found in a series of articles by the playwright Thomas William Robertson published in the London *Illustrated Times* in 1864. Robertson contrasted the "Actor Manager of thirty years ago" with the "Commercial Manager of today," who "takes an entirely commercial view of all things . . . and cuts down salaries and expenses to the very lowest scale" (see "Tom Robertson's Theatrical Types," in Alois M. Nagler, ed., *Sources of Theatrical History* [New York: Theatre Annual, 1952], 490—92).

5. Poe cited in Reynolds, *Beneath the American Renaissance*, 171. See also, for example, Nevins, *Diary of Philip Hone*, 275, entry of 23 Sept. 1837. Other sources are James L.

Crouthamel, *Bennett's New York Herald and the Rise of the Popular Press* (Syracuse: Syracuse University Press, 1989), 20–25; and George Juergens, *Joseph Pulitzer and the New York World* (Princeton, N.J.: Princeton University Press, 1960), viii–ix, for an apt definition of sensationalism.

6. Quote from Dunlap, *History of the American Theatre* 2:237. Kate Field described drama critics of the 1790s as "private individuals who attended the theatre for purposes of conscientious criticism . . . and prepared articles for the press" (see Field, "A Conversation on the Stage," *Atlantic Monthly*, March 1868, 272). See also Miller, *Bohemians and Critics*, 2–4; Wemyss, *Theatrical Biography*, 294–97; Wood, *Personal Recollections of the Stage*, 174–75. A puff thus was either a flattering newspaper notice or a theatre employee who prepared laudatory press releases and wined and dined journalists who might be persuaded then to print them.

7. "Literary aids" in Wood, *Personal Recollections of the Stage*, 175. On Bennett, see Crouthamel, *James Gordon Bennett*; *Walt Whitman of the New York Aurora*, 115; Brown, *History of the New York Stage*, 1:128–29. Bennett's practice as editor of overriding his dramatic critic is mentioned in Miller, *Bohemians and Critics*, 46–47. For Ellsler's charge of extortion, see *Spirit of the Times*, 13 and 20 April 1844, 84 and 96. According to Fanny Kemble, Ellsler had something to hide; see Kemble, *Records of a Later Life*, 194. Bennett's reputation was such that he felt obliged to subsidize a flattering contemporary biography: Isaac Clark Pray, *Memoirs of James Gordon Bennett and His Times* (New York: Stringer and Townsend, 1852).

8. This account of the Bowery is based primarily on Theodore J. Shank, "Theatre for the Majority: Its Influence on a Nineteenth Century American Theatre," *Educational Theatre Journal* 11 (October 1959): 188–99; and Shank's "Bowery Theatre." On working-class audiences, see also Bruce McConachie, "Theatre of the Mob: Melodrama and Riots in Antebellum New York," in McConachie and Friedman, *Theatre for Working-Class Audiences*, 17–46. Providence information is from Blake, *Historical Account of the Providence Stage*, 198–99; "never more popular" from Wood, *Personal Recollections of the Stage*, 196; "American-born mechanics" in Whitman, *Prose Works* 2:595–96; "young girls" in Charlotte Cushman, "A Woman's View of the People's Amusement," n.d., holo., Cushman Papers.

9. Shank, "Bowery Theatre," 304–05. After riots at the Park Theatre in October 1831 against Joshua Anderson, an English actor who was rumored to have maligned the American people, Hamblin moved with remarkable speed to rename his theatre the "American Theatre, Bowery" and to exhibit an American eagle ornament on the pediment of the building. Philip Hone found that all the violence in the Anderson riots was committed by about twenty boys and concluded that they had been hired or encouraged by Hamblin, whom he referred to as "the cloven hoof in relation to the riots at the Park Theatre" (Nevins, *Diary of Philip Hone*, 50–51). The dubious games Hamblin apparently played when the Kembles came to the United States are discussed above in Chapter 2. By the time of the Astor Place riots in 1849, New York audiences were accustomed to acting out nativism in ways that owed a good deal to Hamblin's constant commercial exploitation of the theme.

10. Shank, "Bowery Theatre," 323–30, 258; Whitman, *Prose Works* 2:594.

11. The term "manufactured star" is from Norman J. Myers, "Josephine Clifton: 'Manufactured Star,'" *Theatre History Studies* 6 (1986): 109–23. See Shank, "Bowery Theatre," 274–78, on the long-term contracts. Perhaps Hamblin learned these methods from Charles Gilfert, his predecessor as manager of the Bowery. Early in 1827 Gilfert had the young Edwin Forrest under contract at $40 a week and sent Forrest to star in Philadelphia, where, according to one source, his services brought $200 per night. The difference in pay went into Gilfert's own treasury (Shank, "Bowery Theatre," 75, 83). As a young actress Charlotte Cushman narrowly escaped an exploitative three-year contract with Hamblin when the theatre burned down shortly after she signed (Leach, *Bright Particular Star*, 48, 53, 57).

12. Quote from Hamblin to F. C. Wemyss, March 18, n.y., in Ireland, *Records of the New York Stage*, extra-illustrated version in the Harvard Theatre Collection, vol. 1, pt. 9, p. 148. The portion of the repertoire devoted to melodrama increased steadily under Hamblin's management. By 1836 melodrama was 66 percent of the Bowery's repertoire and accounted for 84 percent of the performances there (Shank, "Bowery Theatre," 600, Appendix B). Figures are exclusive of afterpieces.

13. Quotes in Hamblin to F. C. Wemyss, 10 September, n.y., in Ireland, *Records of the New York Stage*, ibid., vol. 1, pt. 9, p. 149; and Hamblin to James Anderson, New York, 11 Dec. [1838], Harvard Theatre Collection.

14. Hiring practices from Shank, "Bowery Theatre," 450–51, 43. It was symbolically appropriate that supernumeraries at the Bowery were not even considered players: they were under the direction of the property man. Quote is from Skinner and Skinner, *One Man in His Time*, 106.

15. J. M. Weston to William Henry Chippendale, 5 Jan. 1845, Dramatic Museum Collection, Columbia University.

16. Forrest cited in Wilson, *History of American Acting*, 26. For "auditors" to describe playgoers, see Leman, *Memories of an Old Actor*, 11; Wood, *Personal Recollections of the Stage*, 321; *Spirit of the Times*, 9 Sept. 1848; 28 Oct. 1848, 432; Skinner, *Footlights and Spotlights*, 67. "Unalloyed fondness" noted in Lewis O. Saum, *The Popular Mind of Pre–Civil War America* (Westport, Conn.: Greenwood, 1980), 137. "Migrated" from *Spirit of the Times*, 21 Sept. 1839, 348; "entertainments for the eye" from Jefferson, *Autobiography*, 396; "content" from Davidge, *Footlight Flashes*, 202. See also *Spirit of the Times*, 17 Aug. 1839, 288; 9 Dec. 1843, 492; and George Frank Gouley, *The Legitimate Drama: A Lecture Delivered before the Shakespeare Club of Delaware College, November 28, 1856* (Washington, D.C.: William H. Moore, 1857), 19. The nineteenth-century rage for "pictorialism" is mentioned in Booth, *Theatre in the Victorian Age*, 95; and explored at length in Meisel, *Realizations*.

17. *New York Mirror*, 25 July 1835, 30. On Hamblin's production methods, see Shank, "Bowery Theatre," 300–301, 389; and the effective summary in Shank, "Theatre for the Majority," 197–98. Shank also notes that Hamblin experimented with eliminating the traditional afterpiece, concentrating effort and expense on the main attraction, since it was the reason people chose to attend. My comment on ease of consumption

was prompted by Neil Postman's *Amusing Ourselves to Death: Public Discourse in the Age of Show Business* (New York: Viking, 1985). Postman contrasts the skills required for reading and television watching.

18. Sennett, *Fall of Public Man;* Haltunnen, *Confidence Men and Painted Women;* Kasson, *Rudeness and Civility;* Lyn H. Lofland, *A World of Strangers: Order and Action in Urban Public Space* (New York: Basic, 1973); all offer useful insight on the problem of living in an urban world in which it is impossible to know as individuals most of the people we encounter. As Lofland points out, we can apprehend them only as members of social categories, which we assign based on how they look, where we see them, or some combination of the two. Kasson's chapter 3, "Reading the City: The Semiotics of Everyday Life," offers an excellent discussion of the nineteenth-century confrontation with the illegibility of urban street life. Sexual expression was affected by these new conditions, for anonymity, often a distressing condition, does facilitate certain sorts of sexual adventure, especially those involving what cinema critics call "scopophilic" pleasure, the pleasure of looking.

19. On Daguerre's theatre career, see Brockett, *History of the Theatre,* 447–49. Gouley, *Legitimate Drama,* 7, refers to the stage as the daguerreotype of life. J. B. Howe, *A Cosmopolitan Actor* (London: Bedford, 1888), 68, recalls seeing daguerreotypes of actors in the early 1850s in shop windows in the neighborhood of New York City's Chambers Street Theatre. L. Clarke Davis, "Among the Comedians," *Atlantic,* June 1867, 757, compares a fine performance to a photograph or a *camera obscura* projection. On theatrical cartes de visite, see *Spirit of the Times,* 29 March 1862, 64: "Appleton and Co., the well-known book firm in Broadway, have on hand, of their own manufacture and by importation, an immense variety of these popular pictures. You can scarce name an artist, or notable individual of the age, who does not figure in their catalogues. . . . Competition and improvement have brought photographic gems to such an insignificant price that the humblest citizen can ornament his parlor table." The article describes Charles D. Fredericks as another popular carte de visite maker: "almost every prominent resident actor and actress" had been to him. For an example from the late 1860s of avid young theatre fans who still recited lines but put more emphasis on their collections of photographs, see Wright, *My New York,* 188.

20. Quote is from Wemyss, *Twenty-Six Years,* 199–200. The best compendium of information on Clifton is Myers, "Josephine Clifton," 109–23, used as a source for this section. Critics remarked that young men who made their "first appearance on any stage" were seldom successful, but young women, especially if attractive, had a better chance. See "The Drama—A New Debutante," *New York Mirror,* 28 April 1838, 350. We know relatively little about Clifton, and that little, sifted from paid puffery and newspaper sensationalism, should be read cautiously—it is mostly her story *as it appeared to the public of the day.* The same is true of the other young women whose stories will be told in this chapter. It may seem unfair to group them as "Hamblin's women," yet the aspect of their lives about which the historian can feel most confident is precisely their common relationship with this manager, in which a pattern of exploitation was repeated.

21. Quote from Wemyss, *Twenty-Six Years*, 201–02. Probably the most thorough discussion of Naomi Vincent is found in Clarke, *Concise History*, a pamphlet contained in the Rare Book Collection of the Boston Public Library. Mrs. Clarke seems to have been a kind of crusading journalist, and certainly she was a partisan of the first Mrs. Hamblin. For separation, see Thomas S. Hamblin, "Articles of Separation and Settlement," 25 June 1832, Harvard Theatre Collection.

22. Odell, *Annals of the New York Stage* 3:628–29; Ireland, *Records of the New York Stage* 2:55–56.

23. Quote from Nevins, *Diary of Philip Hone*, 271.

24. Clarke, *Concise History*, 21–33; quote is in T. S. Hamblin to F. C. Wemyss, 19 Nov., Stephen W. Phoenix Papers.

25. The best source on Medina is Rosemarie K. Bank, "Theatre and Narrative Fiction in the Work of the Nineteenth-Century American Playwright Louisa Medina," *Theatre History Studies* 3 (1983): 55–67; most of the biographical information is found in an interview in *Spirit of the Times*, 1 Oct. 1836, 258.

26. Quotes from Will of Thomas S. Hamblin, 23 November 1836, Harvard Theatre Collection; and Wallack, *Memories of Fifty Years*, 119.

27. See Odell, *Annals of the New York Stage* 4:161, 224–26; Ireland, *Records of the New York Stage* 1:460. Since Medina was living with Hamblin, her salary and author's benefit would have come to him, and presumably a new debutante would have been bound by a contract like those signed by Clifton and Vincent. Medina also wrote a starring role for Hamblin into the new play.

28. Quotes on Missouri's debut and the subsequent controversy come from the *Spirit of the Times*, 7 April 1838, 57; 23 June 1838, 145; 7 July 1838, 161; 31 March 1838, 49. It seems likely, incidentally, that Missouri was a stage name.

29. Apologetics quoted in Clarke, *Concise History*, 18 (Clarke dismisses them as "very fine rhodomontade"); Clifton quote from "A Card to the Public," *Spirit of the Times*, 7 July 1838, 161.

30. Quotes from Wallack, *Memories*, 117–20. "Miss Missouri," *New York Herald*, 20 June 1838, reproduces the post mortem report. Clarke, *Concise History*, 38–40 reprints an account entitled "Singular Death of Miss Missouri," supposedly written by Louisa Medina, which exculpates Hamblin and casts blame on Missouri's mercenary relatives, especially her "vile and polluted mother." Clarke herself rejects this story, clearly considering Hamblin the culprit.

31. Compare *Spirit of the Times*, 9 Feb. 1839, 409, which reported that nine-tenths of the gentlemen in New York considered Hamblin a "reprehensible cur," with the same paper of 17 May 1851, describing him as an "upright, honorable, trustworthy man of business, who never repudiated a debt, whom no one can accuse of oppression or injustice," or with the obituaries contained in the clipping file at the New York Public Library at Lincoln Center. After Hamblin's death, T. Allston Brown described him as "noted for his correct business habits, promptitude, and open-heartedness" (Brown, *History of the New York Stage* 1:128–29).

32. See Sandra M. Gilbert and Susan Gubar, *The Madwoman in the Attic: The Woman*

Writer and the Nineteenth-Century Literary Imagination (New Haven and London: Yale University Press, 1979). There is an enormous literature on melodrama. Among the most helpful works on its special appeal to women are Martha Vicinus, "'Helpless and Unfriended': Nineteenth-Century Melodrama," in Fisher and Watt, *When They Weren't Doing Shakespeare*, 174—86; Gabrielle Hyslop, "Deviant and Dangerous Behavior: Women in Melodrama," *Journal of Popular Culture* 19 (Winter 1985): 65—77; and E. Ann Kaplan, "Theories of Melodrama: A Feminist Perspective," *Women and Performance* 1 (Spring/Summer 1983): 40—48. Vicinus notes (p. 181) the villain's typical "greed and sensuality." Grimsted, in *Melodrama Unveiled*, 175—78, argues that the villain's motives were revenge, avarice, or ambition, but because virtue was personified in the heroine, the villain's threat to her typically presented itself in "physical, specifically sexual, terms." Feminist film criticism routinely treats melodrama as a "woman's" genre, although the meaning of melodrama has shifted considerably by the late twentieth century. See E. Ann Kaplan, *Women and Film: Both Sides of the Camera* (1983, reprint, New York and London: Routledge, 1988), 25—26, for example.

33. *New York Mirror*, 20 Aug. 1836, 62.

34. The remarkable activity of many melodramatic heroines has been noticed by both traditional and feminist critics. See, for example, Rosemarie K. Bank, "The Second Face of the Idol: Women in Melodrama," in Chinoy and Jenkins, *Women in American Theater*, 238—43; Booth, *English Melodrama*, 18—28; Davies, *Mirror of Nature*, 41; Vicinus, "Helpless and Unfriended," 178, 180; Hyslop, "Deviant and Dangerous Behavior," 65—70. Bank suggests that women became more active in the plays written after the Civil War; Hyslop argues that the French playwright Guilbert de Pixérécourt (1773—1844), a pioneer in the genre, was especially apt to write active and energetic, "deviant and dangerous" heroines into his plays during the first half of his career. Hyslop sees most melodramatic heroines as passive, however, with exceptions providing only a "*frisson* of change," and calls melodrama itself "deeply conservative," but this seems to me too rigid a social-control argument. *Under the Gaslight* is available in a recent anthology: Daniel C. Gerould, ed., *American Melodrama* (New York: Performing Arts Journal Publications, 1983). Grimsted's *Melodrama Unveiled* provides an otherwise excellent discussion of the genre in chapters 8 and 9, but the author repeats the conventional wisdom about the heroine's "total goodness and extreme weakness" (p. 175).

35. See McConachie, "Theatre of the Mob," 17—46, on working-class reception of melodrama. Other possible readings of melodrama might focus on its expression of intergenerational tensions or its defense of the family unit against hostile outside forces.

36. Raymond Williams, "The Popularity of Melodrama," *New Society* 52 (24 April, 1980): 170. Quinn, *History of the American Drama*, 102, makes the point that music is crucial to melodrama's exaggeration and implausibility: "Melodrama calls in the aid of musical accompaniment to incite emotion and thus weaken, even momentarily, the critical judgment and the appeal of reason." John Cawelti, *Adventure, Mystery, and Romance* (Chicago: University of Chicago Press, 1976) explains that the primary

problem for mass entertainment is how to make its offerings at once comfortingly familiar and appealingly novel. (True novelty or unpredictability would be unsettling, as it is in high culture or indeed in life itself.) Cawelti argues that popular culture resolves itself into formulaic stories precisely because they permit variation within predictability. As Cawelti focuses solely on literature, his argument, like many others, seems to me to miss the crucial flexibility of multiple-media works, which provide different registers within which variation can occur, different things for different audience members to look at and listen to while, all the time, already "knowing" how the story will end. Musical accompaniment and visual effects helped theatre reach out to a mass audience in the nineteenth century, and subsequent developments in technology have only deepened their power in modern mass entertainments such as film and television.

As a number of scholars have pointed out, melodrama's popularity was based on more than mere technique: melodrama grappled with a profound and quintessentially modern cultural problem. Behind its relentless insistence on poetic justice lay "the loss of the sacred"—the doubt and spiritual anguish of a secularizing age (Brooks, *Melodramatic Imagination*, 11–16). See Williams, "Popularity of Melodrama," 171, on "the structure of feeling which developed with the loss of an effective God;" and David Grimsted, "An Idea of Theatre History," *Educational Theatre Journal* 26 (Dec. 1974): "The importance of melodrama lay precisely in its creation of a myth that both admitted the threatening emptiness of the modern world and asserted the eventual triumph of justice and pattern" (428).

37. The plays named are nine of the ten melodramas that made the list of the thirty-four most popular plays of 1831 to 1851 in four major cities: Philadelphia, Charleston, New Orleans, and St. Louis. (The tenth melodrama, *Tour de Nesle; or, The Chamber of Death*, was a lurid thriller centered on a wicked queen who invites men to assignations in the Tour de Nesle and then has them killed. Here the possibilities of women's power were cast in wholly negative terms and magnified into a subject of horror.) See Grimsted, *Melodrama Unveiled*, appendix 1, table 5. Grimsted's labeling of plays is in some cases rather arbitrary: *Mazeppa*, for example, is considered an equestrian drama rather than a melodrama for the purposes of his list. But I have accepted Grimsted's decisions for the purposes of this tally. Diana Vernon, a character of astonishing feminist *sang-froid* created by Sir Walter Scott, is discussed in T. E. Kebbel, "Diana Vernon," *MacMillan's Magazine*, August 1870, 185–91. Quoted lines are from W. H. Wallack, *Paul Jones* (n.p., n.p., n.d.), act 3, scene 1.

38. Compare Robert Montgomery Bird, *Nick of the Woods* (Philadelphia: Carey, Lea and Blanchard, 1837), and Louisa Medina, *Nick of the Woods* (Boston: William V. Spencer, n.d.); Edward Bulwer-Lytton, *The Last Days of Pompeii* (London: Routledge, 1834), and Medina, *The Last Days of Pompeii* (New York: Samuel French, n.d.).

39. "Drama," *Ladies Companion*, April 1837, 302.

4. FEMALE AMBITION: CHARLOTTE CUSHMAN SEIZES THE STAGE

1. The best biography of Cushman is Leach, *Bright Particular Star*. See also Clement, *Charlotte Cushman*; Stebbins, *Charlotte Cushman*; Price, *Life of Charlotte Cushman*; Yeater, "Charlotte Cushman"; Merrill, "Charlotte Cushman." Figures on her pay are from *Spirit of the Times*, 2 Nov. 1844, 432. Like other women of unusual accomplishment in that era, Cushman depended upon domestic service to free herself for nondomestic work. Sallie Mercer is discussed in Leach, *Bright Particular Star*, passim, and Stebbins, *Charlotte Cushman*, 37—39. Mercer became Cushman's lifelong "dresser" and housekeeper. African-American women could seldom approach the professional stage in other than backstage, menial roles like this. See Errol Hill, *Shakespeare in Sable: A History of Black Shakespearean Actors* (Amherst: University of Massachusetts Press, 1984), for the story of those few who succeeded.

2. Biographical information here and below is taken from the Leach biography unless otherwise noted. The biography by H. L. Kleinfield in *Notable American Women* mentions the stint in domestic service, which I have not found elsewhere; it may simply refer to her unpaid labor at her mother's boardinghouse. The presence of women in theatre management, which was not uncommon, will be discussed further in Chapter 6.

3. Quoted phrase is from Leach, *Bright Particular Star*, 141.

4. Ibid., 145.

5. Quotes from Charles Cushman to Mary Eliza and Susan Cushman, London, 1 May 1845, Cushman Papers; and *Boston Transcript*, 19 Feb. 1876.

6. Quotes from S. A. E. Walton to Charlotte Cushman, New York, 2 Nov. 1874, Cushman Papers; Clement, *Charlotte Cushman*, 73; Julia Ward Howe to Charlotte Cushman, 20 Sept. [1857], as cited in Leach, *Bright Particular Star*, 278.

7. "Without one personal charm" from Reignolds-Winslow, *Yesterdays with Actors*, 28.

8. An example of the death announcements is found in Cowell, *Thirty Years Passed*, 73. Cowell claimed the theatre was in a "degraded condition" due to "dances, mimes, and mummers." For Texas, Maine, and New Hampshire, see *Spirit of the Times*, 23 March 1839, 36; 20 June 1840, 192 and 216. A similar point about rural areas in the South is made in Dormon, *Theatre in the Antebellum South*, 49, 221—223. For another New England tour in the 1840s that took the players to towns like Bangor, Belfast, Orono, and Oldtown, see Leman, *Memories of an Old Actor*, 212. The estimate of fifty residential stock companies by 1850 is from Wilson, *History of American Acting*, 106.

9. "Ballet dancers" from Wood, *Personal Recollections of the Stage*, 456. Model artists are discussed below, Chap. 5. *Spirit of the Times*, 7 March 1840, 12, blamed the decline of the drama in Boston on competition from lectures and inexpensive concerts. *Spirit of the Times*, 18 March 1843, 36, made a similar point about New York City: "The constant occurrence of lectures, concerts, and other cheap amusements has drawn away the theatre audience." On the possibility that an equestrian troupe could outdraw a star in Shakespeare, see Ludlow, *Dramatic Life as I Found It*, 342.

10. See Halttunen, *Confidence Men and Painted Women*. Halttunen suggests that urban-

ization, which required more and more dealings with strangers, together with the innate elusiveness of sincerity as a social ideal, prompted this cultural shift. Whatever the reason, one of the most fundamental philosophical objections to theatregoing was removed at the same time that theatrical entrepreneurs were pushing harder to sell their entertainment products. Halttunen dates the vogue for private theatricals to the late 1840s, but they may have begun earlier, since a speech delivered at the opening of the Albany Museum in 1841 referred to private theatricals and tableaux as "now more prevalent than ever" (Stone, *Personal Recollections of the Drama*, 234). The diary of Henry Clay Southworth in New York City in 1851 includes entries such as "passed the eve playing different kinds of plays" (Southworth Diary, 12 March 1851, and 29 Jan. 1851). The continuing popularity of parlor theatricals after the Civil War was noted in the *Springfield [Mass.] Republican* as cited in Logan, *Before the Footlights*, 601.

11. The *Ladies Companion* began theatre coverage in October 1836 by remarking, "Theatrical amusements being so very *fashionable* now-a-days, we shall hereafter give in each number light and appropriate reviews of this most refined of all recreations of the present day." Since the very next number included praise of the Bowery, and the magazine was remarkably kind in its treatment of Hamblin himself, it seems likely that Hamblin was paying for favorable treatment. See, e.g., *Ladies Companion*, Oct. 1836, 295; Aug. 1838, 200; June 1837, 95. These last two articles refer to Hamblin's divorce regretfully as a matter of fault on both sides and report that in the Missouri affair Hamblin was made the "scapegoat of a clique of abandoned profligates" and extortionists. Hamblin recognized that he should cultivate the good opinion of respectable women, even though he failed miserably in doing so.

12. The standard source on the third tier and its elimination is Johnson, "That Guilty Third Tier," but Johnson places the date of its disappearance too late, in the 1870s or 1880s, due perhaps to excessive reliance on antitheatrical materials generated by evangelical crusaders. My dating is based on Logan, *Before the Footlights*, 537–40; Ritchie, *Autobiography of an Actress*, 445; Ford, *Peep Behind the Curtain*, 27; John D. Vose, *Seven Nights in Gotham* (New York: Bunnell and Price, 1852), 56; Ludlow, *Dramatic Life as I Found It*, 478–79; *Spirit of the Times*, 6 June 1840, and 22 June 1844; Henry W. Bellows, *The Relation of Public Amusements to Public Morality* (New York: C. S. Francis, 1857), 39; Herrick Johnson, *Plain Talk About the Theater* (Chicago: F. H. Revell, 1882), 62. On the elimination of alcoholic beverages, see Smith, *Theatrical Management in the West*, 209; Leonard Woolsey Bacon, *A Sermon Concerning Theatres and Theatre-Going* (Baltimore: The Sun Book and Job Printing, 1871), 7. Quote is from the *Boston Daily Bee*, 19 Feb. 1852. The difficulty of eliminating the bar was almost certainly a matter of economics, and perhaps the decision lay in the hands of the building owners rather than the theatre managers. In one theatre in Philadelphia in 1840, for example, the bar rent for the previous six years was said to have been $13,250, while the rent for the theatre was $20,000 (Wemyss, *Theatrical Biography*, 260–61).

13. The French-style spelling—*parquette* rather than *parquet*—was in vogue at the time.

The parquette—like its predecessor, the pit—occupied the main floor of the theatre, between the musicians' area and the elevated seating areas to the sides and rear, which were termed, variously: boxes, tiers, circles, parterres, or—the highest, cheapest seats—galleries. Initially it took "some little persuasion" to induce ladies to sit in the parquette (Northall, *Before and Behind the Curtain*, 177). Pittsburgh's first experiment with a parquette tells us why: the gallery persisted in jeering everyone who sat in the new section. The easiest conversions came in new theatres, which, like the new St. Louis theatre in 1837, were built with a parquette (Coad and Mims, *American Stage*, 160, 162). For the conversion of a pit into a parquette in 1840, see Odell, *Annals of the New York Stage* 4:506. One old-fashioned newspaper writer expressed relief that when the Park Theatre was refurbished in 1848 the pit was not transformed into "that modern absurdity, a 'parquette'" (cited in Ireland, *Records of the New York Stage* 2:522). By the late 1860s the pit was referred to as a thing of the past (Logan, *Before the Footlights*, 381). Quoted letter is from William Dinneford to Thomas Hamblin, as cited in Odell, *Annals of the New York Stage* 4:165.

14. Cushman quote in Charlotte Cushman to Mrs. Mann, Massachusetts Historical Society, as cited in Leach, *Bright Particular Star*, 231. Similarly, a Brookline matron told her diary in 1856 that she had gone to the opera alone, "it being the practice of ladies to go unattended afternoons" (Caroline Barrett White Diary, 9 Feb. 1856, White Family Papers). The *Boston Transcript* of 8 Dec. 1906 recalled, "The matinee added a fixed income to the treasuries . . . and also helped abolish the old prejudice against theatrical entertainments." For couples prices in 1847, see Brown, *History of the New York Stage* 1:176; Phelps, *Players of a Century*, 244. William Wood, for instance, saw that *Julius Caesar* was a problem for the new strategy because of the lack of a female lead (see Wood, *Personal Recollections of the Stage*, 105). An article in the *New York Times*, 14 March 1860, 1, referred to a play with "the common defect of insufficient female interest."

15. Playbill, Mobile Theatre, 25 Jan. 1841, Harvard Theatre Collection.

16. George Colman to Charles Kemble, 10 Dec. 1828, Dramatic Museum Collection. See Blake, *Historical Account of the Providence Stage*, 50, 77; Ritchie, *Autobiography of an Actress*, 441; Wood, *Personal Recollections of the Stage*, 460; Logan, *Apropros of Women and Theatres*, 91, 93, 95; George Frank Gouley, *The Legitimate Drama: A Lecture Delivered Before the Shakespeare Club of Delaware College, November 28, 1856* (Washington, D.C.: William H. Moore, 1857), 15. The earlier state of affairs is reflected, for instance, in a reference to an actor who died in 1808 and who had the "constant habit of interlarding the text with small oaths" (Wood, *Personal Recollections of the Stage*, 120).

17. The earliest reference to the term *moral drama* that I have found is in the *Spirit of the Times*, 16 June 1838, which speaks of a series of "Moral Dramas on Duelling, Procrastination, Speculation, Gambling, etc." On *The Drunkard*, see Judith N. McArthur, "Demon Rum on the Boards: Temperance Melodrama and the Tradition of Antebellum Reform," *Journal of the Early Republic* 9 (Winter 1989): 517—40.

18. The first theatres to prosper under euphemistic cover had been garden theatres, most

notably Niblo's Garden in New York, which opened in 1823 and was said to be patronized by "a large class of people who had a holy horror of profane theatres" (Northall, *Before and Behind the Curtain*, 115). For a thorough discussion of museum theatres see Bruce McConachie, "Museum Theatre and the Problem of Respectability for Mid-Century Urban Americans," in his *Melodramatic Formations*. The *Evening Transcript* quote and other details about the Boston Museum are from McGlinchee, *First Decade of the Boston Museum*, 22, 48—50; and Skinner, *Footlights and Spotlights*, 16. The Albany Museum, another early competitor, opened its "museum saloon" in 1841 with a message from the proprietors that, "disclaiming any wish or intention to make theatrical amusement their exclusive object," they would, from time to time, offer "such chaste and pleasing productions as may be free from the charges which have been made against the regular theatre, and in too many instances not without cause." On Albany, see Stone, *Personal Recollections of the Drama*, 232—34. Observer's comment is from Clapp, *Record of the Boston Stage*, 471.

19. James quote from James, *Small Boy*, 155; Barnum boast in A. H. Saxon, *P. T. Barnum: The Legend and the Man* (New York: Columbia University Press, 1989), 107. General sources on Barnum include Buckley, "To the Opera House," chap. 6; Neil Harris, *Humbug: The Art of P. T. Barnum* (Chicago: University of Chicago Press, 1973); Saxon, *P. T. Barnum*; Waldo R. Browne, ed., *Barnum's Own Story* (Gloucester, Mass.: Peter Smith, 1972).

20. Quote from Browne, *Barnum's Own Story*, 120. See extensive protestations in Saxon, *P. T. Barnum*, 107.

21. P. T. Barnum, *Struggles and Triumphs; or, Forty Years' Recollections* (Buffalo: Courier, 1879), 68—69.

22. Quote from Leman, *Memories of an Old Actor*, 122. Another actor described her as "a lover of place and position" (Murdoch, *Stage*, 239).

23. Merrill, "Charlotte Cushman," 47—50. Cushman found herself a post with a company in Albany. Fisher's last letters to her suggest that there had been some flirtation between them, at least on his part. A veteran manager later explained that when Cushman's talents had been underappreciated early in her career, "her masculine mind at once perceived that the only means of success was to cultivate the acquaintance of the gentlemen conducting the newspapers" (Wemyss, *Twenty-Six Years*, 336).

24. Cushman quote in Charlotte Cushman to Park Benjamin, 13 Oct. 1841, Harvard Theatre Collection. On Cushman's suspicions about Hamblin's role in the fire, see Wemyss, *Twenty-Six Years* 2:359: "[Cushman's] suspicions pointed to a party as yet unimpeached, but who could have no motive for such a diabolical act." This admittedly ambiguous remark seems to me to point to Hamblin. Wemyss had just detailed how the "dangerous" rivalry of Burton's theatre had compelled Hamblin to cut his prices and lose money, and so indicated a motive. Because Hamblin was his old friend, Wemyss chose to consider him "yet unimpeached" and claimed to discern "no motive." See also Odell, *Annals of the New York Stage*, 4:467, 469, 473—78; and Wemyss, *Theatrical Biography*, 289.

25. See *Godey's Lady's Book*, Feb. 1837, 70—73; and Wemyss, *Twenty-Six Years*, 336.

26. Leman, *Memories of an Old Actor*, 179—80.

27. "Fine tact" in Murdock, *Stage*, 239; Cushman quotes in Charlotte Cushman to Mother, Liverpool, 2 Dec. 1844, Cushman Papers. On the importance of the letters, see Vandenhoff, *Leaves from an Actor's Notebook*, 198.

28. Charlotte Cushman to Mother, London, 27 March 1845, Cushman Papers.

29. See Charlotte Cushman to Mary (?), Boston, 2 Oct. 1832; and Charlotte Cushman to Mother, London, 17 April 1845, Cushman Papers.

30. Stebbins, *Charlotte Cushman*, 238, 144.

31. Charlotte Cushman to Mother and Sue, London, 1 May 1845, as quoted in Stebbins, *Charlotte Cushman*, 50.

32. See Price, *Life of Charlotte Cushman*, 23—24, for a listing of her early roles; actor's story in Leach, *Bright Particular Star*, 185—86.

33. Gary Jay Williams, "*Guy Mannering* and Charlotte Cushman's Meg Merrilies," in Fisher and Watt, *When They Weren't Doing Shakespeare*, 19—38.

34. Quoted phrases are from Clapp, *Reminiscences of a Drama Critic*, 81; and Auerbach, *Woman and the Demon*. See also Martha Roth's argument: "Most terrifying of all female figures is the self-sufficient old woman. Because the patriarchy cannot hook her, either economically or sexually, hers is the character that binds masculine fears; she is the witch" (Roth, "Notes Toward a Feminist Performance Aesthetic," *Women and Performance* 1:1 [1983]: 10). Auerbach is primarily concerned with British literature and art, Roth with modern performance, but the connection to imaginative life in the nineteenth-century United States is easily made. For example, Meg Merrilies recalls similar characters in American fiction, such as Crazy Sal in Mary Jane Holmes's *The English Orphans*, discussed in Mary Kelley, *Private Woman, Public Stage: Literary Domesticity in Nineteenth-Century America* (New York: Oxford University Press, 1984), 336—42. See also Linda K. Kerber, *Women of the Republic: Intellect and Ideology in Revolutionary America* (Chapel Hill, N.C.: University of North Carolina Press, 1980), 273—74, on Eliza Foster Cushing's *Yorktown* and James Fenimore Cooper's *The Spy*, in which women are given the role of sybil. Patrick Bade argues that the second half of the nineteenth century saw an "extraordinary proliferation" of images of femmes fatales in European literature and art. See his *Femme Fatale* (New York: Mayflower Books, 1979). Compare also Joy Kasson, *Marble Queens and Captives*, chap. 8, "Domesticating the Demonic," who discusses a whole genre of sculpture devoted to arousing anxiety but ultimately resolving viewers' fears in representations of women like Cleopatra, Salome, Delilah, Judith, Clytemnestra, and Cassandra. Kasson notes that William Wetmore Story was among the most persistent explorers of this theme, always showing such women as controllable and controlled. Story knew Cushman, since they were both part of the American community resident in Rome, and he disliked her intensely. See Henry James, *William Wetmore Story and His Friends*, 2 vols. (Edinburgh and London: William Blackwood and Sons, 1903), 1:255, 2:127.

35. Quotes from Merrill, "Charlotte Cushman," 132; and *London Theatrical Times*, 13 Nov. 1847, 355, as cited in Leach, *Bright Particular Star*, 202.

36. Quote from Lawrence Barrett, cited in Clement, *Charlotte Cushman*, 25. See Yeater, "Charlotte Cushman," 40, for the Five Points story. Emma Stebbins, Cushman's friend and biographer, wondered "why the repulsive details of such a picture should be so readily accepted when clothed in all the elaboration of an author's imagination, and yet be found shocking when acted out before the eyes" (Stebbins, *Charlotte Cushman*, 155).

37. Whitman in the *Brooklyn Eagle*, 14 Aug. 1846, and Booth are cited in Leach, *Bright Particular Star*, 91, 130; "portrait" from Wemyss, *Theatrical Biography*, 269; "fearfully natural" from Vandenhoff, *Leaves from an Actor's Notebook*, 195.

38. Quoted in Westland Marston, *Our Recent Actors* (London: Lowe, Marston, Searle, Rivington, 1888), 77—78, as cited in Leach, *Bright Particular Star*, 177.

39. See William Rounseville Alger, *Life of Edwin Forrest, the American Tragedian*, 2 vols. (1877, reprint, New York: Benjamin Blom, 1972), 161, 251, and 196, on Forrest's portrayal of "the democratic ideal of universal manhood." See also Richard Moody, *Edwin Forrest* (New York: Alfred A. Knopf, 1960); and Bruce McConachie, "The Theatre of Edwin Forrest and Jacksonian Hero Worship," in Fisher and Watt, *When They Weren't Doing Shakespeare*, 3—18.

40. The common experiences of the female body can be a bond of solidarity among women, as Judith Walzer Leavitt's *Brought to Bed: Child-Bearing in America, 1750—1950* (New York: Oxford University Press, 1986) demonstrates. But nothing like this seems to result when women's bodies become an element in entertainment for male-dominated audiences. Both friends and enemies commented that Cushman tended to be a performer offstage as well as on. See William James Stillman, *Autobiography of a Journalist*, 2 vols. (Boston and New York: Houghton Mifflin, 1901), 1:362; and Diary of Annie Adams Fields, 12 Sept. 1863, Massachusetts Historical Society.

41. "Pantheress" in *New York Times*, 19 Feb. 1876, as cited in Leach, *Bright Particular Star*, 44; actor's complaints in Vandenhoff, *Leaves from an Actor's Notebook*, 196; winedrinking in Clement, *Charlotte Cushman*, 82—83; "grandfather" in *New York Mirror*, December 1907, as cited in Yeater, "Charlotte Cushman," 97.

42. Quote from Stebbins, *Charlotte Cushman*, 215.

43. The story of the young man in Albany is found in Geraldine Jewsbury to Emma Stebbins, 6 Feb. 1877, Cushman Papers. See also Yeater, "Charlotte Cushman," 16, n. 2.

44. The letter is Burton to Benjamin Webster, Philadelphia, n.d., in the extended copy of Clement, *Charlotte Cushman*, in the Harvard Theatre Collection. Critical opinions in George C. D. Odell, *Shakespeare from Betterton to Irving*, 2 vols. (New York: Charles Scribner's Sons,), 2:272; and Ludlow, *Dramatic Life as I Found It*, 316, who says he saw only two great Romeos—John Howard Payne and Charlotte Cushman. The London *Times* declared Cushman "far superior to any Romeo that has been seen for years." London *Times*, 3 January 1846, as cited in Merrill, "Charlotte Cushman," 109. "Of so erotic" is from John Coleman, *Fifty Years of an Actor's Life*, 2 vols. (New York: James Pott and Co, 1904), 1:363.

45. "Private virtue" in Kemble, *Records of a Later Life*, 459—60. Knowles cited in Clement, *Charlotte Cushman*, 45. Whitehead, in "Fancy's Show Box," 120, indicates that Cushman played Romeo for the last time in 1854 at the age of thirty-eight.

46. Estimates of thirty and sixteen from Yeater, "Charlotte Cushman," 45, 117. See Yvonne Shafer, "Women in Male Roles: Charlotte Cushman and Others," in Chinoy and Jenkins, *Women in American Theatre*, 74—81; Price, *Life of Charlotte Cushman*, 123—29.

47. Coverage of her behavior and the quote in *Boston Daily Bee*, 27 Nov. 1852, 1 Jan. 1853.

48. Quotes from Vandenhoff, *Leaves From An Actor's Notebook*, 4; and Odell, *Annals of the New York Stage* 4:121. "Most respectable female audiences" from Benjamin Brown French, *Witness to the Young Republic: A Yankee's Journal, 1828—1870*, ed. Donald B. Cole and John J. McDonough (Hanover, N.H.: University Press of New England, 1989), 58, on a Philadelphia performance by the French actress Madame Celeste in November 1835. Madame Vestris' excellence as a breeches character on the British stage in the 1820s and 1830s was memorialized by plaster models of her legs, which were sold in London (William W. Appleton, *Madame Vestris and the London Stage* [New York: Columbia University Press, 1974], 63). In revealing their knees and calves, women were imitating male display; in the era of knee breeches, men's calves were considered one of their most attractive elements. See also Laurence Senelick, "The Evolution of the Male Impersonator on the Nineteenth-Century Popular Stage," *Essays in Theatre* 1 (Nov. 1982): 32—33. Senelick argues that the prime attraction of women in male roles was the display of their legs and that there was a tacit refusal on the part of the public to accept a woman on the popular stage as a "real man." For a recent version of this same judgment, see Tracy Davis, "Questions for a Feminist Methodology in Theatre History," in Postlewait and McConachie, *Interpreting the Theatrical Past*, 75. Davis argues that "the cross-dressed actress did not have the opportunity to impersonate the other sex but could only indicate her own." She cites Cushman as the exception that proves the rule, but I would argue Cushman represents a different case that must be dealt with on its own terms, especially given Cushman's enormous popularity.

49. See Carroll Smith-Rosenberg, "The Female World of Love and Ritual: Relations Between Women in Nineteenth-Century America," in Nancy F. Cott and Elizabeth H. Pleck, eds., *A Heritage of Her Own* (New York: Simon and Schuster, 1979), 311—42; Lillian Faderman, *Surpassing the Love of Men: Romantic Friendship and Love Between Women from the Renaissance to the Present* (New York: William Morrow, 1981), especially the introduction and pp. 147—230; and John D'Emilio and Estelle Freedman, *Intimate Matters: A History of Sexuality in America* (New York: Harper and Row, 1988), 121—30, 223—29. Once lesbianism was named and stigmatized, even theatrical cross-dressing was condemned: Richard von Kraft-Ebing wrote that "Uranism [lesbianism] may nearly always be suspected . . . in opera singers and actresses who appear in male attire on the stage by preference" (*Psychopathia Sexualis*, trans. F. J. Rebman [1886; Brooklyn: Physicians and Surgeons Book Co., 1908],

334—35. Senelick explicitly associates male impersonation with "lesbian wish-fulfillment" ("The Evolution of the Male Impersonator," 33).

50. The best overview of Cushman's relationships is found in Faderman, *Surpassing the Love of Men*, 220—25. Quotes are from Leach, *Bright Particular Star*, 126, 210; and William W. Story to J. R. Lowell, Rome, 11 Feb. 1853, in James, *William Wetmore Story* 1:254. For an example of Cushman's discretion, see her letter to "My dear little love" [Emma Stebbins?] (Nashville, 31 March 1858, Charlotte Cushman Papers), in which she cautions her friend against coming to the hotel to sleep with her. It is important to distinguish between writing off breeches parts as the activities of women whose "abnormal" psychology made them want to be men and a serious recognition that lesbian performers and audiences alike have a particular interest in deconstructing gender through theatrical roles, gesture, dress, and manner. See Jill Dolan, "Gender Impersonation Onstage: Destroying or Maintaining the Mirror of Gender Roles?" *Women and Performance* 2:2 (1985): 5—11; and Sande Zeig, "The Actor as Activator: Deconstructing Gender Through Gesture," *Women and Performance* 2:2 (1985): 12—17.

51. Quotes from [actor] John Coleman, *Fifty Years of an Actor's Life* (New York: James Pott, 1904) 1:362—63; [woman] "Theatricals in Boston," *Spirit of the Times*, 12 June 1858; and [drama critic] *London Britannia*, 3 Jan. 1846, as cited in Merrill, "Charlotte Cushman," 111.

52. Quote from Dickens to John Forster, 1858, cited in Auerbach, *Ellen Terry*, 59. The most extensive and persuasive discussion of the cultural meanings of transvestism is Garber, *Vested Interests*. Garber ranges across a variety of cultural settings and episodes in arguing that cross-dressing "tells the truth about gender"—namely, that gender is performative rather than natural, and exists only in representation. See also E. Ann Kaplan's discussion of how a female in male attire can become a "*resisting* image for the female spectator" (*Women and Film: Both Sides of the Camera* [New York and London: Routledge, 1988], 5, 50); Judith Butler, "Performative Acts and Gender Constitution: An Essay in Phenomenology and Feminist Theory," in Case, *Performing Feminisms*, 270—82; and Candace West and Don H. Zimmerman, "Doing Gender," *Gender and Society* 1 (1987): 125—51. There are hints that women recognized that pants stood for male privilege and power. For example, to go to the theatre as freely and as cheaply as the boys, at least one young girl disguised herself in male garb (Phelps, *Players of a Century*, 348). But the basis of my argument here is admittedly theoretical, as there are few historical sources in which women explicitly expressed such motives or understandings.

53. Declining tolerance for breeches parts in legitimate theatre is noted in Wood, *Personal Recollections of the Stage*, 69. Michael Booth notes the decline of breeches parts for women in the late Victorian theatre in England; see his *Theatre in the Victorian Age*, 130—31. On the impersonators of the minstrel and burlesque stage, see Toll, *Blacking Up*, 139—44; Odell, *Annals of the New York Stage* 8:220; Senelick, "Evolution of the Male Impersonator," 33—40; Lillian Schlissel, *Bawdy Women* (forthcoming from Pantheon); and Allen, *Horrible Prettiness*. In her 1874 farewell to the New York stage,

Cushman attributed her success to the fact that she was always "thoroughly in earnest" (Leach, *Bright Particular Star*, 377).

54. For an example of bloomer spoofing see *Spirit of the Times*, 22 Nov. 1851, 469. The changing content of burlesque is discussed below, in Chaps. 5 and 7.

55. Quotes from [jealous actor] Vandenhoff, *Leaves from an Actor's Notebook*, 217; [press notice] London *Theatrical Times* cited in Leach, *Bright Particular Star*, 196; [acquaintance] Gamaliel Bradford, *Biography and the Human Heart* (Boston: Houghton Mifflin, 1932), 114–15; [Macready] *Journal of William Charles Macready*, 223, as cited in Merrill, "Charlotte Cushman," 153; [detractor] Stillman, *Autobiography of a Journalist* 1:361.

56. As the first native-born woman to become a great star, Cushman might have been something of a heroine to working-class women who harbored dreams of theatrical success. In 1837 one New York editor gave it as a general opinion that "the reason half the journeymen printers and milliners in town are not upon the stage is owing to the heartless opposition of managers who are prejudiced against native genius" (*Spirit of the Times*, 12 Aug. 1837). Cushman showed them that native genius could make it, but her relentless social climbing and her decision to live in Europe once she had achieved success cannot have endeared her to milliners or journeyman printers. Cushman demanded huge fees, which translated into ticket prices as high as $1 a seat, well beyond most working-class budgets. Working people might even have been aware that her hefty fees, like those of all stars, tended to depress the wages of ordinary players (Ford, *Peep Behind the Curtain*, 77–78). On how Marie Curie's achievements were used to create a double standard whereby American women scientists had to be not only better than men but "Madame Curies," see Margaret W. Rossiter, *Women Scientists in America: Struggle and Strategies to 1940* (Baltimore: Johns Hopkins University Press, 1982), 130 ff.

57. Cushman's letter is cited in Merrill, "Charlotte Cushman," 26. Miss Cameron lines are from Alcott, *Jo's Boys and How They Turned Out* (Boston: Roberts Bros., 1886), 162. In 1850, when she was seventeen and beginning to recognize her father's incompetence as a breadwinner, Alcott dreamed of a stage career. "Anna wants to be an actress, and so do I," she wrote in her journal. "We could make plenty of money perhaps, and it is a very gay life" (Entry for August 1850, in Joel Myerson and Daniel Shealy, eds., *The Journals of Louisa May Alcott* [Boston: Little, Brown, 1989]). Bronson Alcott had his children dramatize moral allegories so that they might internalize moral precepts, just as in Alcott's fictional March family the youngsters learned self-restraint through amateur theatricals. This acting was private, for moral purposes, not public and not for profit, yet Alcott never lost her fascination with the stage. The connection between the real-life parlor theatricals in Bronson Alcott's family and the performances in Louisa May Alcott's fiction is noted in Karen Halttunen, "The Domestic Drama of Louisa May Alcott," *Feminist Studies* 10 (Summer 1984): 233–54. Alcott was a devoted amateur actress, frequent theatregoer, and the author of one farce that was actually produced in Boston. She was also drawn to the darker side of performance, and in her melodramatic thrillers, published pseudonymously, virtually all her hero-

ines are actresses onstage or off; often they are evil women who use their acting ability to deceive others and gain selfish goals. On the thrillers, see Madeleine Stern, ed., *Behind a Mask: The Unknown Thrillers of Louisa May Alcott* (New York: William Morrow, 1975); and Madeleine Stern, ed., *Plots and Counterplots: More Unknown Thrillers of Louisa May Alcott* (New York: William Morrow, 1976). It is quite possible that Alcott recognized both aspects of Cushman's career project—capturing and taming theatre for the purpose of moneymaking and the approving nods of respectability, while never losing sight of the "divine-demonic" that female performance might contact or unleash.

5. SEGMENTATION: MANY THEATRES

1. The best sources on this and other Mose plays are Turner, "City Low-Life," and Dorson, "Mose the Far-Famed."
2. Information on the play is taken from the revised version, which was published: Benjamin Baker, *A Glance at New York* (New York: Samuel French, n.d.). I am assuming Mose's activities were substantially the same in the original version. (For the spelling "b'hoy," see Dorson, "Mose the Far-Famed.") Mose brought the representation of contemporary class divisions to the American theatre, as William Dean Howells noted. "The first successful attempt to represent the life of our streets was in dramatic form," he wrote, recalling that at the time "there was hardly anywhere a little blackguard boy who did not wish to act and talk like Mose" (see Howells, "New York Low Life in Fiction," in *Criticism and Fiction and Other Essays*, ed. Clara M. Kirk and Rudolf Kirk [Westport, Conn.: Greenwood, 1977], 271. This essay appeared originally in the *New York World*, 26 July 1896.)
3. On Mary Taylor see Odell, *Annals of the New York Stage* 6:130; Turner, "City Low-Life," 47, 54; and Rinear, *Temple of Momus*, 83—85.
4. Turner, "City Low-Life," 73; Odell, *Annals of the New York Stage* 5:363; Dorson, "Mose the Far-Famed," 296—97. Richard B. Stott, *Workers in the Metropolis: Class, Ethnicity and Youth in Antebellum New York City* (Ithaca, N.Y.: Cornell University Press, 1990), 270—71, notes that Lize is a minor figure compared to Mose and significantly so, Stott argues, because working-class culture as a whole was decidedly masculine. Christine Stansell, in contrast, emphasizes the novelty and the impact of working-class women's presence in the city (*City of Women: Sex and Class in New York, 1789—1860* [New York: Alfred A. Knopf, 1986], chap. 5) but nevertheless concedes most aspects of the marginality that Stott and the Mose plays indicate.
5. Northall, *Before and Behind the Curtain*, 91—92; Coad and Mims, *American Stage*, 112.
6. *Spirit of the Times*, 6 April 1844, 72; Levine, *Highbrow Lowbrow*. Levine suggests (based on the history of opera, symphonic music, and art museums as well as theatre) that the bifurcation of nineteenth-century entertainment audiences, which led to stylistic bifurcation, was largely due to a deliberate effort by elites determined to set themselves above the herd.
7. In contrast to Levine, I suggest that the change was largely an unanticipated result of

the dynamics of commercialization; the emerging audience segmentation probably corresponded to some preexisting, if minor, differences in taste among different social groups, which market segmentation had the effect of emphasizing and expanding. See Ronald E. Frank, William F. Massy, and Yoram Wind, *Market Segmentation* (Englewood Cliffs, N.J.: Prentice-Hall, 1972); and Michael J. Piore and Charles F. Sabel, *The Second Industrial Divide* (New York: Basic, 1984), 56–57.

8. See Buckley, "To the Opera House," for a thorough and sophisticated account of the riot that links it to class formation and the emergence of forms of urban public culture, especially the penny press and the theatre, inflected by class.

9. *Spirit of the Times*, 4 Nov. 1865. Significantly, Whitman's description of the Bowery audience mentioned the sorts of skilled workers—shipbuilders, cartmen, butchers— who were apt to have decent incomes (Whitman, *Prose Works* 2:595–96).

10. Stott, *Workers in the Metropolis*, 216, 245, and chap. 8 generally. Detailed studies of working-class family budgets done around the turn of the century revealed that household budgets allowed only small sums for family recreation but that the bread-winner customarily held back about 10 percent of his income for his personal use, most of it going to alcohol, tobacco, and movie and theatre tickets. There is no reason to assume that workingmen behaved differently with their money in the earlier period. See Kathy Peiss, *Cheap Amusements: Working Women and Leisure in Turn-of-the Century New York* (Philadelphia: Temple University Press, 1986), 23. Peiss terms the world of working-class amusements "homosocial," just as Stott concludes that working-class culture in the earlier period was "strongly masculine" (p. 253).

11. *Worcester Weekly Transcript*, 6 March 1852 and 7 Feb. 1852, clippings contained in "Early Drama in Worcester, 1781–1854," in the Benjamin Thomas Hill Papers.

12. Quotes from "The New Bowery Theatre—Opening Night," *New York Herald* 6 Sept. 1861, 1. On "walking out" and the risky or compromising possibilities involved in meeting men in the antebellum city, see Stansell, *City of Women*, 86, 98, and chap. 5 generally. Stansell emphasizes that the Bowery girls constituted a new and significant public presence on the city streets and in places of commercial amusement. She argues that there was an excess of young women over young men in New York after 1830, and that about half of a sample of working women she investigated lived apart from the supervision of parents, aunts and uncles, or grandparents. But her sample seems to be drawn from two working-class wards, and therefore neglects the situation of the typical working woman, a domestic servant, who lived and worked under very tight supervision, albeit not by her parents. And Stansell herself cautions, "Bowery men saw public life—in their case, working-class life—as a place where men were the main show and women the supporting cast" (p. 96). On the history of dating and "treat-ing," which became common after 1880, see Peiss, *Cheap Amusements*, 51–55, 108–14, and chap. 6; Beth L. Bailey, *From Front Porch to Back Seat: Courtship in Twentieth-Century America* (Baltimore: Johns Hopkins University Press, 1988), 17–20. I have found scattered earlier cases of a young man taking "his girl" to the theatre. In 1866 seventeen-year-old Samuel Gompers took his future wife there occasionally. See Gompers, *Seventy Years of Life and Labor*, 2 vols. (New York: E. P. Dutton, 1925),

1:36. On the end of the pit at the New Bowery Theatre, see *Spirit of the Times*, 26 Oct. 1861, 128, which ascribes the change to the demands of "upper twenty-five-cent-dom" wanting to take his wife and daughter to the plays. Even after the pit was eliminated, sections of the cheap seats upstairs at the New Bowery were almost completely occupied by men and boys.

13. See "The Old Bowery," in Whitman, *Prose Works* 2:595; and Charlotte Cushman, "A Woman's View of the People's Amusement," n.d., Cushman Papers. Quotes from *New York Herald*, 6 Sept. 1859, 1; *Spirit of the Times*, 4 Nov. 1865, 160. See Wallack, *Memories of Fifty Years*, 129, for women in the Astor Place crowd.

14. Quotes from *Spirit of the Times*, 30 March 1844, cited in Odell, *Annals of the New York Stage* 5:47; Rinear, *Temple of Momus*, 119, 127—28. Mary Taylor eventually emerged as the overall favorite, thanks in part to Miss Clarke's falling ill, but not before Mitchell burlesqued the rivalry in his own house in a play called *Peytona and Fashion*, in which he cast the two actresses as rival belles. Mary Taylor's appeal is discussed in Northall, *Before and Behind the Curtain*, 70—71, 80—81.

15. See Odell, *Annals of the New York Stage* for the first German-language theatre in 1840 (4:393), and the Stadt Theatre (6:398—402). The progress of the German theatre can be followed elsewhere in the Odell, for example, 8:68—70. See also LaVern J. Rippley, *The German-Americans* (Boston: Twayne, 1976), chap. 10; Christa Corvajal, "German-American Theatre," in Seller, *Ethnic Theatre in the United States*, 175—89; Friedrich A. H. Leuchs, *The Early German Theatre in New York* (1928; New York: AMS Press, 1966).

16. See Odell, *Annals of the New York Stage* 3:655—56, 660; 5:425, 513; Samuel Lover, *Rory O'More* (London: Chapman and Hall, n.d.); Tyrone Power, *Born to Good Luck; or, The Irishman's Fortune* (London: Thomas Hailes Lacy, n.d.); Maureen Murphy, "Irish-American Theatre," in Seller, *Ethnic Theatre in the United States*, 221—23.

17. Quote from Odell, *Annals of the New York Stage* 5:389. See Toll, *Blacking Up*; Carl F. Wittke, *Tambo and Bones: A History of the American Minstrel Stage* (1930; reprint ed: New York, Greenwood, 1968); Alexander Saxton, *The Rise and Fall of the White Republic* (London and New York: Verso, 1990), chap. 7; Lott, "'The Seeming Counterfeit.'" There is also a useful discussion of minstrelsy in Jean H. Baker, *Affairs of Party: The Political Culture of Northern Democrats in the Mid-Nineteenth Century* (Ithaca, N.Y.: Cornell University Press, 1983), chap. 6. Many of these sources suggest that few or no women attended minstrel shows. The working-class origins of minstrelsy did indeed produce predominately (though not wholly) male audiences, but for evidence of middle-class and female patronage of minstrelsy, see the diary of N. Beekley, a Philadelphia bookkeeper. On occasion he acted as escort to groups of women, probably family friends or relatives, attending a performance, for instance on 27 September 1849, when he took the Miss Sandersons(?) to hear the New Orleans Serenaders, a minstrel show. See also Baines, "Samuel S. Sanford and Negro Minstrelsy." Sanford's minstrel troupes always appealed to respectable middle-class audiences, including many ladies.

18. On separate colored galleries, see, e.g., Odell, *Annals of the New York Stage* 5:330,

6:238. The line "No colored persons admitted" is found on the playbill of the Franklin Theatre in New York for 14 Sept. 1835 (Harvard Theatre Collection). See also Edward G. Smith, "Black Theatre," in Seller, *Ethnic Theatre in the United States*, 39. Fanny Kemble remarked in 1874 on the anomalous situation that African-Americans could vote but could not be admitted to the gallery of the Philadelphia theatre she visited. (See her *Further Records* 1:45.) For African-Americans attending minstrel shows, see Baines, "Samuel S. Sanford and Negro Minstrelsy," 248, 277, on Harrisburg, Pa.

19. The *New York Herald* in 1841 noted bad times in the theatre business, adding: "The shilling theatres, it is true, with their everlasting burlesques of everything—good, bad and indifferent beneath the sun, keep their heads above water, please the million, and put money in the purse of the manager" (quoted in Odell, *Annals of the New York Stage* 4:458). The best source on both burlesque and the Olympic is Rinear, *Temple of Momus*.

20. Brougham's script is quoted in Rourke, *American Humor*, 123. On the rapid-fire pace, see *Spirit of the Times*, 28 Oct. 1848, 432: "In all doggerel burlesques the auditor should never have time for reflection." Examples cited are from Rinear, *Temple of Momus*, 50–51, 104–05, 157, 23, 28–29.

21. Rinear, *Temple of Momus*, 43, 62.

22. See *Spirit of the Times*, 25 Sept. 1852, on the Chatham. Examples of minstrelsy burlesques are found in Gary D. Engle, *This Grotesque Essence: Plays from the American Minstrel Stage* (Baton Rouge: Louisiana State University Press, 1978). Quote is from Rourke, *American Humor*, 119. Compare a comment in *Spirit of the Times*, 17 Aug. 1839, 288: "The griefs of lovers and the sorrows of their mistresses have now become matters of jest." That earnest nineteenth-century drama flourished in the immediate presence of its own burlesque is noted in Davies, *Mirror of Nature*, 55, and Levine, *Highbrow Lowbrow*, 13–15.

23. For *Don Cesar*, adapted from Victor Hugo's *Ruy Blas*, see the clippings file at the Harvard Theatre Collection; and Rinear, *Temple of Momus*, 123–24. On Chanfrau's management and *Rosina Meadows*, see Odell, *Annals of the New York Stage* 5:94, 455–61, 6:318; and Grimsted, *Melodrama Unveiled*, 241–48.

24. J. A. Amherst, *Ireland as It Is* (New York: S. French, 1861?). See Michael Denning, *Mechanic Accents: Dime Novels and Working-Class Culture in America* (London and New York: Verso, 1987), 93–99, for a discussion of the complexities of "seduction-rape" plots in the presence of class differentiation.

25. Toll, *Blacking Up*, 162–63. Lize's song in Baker, *Glance at New York*, act 2, sc. 2; Lott, "'Seeming Counterfeit,'" 247.

26. "Carried away" in *Spirit of the Times*, 22 April 1848, 108; "assumed the prerogatives" in *Albion*, 4 (25 Jan. 1845), 48; prologue to *Fashion* quoted in Odell, *Annals of the New York Stage* 5:99. For other examples of burlesques of women's rights, see ibid., 6:326, on Wood's minstrels in 1853; and *Spirit of the Times*, 13 Dec. 1851, 516, on Kate Horn at the Broadway Theatre in a burlesque of *Woman's Rights*. Rourke is from Rourke, *American Humor*, 142.

27. On the model artist exhibitions, see McCullough, *Living Pictures*; McCullough, "Model Artists vs. the Law"; Meade Minnigerode, *The Fabulous Forties* (New York: G. P. Putnam's Sons, 1924), 142–46; Odell, *Annals of the New York Stage* 5:378–81, 397, 495; John D. Vose, *Seven Nights in Gotham* (New York: Bunnell and Price, 1852), 43–50; Clemens, *Mark Twain's Travels with Mr. Brown*, 84. This same decade, the 1840s, saw the beginnings of sexually oriented literature and the American pornography industry. See Reynolds, *Beneath the American Renaissance*, chap. 7, but beware Reynolds' overheated description of the model artist shows: he alleges, without evidence, that they occurred in taverns "nationwide" and were imitated at home by upper-class dinner-party hostesses. He seems to confuse model artist exhibits with tableaux vivants; at the time the managers of the model artists often took refuge behind such a confusion.

28. Quote from *New York Herald*, 2 Feb. 1848. See Odell, *Annals of the New York Stage* 5:378–79. See Meisel, *Realizations*, on the popularity of tableaux vivants and other visual representations of narrative in the nineteenth century. Kasson, in *Marble Queens and Captives*, provides a thorough and thoughtful discussion of the popularity of Powers' statue and others like it. She argues that respectable middle-class audiences flocked to see the figure of a nude woman in chains in part because commentators emphasized the sentiment and spirituality inherent in the piece. Pamphlets distributed to viewers embedded the figure in a narrative that distracted attention from the female body in itself and focused concern on the story of a woman torn from home and family. There were, however, at least two other, probably concurrent, sources of audience interest: the eroticism (however suppressed) evoked in male viewers, and the motif of the triumph of faith over adversity and hence the possibility of role reversal, and empowerment of the powerless. See also William H. Gerdts, *American Neo-Classical Sculpture* (New York: Viking, 1973), 32–33, on how Powers' statue broke the strictures against the representation of the nude.

29. See *New York Herald*, 2 Feb. and 4 March 1848.

30. Quotes from *New York Herald*, 2 Feb. 1848. The connection between ticket prices and degrees of undress in *New York Herald*, 5 and 18 March 1848; audience behavior in Vose, *Seven Nights*, 44; the near-riot in Minnigerode, *Fabulous Forties*, 145; and *New York Herald*, 5 March 1848.

31. McCullough, "Model Artists vs. the Law;" *New York Herald*, 24 Feb. 1848. The young women arrested in an 1856 raid were reportedly paid four or five dollars a week (McCullough, *Living Pictures*, 45–46).

32. Odell, *Annals of the New York Stage* 6:258; Toll, *Blacking Up*, 137. Female minstrels of this description are pictured in the playbill for the Franklin Museum, New York City, 1 April 1851, Harvard Theatre Collection (fig. 29), and often are announced in other model artist playbills. The year 1859 seems to have been the last season for the model artists before the variety shows offered in concert saloons "snuffed out its existence" (Odell, *Annals of the New York Stage* 7:284).

33. Guy Debord, *Society of the Spectacle* (Detroit: Black and Red, 1983), notes that spectacle is an ideal consumer product, as the viewer is never sated.

34. *Philadelphia Public Ledger*, 15 and 16 Feb. 1848; *Boston Daily Bee*, April 6, 1850, 11 and 13 Feb. 1852; *Spirit of the Times*, 29 Sept. 1860.

35. On ranting see *Spirit of the Times*, 4 Nov. 1865. See Odell, *Annals of the New York Stage* 7:203 on a shorter program at middle-class theatres in the 1859—60 season. On frequent change of bill at the New Bowery in 1865, see *Spirit of the Times*, 4 Nov. 1865. See Stott, *Workers in the Metropolis*, 257—60, on the working-class accent that had emerged by the 1840s. The story about Kirby is from *Spirit of the Times*, 21 Dec. 1844, 516.

36. *Spirit of the Times*, 4 Nov. 1865.

37. James, *Small Boy*, 160, 162, 163.

38. The importance of female readership in the literary marketplace sprang from the fact that by 1840 literacy rates among women equaled those among men; the leisure time available to middle-class women made them an especially important part of the reading public. I would suggest that the act of reading could be incorporated into traditional feminine roles more easily than could the act of theatregoing because it took place within the privacy of the home.

6. MANAGING: THE DECLINE OF LAURA KEENE

1. An excellent modern biography is Ben Henneke, *Laura Keene*. Henneke has settled issues long in doubt, including Keene's real name and her date of birth. Biographical information on Keene in this chapter is from Henneke unless otherwise noted. Another valuable source is Taylor, "Laura Keene in America," and also useful is Dorothy Jean Strickland, "Laura Keene, Nineteenth-Century Actress-Manager," M.A. thesis, University of Arizona, 1961. The description of Keene's husband is from the sympathetic work by Creaghan, *Life of Laura Keene*, 168, quoting her younger daughter Clara: "I never knew my father. I only know that he was a loafer." The conjecture that he was a criminal arises from his having turned up in Australia at one point. Vestris, born Lucia Elizabetta Bartolozzi, was always known as "Madame" Vestris in her career, which developed after her marriage to a dancer named Armand Vestris. She pioneered the use of realistic sets and props, and concerned herself with production as an integrated whole. For an overview of her significance in theatre history, see Brockett, *History of the Theatre*, 467—68.

2. "Their name was legion" is from Reignolds-Winslow, *Yesterdays with Actors*, 72. On Elizabeth Blanchard Hamblin, see Ireland, *Records of the New York Stage* 1:462; on Clifton, see Wemyss, *Theatrical Biography*, 293; refs. to petticoat government in Wemyss, *Twenty-Six Years*, 378; and Wood, *Personal Recollections of the Stage*, 435. On Mrs. Bowers, see *Spirit of the Times*, 15 May 1858 and 29 Jan. 1859. On Matilda Vining (Mrs. John) Wood see Odell, *Annals of the New York Stage* 7:471—72, 547—52. For Louisa Lane Drew, see Drew, *Autobiographical Sketch*.

3. Jefferson, *Autobiography*, 206.

4. *Spirit of the Times*, 16 March 1861, 20, on the "played out" repertory, which included *Macbeth*, *Lady of Lyons*, *Guy Mannering*, and *Othello*. For the decline of tragedy, see

Rede, *Guide to the Stage*, 22. "Line of policy" from Taylor, "Laura Keene in America," 184.

5. It seems that her husband, Henry Wellington Taylor, was in Australia; apparently they met, and according to one report he refused her request for a legal separation. In any case she starred opposite the young Edwin Booth in a number of Australian theatres before returning to San Francisco to take up theatre management again.

6. Corbyn Wardle to John Povey, 16 Jan. 1855, Dramatic Museum Collection [location unconfirmed]. The date is certainly in error: it was 1856. Wardle reports, "She is backed it is said by the leading gamblers of this city to the tune of $20,000. Five of this she spent in altering the theatre." The figures may have come from the *New York Evening Express* article of 22 Dec. 1855, discussed below in n. 8.

7. On the soaring value of Manhattan real estate, see for example, Edward K. Spann *The New Metropolis: New York City, 1840–1857* (New York: Columbia University Press, 1981), 112, 208; and Elizabeth Blackmar, *Manhattan for Rent, 1785–1850* (Ithaca, N.Y.: Cornell University Press, 1989). The description of Lutz as "not precisely a Grandison" is from Winter, *Vagrant Memories*, 58. Winter had mellowed on the subject of Lutz and Keene by the time he wrote this. His earlier treatments had been slighting or savagely dismissive. Louisa Lane Drew also began her career as a manager on the strength of a loan, which she did not finish paying back until the end of her third year of management. We do not know who loaned her the money or why that person was willing to trust her, for Mrs. Drew was very good at keeping her own secrets. See her *Autobiographical Sketch*, 113, and the very readable portrait of Louisa Lane Drew in the early chapters of Margot Peters, *The House of Barrymore* (New York: Alfred A. Knopf, 1990). It may be instructive to recall Edith Wharton's *The House of Mirth*, in which Lily Bart's having accepted money from Gus Trenor is interpreted in the worst possible terms.

8. The ads for Keene's new theatre indicate the market in which she expected to compete by boasting that the playhouse compared favorably to "any first-class theatre in the country." In New York that meant her competitors would be Wallack's, Niblo's Garden, the Broadway Theatre, and Burton's Chambers Street Theatre. The letter is found in *New York Evening Express*, 22 Dec. 1855, 4. The same letter, as quoted in Taylor, "Laura Keene in America," 91–92, contains a particularly obnoxious line about "blacklegs and indecent persons," an evident reference to Lutz and Keene. Perhaps this was cut from a later edition; I examined a photocopy from the microfiche of the National Newspaper Project, in which it did not appear. Manager William Burton was later linked to the vandalism of a rival's scenery in Baltimore (Wemyss, *Theatrical Biography*, 286–88, 302). Perhaps Burton had learned about such methods the hard way: his was the theatre torched in 1841 by arsonists—arsonists Charlotte Cushman thought had been hired by Thomas Hamblin.

9. One of the best sources on the different currents within feminism at mid-century is William R. Leach, *True Love and Perfect Union: The Feminist Reform of Sex and Society* (New York: Basic, 1980).

10. *New York Times*, 24 Dec. 1855.

11. Letter is in *New York Herald*, 12 June 1856; curtain speech was printed in *New York Tribune*, 23 June 1856; critique is in *New York Times*, 23 June 1856.

12. The history of the emergence of independent dramatic criticism is found in Miller, *Bohemians and Critics*. The comment on Keene is from *Spirit of the Times*, 10 Sept. 1859, as cited in Henneke, *Laura Keene*, 109. The essentially masculine character of dramatic criticism is revealed in a comment from Clapp, *Reminiscences of a Dramatic Critic*, 30–31: "Every decent outspoken critic raises up against himself a body of hostile unprofessionals, *principally of the more excitable sex*—strong in numbers, too, if weak in brain—to whom he is *persona* excessively *non grata*, simply because he has dispraised, or even not sufficiently praised, their favorite performer" (emphasis added). See also Thomas K. Wright, "Nym Crinkle: Gadfly Critic and Male Chauvinist," *Educational Theatre Journal* 24 (1972): 370–82, on Andrew Carpenter Wheeler, who was the theatre critic for the *New York World* beginning in 1864. My characterizations of Wilkes and Winter and account of the biases of the major dailies and their rivalries are based on Miller, *Bohemians and Critics*, chaps. 3 and 4, and on my own reading of their theatre coverage. It should be noted that New York City press rivalries did Keene no favors: on the one hand, the *Tribune* and the *Times*, bastions of middle-class respectability, tended to view her negatively out of loyalty to Wallack's, and on the other, the *Herald* was particularly ferocious in its condemnations of women. Keene found no allies among the major dailies.

13. *New York Herald*, 19 Nov. 1856. The presence of more women than usual is noted in Taylor, "Laura Keene in America," 95.

14. Quote is from Charles M. Walcott, cited in Creahan, *Life of Laura Keene*, 128. The *New York Times*, 19 Nov. 1856, gave the capacity of Laura Keene's Theatre at "about 1800" and the *New York Herald*, 16 Nov. 1856, gave it as 2500.

15. *Uncle Tom's Cabin* ran for some three hundred performances when it was first dramatized in 1852–53. Henneke, *Laura Keene*, chap. 5, is especially informative on the *Our American Cousin* phenomenon.

16. Henneke is very good on this issue. See also a pamphlet on *Laura Keene v. Wheatley and Clarke*, reprinted from the *American Law Register*, November and December 1860, in the Laura Keene Papers. For a slightly different account, which emphasizes other cases in the ongoing *Cousin* litigation, see Taylor, "Laura Keene in America."

17. The fact of Henry Wellington Taylor's existence, otherwise well guarded, probably came to Clarke through his wife, Asia Booth, the sister of Edwin. Edwin Booth had been on tour in Australia with Laura when she saw Taylor there. The best guide to this issue is Henneke, *Laura Keene*.

18. Laura Keene to Augustin Daly, August 1863, Augustin Daly Papers.

19. For critic, see *Albion*, 17 May 1856, cited in Taylor, "Laura Keene in America," 106. The play under discussion was *Diane*, which featured a mercenary husband and a neglected wife. For curtain speech, see *New York Times*, 23 June 1856, 8.

20. "So many delineators" in *Spirit of the Times*, 17 Jan. 1857, cited in Humble, "Matilda Heron, American Actress," 105–06. Humble's dissertation is the best source on Heron and incidentally contains a good deal of information on *Camille*. The play's

enduring popularity is discussed in Stephen S. Stanton, ed., *Camille and Other Plays* (New York: Hill and Wang, 1957), viii–xxx. As Stanton points out, *Camille* has been described as one of the two most popular plays in late nineteenth-century America (along with *The Two Orphans*). See Marvin Felheim, *The Theatre of Augustin Daly: An Account of the Late Nineteenth Century American Stage* (Cambridge, Mass.: Harvard University Press, 1956), 204.

21. See the excellent discussion of the 1936 film version of *Camille* in Kaplan, *Women and Film*, chap. two generally, and especially p. 39.

22. On the label "immoral drama," see *New York Herald*, 20 Jan. 1857, 4; Humble, "Matilda Heron, American Actress" 137–38. See Hutton, *Plays and Players*, 158, for a reference to *Camille* as "the grand prototype of the whole sensational school of drama and acting; the father, or mother, of all the *Formosa*s and *Frou-Frou*s, and *Jezebel*s, and *Women Without Hearts*, that have followed it *ad nauseum*." But "sensation drama" also had another meaning in this period, referring to plays involving physical peril and rescue (see, for example, Daly, *Life of Augustin Daly*, 75). William Winter comments on the "hydraulic emotional school" in his obituary of Keene, *New York Tribune*, 7 Nov. 1873; and on "problem plays" in Winter, *Vagrant Memories*, 497. See also Stanton, *Camille and Other Plays*, viii, for a reference to *Camille* as an example of the "social play (*pièce à thèse*)". Male reviewers often had difficulty with the "immoral drama," despite its popularity. For example, the critics were inclined either to condemn *Camille* as unseemly or praise it for breaking taboos, but they could seldom actually sympathize with the heroine: apparently they took the double standard so much for granted that they could only see a "fallen" woman as despicable. Examples of hostile critical reaction to *Camille* appear in the *New York Herald*, 12 April 1857 (the play is described as "a deification of prostitution"), and 21 April 1857 (the heroine is described as "an unfortunate woman without a redeeming trait but her merited affliction"). As both commentaries appeared on the editorial page, they were probably written by James Gordon Bennett himself. On the other hand, Henry Clapp, Jr., an independent critic and editor of the *Saturday Press*, was delighted with *Camille* because it offended the moralists, and E. G. P. Wilkins praised it as "unconventional." See Miller, *Bohemians and Critics*, 30–31, 60–62.

23. See *Spirit of the Times*, 31 May 1856, 192 on *Jane Eyre* as the "most legitimate hit of the season." *Spirit of the Times*, 13 June 1857, 208, calls "plays like *Camille*, *The Marble Heart*, or *The Demi-Monde*" characteristic of the times. *The Marble Heart* by Charles Selby (New York: S. French, n.d.) was first played in the United States in San Francisco in 1855.

24. On *East Lynne*'s success, see Odell, *Annals of the New York Stage* 7:479. "Well-worn" is from *New York Times*, 24 March 1863; see also *Spirit of the Times*, 4 April 1863, 80, on "wicked wife" plays.

25. Tom Taylor and Charles Reade, *Masks and Faces* (New York: Samuel French, n.d.), act 2, sc.1, p. 57.

26. For benefit, see Elizabeth Ellet, *The Queens of American Society* (New York: Charles Scribners, 1867), 394.

27. For *The King's Rival* and *World and Stage*, see Strickland, "Laura Keene," 90, 168–69; for *Nature and Art* see Taylor, "Laura Keene in America," 136. Rachel Félix was known on the stage by her first name only. For *Adrienne Lecouvreur* and *Actress by Daylight*, see Odell, *Annals of the New York Stage* 6:280, 448; 7:389, 471; for *Grimaldi*, see Quinn, *History of the American Drama*, 368.

28. *Boston Daily Bee*, 1 Nov. 1850.

29. Quote is from Russell Nye, *The Unembarrassed Muse: The Popular Arts in America* (New York: Dial, 1970), 159. See Julia Ward Howe, *Leonore; or, The World's Own*, in Arthur Hobson Quinn, ed., *Representative American Plays* (New York: Century, 1917), 387–427. Howe was a wealthy and prominent woman with antislavery sympathies and social connections in New York and Boston. She also wrote poetry and is now remembered as the author of "Battle Hymn of the Republic."

30. Quotes from *Frank Leslie's Illustrated Newspaper*, 18 April 1857 (cited in Humble, "Matilda Heron, American Actress" 127, n. 52); and *Albion* 35, 28 March 1857, 152 (emphasis added). There is little doubt that Howe meant her play as a critique of male behavior; her brother urged her to answer the critics with the argument that "you stand up for woman's rights and had a view how abominable our sex can be and how ill-used yours" (Sam Ward to Julia Ward Howe, 30 March 1857, cited in Deborah Pickman Clifford, *Mine Eyes Have Seen the Glory* [Boston: Little, Brown, 1978], 126).

31. See Kemble, *Records of a Later Life*, 73–74; and Furnas, *Fanny Kemble*, 312, 426–28. See Bobbé, *Fanny Kemble*, 275; and Odell, *Annals of the New York Stage* 7:579, on the production of *English Tragedy* at the Broadway Theatre in New York in 1864.

32. "Morbid fictions" in *Spirit of the Times*, 9 Dec. 1865, 240. For evidence that differences between the tastes of male and female audiences were noticed, see *Spirit of the Times*, 20 Dec. 1856, in the Laura Keene clipping file of the New York Public Library at Lincoln Center. See *New York Herald*, 12 April 1857, 4, on "immoral plays," and "The Women's Rights Conventions," *New York Herald*, 10 July 1858 for "gross indecency."

33. The unusually large number of women at her benefit is mentioned in Henneke, *Laura Keene*, 81.

34. *Novelty* had been popular at Keene's theatre in San Francisco. In New York it ran from Washington's Birthday to the middle of April (*San Francisco Alta*, 20 Sept. 1855, cited in Strickland, "Laura Keene," 79–80; description of content is from ibid., 91). No script of the play survives, but we can gain some sense of it from the extensive descriptions of scenes and characters that accompanied newspaper ads. This is a problem common to nearly all such burlesque productions, where the emphasis was on the visual and the lines consisted of oft-updated topical humor.

35. On *Young Bacchus* see Taylor, "Laura Keene in America," 129. Reignolds-Winslow, in *Yesterdays with Actors*, 67–68, wrote that "Laura Keene was driven in dark days to a variety show." For a description of *Variety*, see Strickland, "Laura Keene," 114–16. Quoted passages are from *Spirit of the Times*, 16 May 1857, 176, as cited in McCullogh, *Living Pictures*, 57–58.

36. The Southerners' behavior is mentioned in the *New York Clipper*, 20 April 1861, as cited in Henneke, *Laura Keene*, 159. For indications that hissing was frowned upon in the 1860s, see *Spirit of the Times*, 26 Sept. 1863, 64; and Logan, *Apropos of Women and Theatres*, 104. Later references to silent audiences include Jefferson, *Autobiography*, 49; Joseph Hatton, "American Audiences and Actors," *The Theatre*, 3rd ser., vol. 3 (1 Aug. 1881): 257. For an excellent overview of this process, see Bruce A. McConachie, "Pacifying American Theatrical Audiences, 1820—1900," in Butsch, *For Fun and Profit*, 47—69.

37. It may be significant that changing political styles also were moving in the direction of greater passivity. See Michael McGerr, "Political Style and Women's Power, 1830—1930," *Journal of American History* 77 (Dec. 1990):864—85.

38. For an overview of the popularity of "burlesque extravaganza," see Brockett, *History of the Theatre*, 520; Booth, *Theatre in the Victorian Age*, 194—98.

39. Brown, *History of the New York Stage* 1:255; Odell, *Annals of the New York Stage* 7:545. See also Reignolds-Winslow, *Yesterdays with Actors*, 112, on Matilda Heron as one of the first actresses who "made a point of her wardrobe and had her costumes described in the newspapers." Booth, *Theatre in the Victorian Age*, 114—15 comments that British actresses' pay was eroded by the custom of having to provide their own costumes. A new emphasis on theatregoing as an occasion for women to dress up and show themselves off may also date from this period. Richard Grant White noted the development of a new style of evening wear at the Astor Place Opera House. See his "Opera in New York," *Century*, April 1882, 881, on the emergence of "a demi-toilette of marked elegance and richness, and yet without that display, either of apparel and trimmings or of the wearer's personal charms, which is implied by full evening dress in fashionable parlance." A contemporary comment on women's theatre attendance as an opportunity to dress up, "glitter," and do credit to male escorts by their appearance, is found in Marie-Claire Pasquier, "Women in the Theatre of Men: What Price Freedom?" in Judith Friedlander et al., *Women in Culture and Politics: A Century of Change* (Bloomington, Ind.: Indiana University Press, 1986), 195.

40. "Most cultured woman" from Creahan, *Life of Laura Keene*, 99; mistakes in play selection from Jefferson, *Autobiography*, 184. A copy of her "Rules and Regulations" is found in the Laura Keene Papers. "Immoralities" in *Spirit of the Times*, 6 Feb. 1858. See also ibid., 17 Oct. 1857, 432: "Nothing is ever said or done on the stage [at Laura Keene's] to offend the most straight-laced."

41. Quote from *Spirit of the Times*, 19 Jan. 1856, 588, on "number and fashion" in this most comfortable and elegant theatre. I conclude there was no bar at Laura Keene's because the theatre was conspicuously absent from a very complete list published in the *New York Herald* on 25 April 1862 in an article on the new law against serving alcohol in theatres. The bars at Niblo's, the Winter Garden, and Wallack's were closed. Comparative ticket prices are taken from *New York Times*, 17 Dec. 1855.

42. See *Spirit of the Times*, 8 Jan. 1859, clipping in the Laura Keene file, New York Public Library at Lincoln Center; Creaghan, *Life of Laura Keene*, 143; Taylor, "Laura

Keene in America," 133–35; and Rev. Henry Bellows, *The Relation of Public Amusements to Public Morality, especially of the Theatre* (New York: C. S. Francis, 1857).

43. Henneke, *Laura Keene*, chap. 6, is especially good in explaining how these legal problems sprang from the inherent contradictions between stock company traditions and the long run. Quote from Nevins and Thomas, *Diary of George Templeton Strong* 2:422, entry of 20 Nov. 1858.

44. Her falling out with Wilkins is detailed in Miller, *Bohemians and Critics*, 52–58.

45. Comments on Boucicault are from *Spirit of the Times*, 27 Sept. 1890; and 10 Oct. 1874. His roguery is attested to by the stories that circulated about his first wife, a wealthy widow who died conveniently while they were on a tour of the Alps. Boucicault said she fell off a precipice, but he was doubted. Dickens seems to have written this history into the villain Rigaud in *Little Dorrit*, who in a similar place disposed of an inconvenient and wealthy wife.

46. See *New York Herald* ad of 27 Nov. 1860 as cited in Taylor, "Laura Keene in America," 203. Descriptions of the play based on newspaper notices are found in Strickland, "Laura Keene," 192–93, and Henneke, *Laura Keene*, 147–48. It was "something after the melange of the minstrels, and adopts the war news from day to day," according to the *Spirit of the Times*, 25 May 1861. Such topicality was common in burlesque spoofing; it appealed to audiences and it kept the production a step ahead of any rivals tempted to piracy.

47. Quotes from *Spirit of the Times*, 29 Dec. 1860; *New York Tribune*, 27 Nov. 1860; Odell, *Annals of the New York Stage* 7:313. The costumes of the corps de ballet in *Seven Sisters* are described in detail in Morris, *Life on the Stage*, 22–23. They included flesh-colored slippers and tights, very full skirts that came a little below the knee, and flesh-colored "waists" with necklines cut two or three inches below the collarbone. There was also a drill and march in which the performers wore "regular Fire Zouave uniforms."

48. Critic's quote is from *New York Herald*, 2 Sept. 1860. On the concert saloons, see Zellers, "Cradle of Variety: The Concert Saloons;" Odell, *Annals of the New York Stage* 7:284–85, 287. For a matter-of-fact explanation of why the waiter girls were presumed to be impure, see Edward Winslow Martin, *Secrets of the Great City* (Philadelphia: National Publishing, 1868), 256–57. Martin explains that although the pay was good, the cost of dress and lodging was apt to be ruinously high, subjecting the women to temptation to profit after hours from the solicitations of their customers. The same work (pp. 308–12) gives a description of the scene inside a concert saloon. These saloons became so popular that a state law was passed in 1862 to shut them down by outlawing the sale of alcoholic beverages in theatres (*New York Herald*, 25 April 1862). The bars in Wallack's and Niblo's Garden closed, but the proprietors of the concert saloons managed to evade the law. They could stop charging admission, becoming a "free and easy," and make their profits on the price of the drinks. Or, if they dispensed with a curtain separating audience and performers, they could claim they were barrooms, not theatres. It was estimated that by 1869

there were more than 600 concert saloons in New York City (Henderson, *City and the Theatre*, 108). Zellers, "Cradle of Variety: The Concert Saloons," also indicates they continued essentially unchecked.

49. For concert saloons putting model artist shows out of business, see Odell, *Annals of the New York Stage* 7:359. Ad is from the *New York Herald*, 6 Jan. 1862.

50. That concert saloons attracted male patrons away from legitimate theatres was noted in the *New York Clipper*, 30 Nov. 1861, 262; and 28 Dec 1861, 294. It is also suggested in "The American Drama," *New York Herald*, 28 Oct. 1866, in a reference to the drama having to compete with model artists and waiter girls.

51. Ad in *Spirit of the Times*, 14 Sept. 1861, 32; critic in *New York Times*, 24 Sept. 1861.

52. *New York Times* and the *New York Herald*, cited in Strickland, "Laura Keene," 210.

53. *New York Tribune*, 1 Dec. 1862.

54. Laura Keene to William Booth, as cited in Henneke, *Laura Keene*, 172. She had purchased a saltwater farm near New Bedford, Massachusetts, where she could spend her summers, and Lutz had carefully placed her nest egg out of easy reach, in a trust. One source indicates that she left New York just as soon as she had completed paying off the obligation she had incurred for the construction of her theatre—$12,000 per year for seven years. (See the biographical sketch by Vera Mowry Roberts in Robinson, Roberts and Barranger, *Notable Women in the American Theatre*, 492.) This would explain why Keene was willing to remain in New York experimenting with the leg business in the early 1860s, but I have not found any confirming source.

55. *Fine Arts* 1 (March 1872):7.

56. *Fine Arts* 1 (Sept. 1872): 123, 125.

57. *Spirit of the Times*, 26 March 1864, as cited in Henneke, *Laura Keene*, 171–72; Bayard is identified as Ottarson in Miller, *Bohemians and Critics*, 42.

58. *New York Tribune*, 7 Nov. 1873, 5.

59. See Lawrence J. Oliver, "Theodore Roosevelt, Brander Matthews, and the Campaign for Literary Americanism," *American Quarterly* 41 (March 1989): 93–111. For theatre clubs, see Tina Louise Margolis, "A History of Theatrical Social Clubs in New York City" (Ph.D. diss., New York University, 1990). On the Lambs' Club, see also Skinner, *Footlights and Spotlights*, 161. Henry James repeated the judgment of polite society when he wrote that Laura Keene had belied her promise, had become "hard and raddled," and had forfeited "all claim to the higher distinction" (James, *A Small Boy*, 111).

Chinoy and Jenkins, *Women in American Theatre*, 4–5, make the point strongly that women were "really the 'doers' in the development of the modern art theatre," and that, less concerned than men with power and status, women tended to turn their backs on Broadway: "The association of women with regional, institutional, little, art, and alternative theatre is striking." In 1891 the actress Elizabeth Robins wrote of the insight that had taken her and her friend Marion Lea to London and *Hedda Gabler*: "We had further seen how freedom in the practice of our art, how the bare opportunity to practise it at all, depended, for the actress, on considerations humiliatingly different from those that confronted the actor. The stage career of an actress was inextricably involved in the fact that she was a woman and that those who were masters of the theatre were men. . . . We dreamed of an escape, through hard work, and through deliberate abandonment of the idea of making money—beyond what would give us the wages of going on" (*Theatre and Friendship: Some Henry James Letters* [New York: G. P. Putnam's Sons, 1932], 33—34).

7. THE RISE OF THE LEG SHOW

1. See Matlaw, *Black Crook*, esp. the preface on pp. 319—22; Harris, "Extravaganza at Niblo's"; Odell, *Annals of the New York Stage* 8:152—56; Toll, *On With the Show*, 167—76, 214—17; Hughes, *History of the American Theatre*, 199—200; Whitehead, "Fancy's Show Box," chap. 8. For an effective argument against *Crook*'s claims as a musical, see Mates, "Black Crook Myth." *The Black Crook* as ballet is analyzed in Gintautiene, *"Black Crook."* Both this play and the general problem of female undress as an entertainment form are treated in Allen, *Horrible Prettiness*, esp. 108—17.

2. *New York Tribune*, 17 Sept. 1866, cited in Odell, *Annals of the New York Stage* 8:154.

3. Allen, *Horrible Prettiness*, 108—17, compares the costuming to the prevailing standards for ballet dancers.

4. The story of ballet and ante-bellum American audiences is summarized in Allen, *Horrible Prettiness*, 87—92, and treated at greater length in Swift, *Belles and Beaux on Their Toes*. The early reaction of horror is found in a letter from J. Fisher Leaming to his wife from New York City, 19 Nov. 1827 (Spicer-Leaming Papers, Historical Society of Pennsylvania). Leaming had seen the French dancers and reported he had been "rather disgusted" with dancers whose skirts did not pretend to come below the knee, and who wore "tight silk pants" (but no petticoats) beneath. An indication of the change in audience reception is found in the *New York Herald*, 5 June 1838, 2. "What a vast difference a few years makes in manners and morals," the *Herald* commented, recalling how a sensation was created by Madame Hutin's dancing ten years before, including "crimson cheeks and instantaneous departure of every female in the lower tier." On Ellsler's tour, see Whitehead, "Fancy's Show Box," 169—81; and *Fanny Ellsler in America. Comprising Seven Facsimiles of Rare Americana* (New York: Dance Horizons, 1976). On the importance of the narrative, or story-telling, element in the acceptability of otherwise questionable art, see Kasson, *Marble Queens and Captives*. Ellsler's performances included, for example, "La Tarantelle," which told the story of a woman bitten by a tarantula. There were also some reports that Ellsler lengthened her skirts before she danced in this country (see Swift, *Belles and Beaux*, 214). The Ralph and Margaret joke is reproduced in Charles T. Congdon, *Reminiscences of a Journalist* (Boston: James R. Osgood, 1880), 196. Ballet was further domesticated by the Viennese Children, a troupe of forty-eight little ballerinas aged six to fourteen, who danced their way into American hearts in an 1846—47 tour.

5. Bennett's strictures are from the editorial page of the *New York Herald*, 27 Nov. 1866. The story of Bennett's "opposition" to *The Black Crook* began with Bennett and P. T. Barnum falling into a feud over the sale of some land. Eventually all the major theatre

managers met and decided by majority vote to back up Barnum by withdrawing their advertising and printing business from the *Herald*. But Wheatley, the principal manager of *Crook*, voted against the boycott, and Bennett knew of his vote. Although Bennett could not with consistency puff the play, he took a course he thought would be effective in stimulating business for the production. See Odell, *Annals of the New York Stage* 8:1–2; Whitton, *Wags of the Stage*, 252–57. Smyth is mentioned in ibid., 260–63; the Reverend Charles Burnham is cited in Wills, "Riddle of Olive Logan," 130. Similarly, the *Tribune*'s critic, William Winter, hearing police reports that vice had increased in the neighborhood of the theatre, felt it his duty to denounce the play, whereupon attendance surged and he received a note from Harry Palmer: "Go on my boy; this is exactly what we want" (Winter, *Press and the Stage*, 35). The usefulness of such controversy was not lost on Dion Boucicault, who deliberately created it for his play *Formosa* in 1869: he had one set of correspondents write to the papers denouncing the play, another set in defense of it, so that "everybody is rushing to see *Formosa* at Niblo's, just to discover how vicious it is" (*Appleton's Journal*, 2 Oct. 1869, clipping in the Dion Boucicault file, Billy Rose Theatre Collection).

6. Twain quote in Clemens, *Mark Twain's Travels with Mr. Brown*, 85, from a travel piece written for the San Francisco *Alta California* in 1867. For Strong's wife, see Nevins and Thomas, *Diary of George Templeton Strong* 4:164, entry of 4 Nov. 1867. See Gertrude Kellogg Diaries, 24 Nov. 1866, 8 June and 17 Sept. 1867, New-York Historical Society. See also 18 March 1867: "Mother and Uncle Allen went with the Otises to see the *Black Crook*." Kellogg and all her family were great theatre enthusiasts, and she herself later became an actress, so her reaction cannot be typical. On the other hand, she and her mother were quite fastidious about what they considered the immoral aspects of theatre, so their attendance may be taken as indication they saw nothing amiss. Jarrett claimed to have counted the house in a letter to a newspaper editor, Augustin Daly, in order to refute charges that the play was unfit for ladies (cited in Daly, *Life of Augustin Daly*, 42). For other indications that women attended, see *Spirit of the Times*, 15 Sept. 1866, 64; 6 Oct. 1866, 96; and 16 Feb. 1867, 400. Children's matinees and toy theatres are mentioned in Wright, *My New York*, 125. She also notes the popularity of the music (p. 194). The Union Club's box rental is mentioned in Gintautiene, "*Black Crook*," 93; arrivals at 9:30 are noted in the *New York Clipper*, 29 Sept 1866, cited in ibid., 98. The canoe trip recital is from Matthews, *These Many Years*, 117–18.

7. The only dancers who achieved name recognition seem to have been Marie Bonfanti, Betty Rigl, and Rita Sangali. Perhaps management's hand was strengthened by the fact that these women did not speak enough English to manipulate the press on their own behalf. Bonfanti was a classically trained ballerina who was young and shy and was closely chaperoned by her mother (Barker, "Maria Bonfanti"). The report of her salary, possibly exaggerated, is found in James D. McCabe, Jr., *Lights and Shadows of New York Life* (Philadelphia: National Publishing Company, 1872), 789–91. The card of salary protest appeared in the *New York Herald*, 20 Nov. 1866, 7. On cast

changes during the run, see Gintautiene, *"Black Crook,"* 135—47; Odell, *Annals of the New York Stage* 8:155, 283. Gintautiene takes a different view of the women involved, asserting that the leading dancers became "superstars" (p. 100), but her frame of reference is the world of classical dance, within which such commercial success was indeed unprecedented.

8. Allen, *Horrible Prettiness,* 77. Allen also notes Keene's influence, pp. 105—06. An editorial in Bennett's *Herald* described *The Black Crook* as the product of competition between the drama and "the impudicities" of model artists and waiter girls (see "The American Drama," *New York Herald,* 28 Oct. 1866).

9. Whitton, *Wags of the Stage,* 82—83, 255—56. See also "Theatrical Managers' Association," clipping from the *New York Tribune,* 18 July 1876, in the John Thompson Ford Papers. The purposes of the organization are here described as improving the theatre, moderating stars' terms, and countering destructive competition. The Managers' Association is also mentioned in the *New York Herald,* for example in "The True and False in Dramatic Representation," 30 Sept. 1866, 4. Here Bennett blasts it as a despotic organization, formed "with a view to control the price of labor among the poor musicians and actors." See also *New York Herald,* 20 Nov. 1866, "Breaking Up of the Theatrical 'Ring' of Associated Managers," in which Bennett compares it to the Tweed Ring. On the development of the Syndicate in the 1890s, see Brockett, *History of the Theatre,* 581—83; Poggi, *Theater in America;* McArthur, *Actors and American Culture,* chap. 9. There is also a good deal of information in Archie Binns, *Mrs. Fiske and the American Theatre* (New York: Crown, 1955).

10. Eleanor Ruggles, *Prince of Players: Edwin Booth* (New York: W. W. Norton, 1953), 212, 216, 219, 242—44; Gintautiene, *"Black Crook,"* 48, n. 3, distinguishing between Harry D. Palmer and A. M. Palmer. Augustin Daly's father-in-law was John A. Duff, owner of the Olympic Theatre. The *Dictionary of American Biography* entries on Booth and Daly are still quite serviceable.

11. On the decline in salaries, see "Ben de Bar," an obituary from the *St. Louis Globe-Democrat,* 4 June 1876, in Ireland, *Records of the New York Stage* 2 (pt. 5): 184, extra-illustrated copy in the Harvard Theatre Collection. See also *Spirit of the Times,* 21 Dec. 1861, 272, which refers to managers having cut by 50 percent the salaries of the "little people," and 19 April 1862, 112, referring to salaries having come down. On the increasing prevalence of job acting, see Davidge, *Footlight Flashes,* 239, 242; Smith, *Theatrical Management in the West,* 238; Wardle Corbyn, "The Stage in America," *The Era Almanack and Annual,* ed. Edward Ledger (London: n.p., 1875), 45; Mammen, *Old Stock Company,* 20. On the elimination of the benefit performance, see Wallack, *Memories of Fifty Years,* 54, where Wallack the younger claims to have eliminated what he considered the "degrading" benefit after he took over his father's theatre in the 1860s, prompting the other managers to follow suit. On the rise of the combination system, see Hughes, *History of the American Theatre,* 207; Brockett, *History of the Theatre,* 520—21; Peter A. Davis, "From Stock to Combination: The Panic of 1873 and Its Effects on the American Theatre Industry," *Theatre History Studies* 8 (1988): 1—9.

12. Hawes, "Much Ado about John Brougham and Jim Fisk." Fisk himself managed a season of *opera bouffe*. By the time he leased the theatre to Augustin Daly he was ready to accept a straight rental payment, although he demanded $25,000 a year. See Daly, *Life of Augustin Daly*, 83, 87. Matthew Josephson, *The Robber Barons* (1934; reprint, New York: Harcourt Brace Jovanovich, 1962), chap. 6, "The Fight for Erie."

13. Menken's history is the subject of some confusion, as she freely made up stories about her own past, inventing and reinventing her life as if it were a stage play. Two reasonably reliable biographies on which I have based this sketch are Lesser, *Enchanting Rebel*, and Falk, *The Naked Lady*. See also Lois Adler, "Adah Isaacs Menken in *Mazeppa*," in Chinoy and Jenkins, *Women in American Theatre*, 81–87. The best single treatment promises to be contained in Lillian Schlissel's *Bawdy Women* (forthcoming from Pantheon); she presented research on Menken at the Eighth Berkshire Conference on the History of Women, Rutgers University, June 1990.

14. Lesser, *Enchanting Rebel*, 25–26, 52.

15. Ibid., 52–60.

16. Lesser, *Enchanting Rebel*, 75–80; Phelps, *Players of a Century*, 313–15, quoting an account by Smith that appeared in the *Albany Mirror*, 25 Oct. 1879.

17. *New York Tribune*, 1 May 1866, cited in Odell, *Annals of the New York Stage* 8:34–35. The *Herald*, which seldom agreed with the *Tribune* about anything, concurred that Menken had "a very poor voice," "decidedly bad delivery and pronunciation," and depended entirely upon her "attitudinal capacity" for audience appeal (*New York Herald*, 1 May 1866, 5).

18. *Spirit of the Times*, 12 May 1866, 176. *New York Herald*, 1 May 1866, 5. Baltimore and Sacramento papers cited in Lesser, *Enchanting Rebel*, 97, 113, and the *New York Herald* of 16 May 1866, 5, note the presence of some women.

19. Lesser, *Enchanting Rebel*, 194, 200–202. There is a brief history of the adoption of photographs by early performers in Frederick J. Hunter, "Passion and Posture in Early Dramatic Photographs," *Theatre Survey* 5 (May 1964): 43–63. A useful summary of the changing photographic technologies and their popularization is found in William C. Darrah, *Cartes de Visites in Nineteenth Century Photography* (Gettysburg, Pa.: W. C. Darrah, 1981), 4–10. See also Ben L. Bassham, *The Theatrical Photographs of Napoleon Sarony* (Kent, Ohio: Kent State University Press, 1978). The selling of cartes de visite outside theatres is mentioned in Logan, *Before the Footlights*, 241. Wright, *My New York*, 188–89, recalls stage-struck young ladies collecting photos of their stage favorites. Late in her career, Menken had some pictures taken of herself embracing the aging Alexandre Dumas. The photos became the talk of Paris, with everyone concluding from the pose that the two were lovers. Almost immediately, altered and faked photos in more suggestive poses began to be offered for sale, and both Menken and Dumas were made to look slightly ridiculous, and pitiable (Falk, *Naked Lady*, 171–82; Clemens, *Mark Twain's Travels with Mr. Brown*, 169–71).

20. Falk, *Naked Lady*, 255; Lesser, *Enchanting Rebel*, 68–69, 242.

21. The "army of Mazeppas" included Charlotte Crampton, Kate Fisher, Addie Anderson, Kate Raymond, and Leo Hudson (Lesser, *Enchanting Rebel*, 139). In Menken's affair with Swinburne she already found herself satirically labeled "the Ancient Dame" (Lesser, *Enchanting Rebel*, 230–31).

22. Of the *Black Crook* dancers an observer wrote, "They were clad and they were clad so as to convey the impression and conviction that they were clad" (clipping file, Harvard Theatre Collection, as cited in Whitehead, "Fancy's Show Box," 227).

23. The best sources on the British Blondes are Allen, *Horrible Prettiness*, chaps. 1 and 5; and Buckley, "The Culture of 'Leg-Work.'" See also Marlie Moses, "Lydia Thompson and the 'British Blondes,'" in Chinoy and Jenkins, *Women in American Theatre*, 88–92. Also useful, though unduly apologetic in tone, is Moses, "Lydia Thompson."

24. Allen, *Horrible Prettiness*, 16–17; Howells, "New Taste in Theatricals."

25. "The Burlesque Madness," *New York Times*, 5 Feb. 1869; Howells, "New Taste in Theatricals," 639–41; Allen, *Horrible Prettiness*, 134–35.

26. Buckley, "Culture of 'Leg-Work,'" 119; Allen, *Horrible Prettiness*, chap. 5; quote from Moses, "Lydia Thompson," 118.

27. The "Girl of the Period" was Linton's term. See Peter Gay, *Education of the Senses*, vol. 1 of *The Bourgeois Experience: Victoria to Freud* (New York and Oxford: Oxford University Press, 1984), 210–12, on the Linton article and its "astonishing vogue." There is a photograph of Thompson as the Girl of the Period in the Billy Rose Theatre Collection. Alcott's *Old Fashioned Girl* was written in 1869 and offered as "a possible improvement upon the Girl of the Period" (Alcott, *Old Fashioned Girl*, preface). See also Allen, *Horrible Prettiness*, 18, 140. My interpretation of the Blondes' exploitation of this theme differs from Allen's.

28. Logan, *Apropos of Women and Theatres*, 133; Howells, "New Taste in Theatricals," 641. Robert Allen argues that the content of Thompsonian burlesque made it the most "feminized" form of theatre ever seen on the American stage, and that it was fundamentally "transgressive" in its implicit challenges to patriarchal gender roles and to bourgeois social order in general (*Horrible Prettiness*, 147–48). See Buckley, "Culture of 'Leg Work,'" 121, for a different interpretation noting the presence of anti-feminist satire in burlesque.

29. One critic, Richard Grant White, discovered "comfortable, middle aged women" from the suburbs and the country in a matinee audience for *Ixion* (White, "Age of Burlesque," 260). But matinees were always likely to include more women and children; what is more, as Allen has pointed out, White's review was a gentle satire and cannot be read "straight": White says, for example, that he likes Thompson's acting better than Forrest's *Hamlet*. (This was something like saying that Thompson was better than Arnold Schwarzenegger playing the Prince of Denmark.) White also suggests that opposition to burlesque probably arises from the parents of ugly or ill-formed daughters who resent the display of pretty women that makes their girls look bad by comparison. He goes on to argue that "the points of a fine woman" should be better known, as they are "quite as interesting as those of a fine horse."

Olive Logan confirms that women did attend burlesque, at least initially. In *Apro-*

pos of Women and Theatres, 133, she argues that until the leg shows began, such material was seen only in low variety halls, where "women were not seen in the audience." See also Louisa May Alcott's *An Old-Fashioned Girl* (Boston: Roberts Brothers, 1870), 13–18, where the main character and her friend, fourteen-year-old girls, attend a Thompson-style spectacle, "very gorgeous, very vulgar, and very fashionable." In Alcott's fictional account, the women performers sing "negro melodies," talk slang, tell jokes, wink at the audience, and appear in scanty costumes, much to the embarrassment of the "old-fashioned" heroine. Repeat attendees are discussed in Matthews, *These Many Years*; and Howells, "New Taste in Theatricals," 642–43; those who "have the appearance of coming every night" seem to be associated with the most prurient interests.

30. Allen, *Horrible Prettiness*, 129–31, contains an account of the affair. See also *New York Times*, 6 and 7 June 1869; *Spirit of the Times* 22 and 29 May 1869. None of the reporting pretended to reproduce Henderson's exact words, but he was clearly offensive: one critic felt moved to accost him later and administer a beating, after which Henderson in turn hauled him into court.

31. *Spirit of the Times*, 22 May 1869, and 29 May 1869; *New York Times*, 7 June 1869 and 2 July 1869.

32. This story is summarized in Allen, *Horrible Prettiness*, 129–30, 132, 160, 240. Thompson is quoted in Lois Banner, *American Beauty* (New York: Alfred A. Knopf, 1983), 121. Thompson's Blondes did not create a market but rather a fit into one that dated back to the model artist shows. For example, James Parton found one of Pittsburgh's theatres in 1868 patronized exclusively by working men and boys. Released from a ferocious week of work in the mills, the men flocked to a show composed of farces, comic songs, and "legs"—all before the arrival of the British Blondes ("Pittsburgh," *Atlantic Monthly*, Jan. 1868, 35).

33. Allen, *Horrible Prettiness*, 156; Howells, "New Taste in Theatricals," 642.

34. The shift in standards of beauty is explained in Banner, *American Beauty*, 120–27. The sheer volume of photographic materials that survive are testament to the new way in which Menken, the *Crook* dancers, and the Blondes were apprehended—seen, studied, collected, and exhibited—in ways that no earlier performers had been.

35. Moses, "Lydia Thompson," 127, and 114–15 on Thompson's marriage.

36. Logan, "Leg Business," 442. See also Wills, "Riddle of Olive Logan."

37. Logan, "Leg Business," 442. Wills, "Riddle of Olive Logan," 84, identifies the woman as Menken, but Logan quotes her informant's reference to "Leo"—perhaps Leo Hudson, a young woman who was part of the "army of Mazeppas" eagerly imitating Menken.

38. Logan, "Leg Business," 442–43; Wills, "Riddle of Olive Logan," 134.

39. Biographical information here and below is drawn from Wills, "Riddle of Olive Logan."

40. *Revolution*, 20 May 1869, 308. The speech is also reprinted in full in the appendix to Wills, "Riddle of Olive Logan," 312–17.

41. *New York Times*, 15 May 1869, 5. In response, a letter from "an American Actress" dismissed Logan as having been a failure in the profession long before the Blondes arrived (see "Reply to Olive Logan's Letter on the Theatrical Profession," *New York Times*, 30 May 1869, 5).

42. Logan, *Apropos of Women and Theatres*, 131–33, 135, 119–20; Logan, *Before the Footlights*, 128.

43. Wills, "Riddle of Olive Logan," 39, 131; Moses, "Lydia Thompson," 112.

44. Mott as cited in Buckley, "Culture of 'Leg-Work,'" 121.

45. Gilbert, *Stage Reminiscences*, 10. Anne Hartley Gilbert was born in 1821 and began in the corps de ballet at the Haymarket Theatre when she was about twelve.

46. Howells, "New Taste in Theatricals," 644; Willoughby Jones, *The Life of James Fisk Jr.* (Philadelphia: Union, 1872), chap. 13. See also Daly, *Life of Augustin Daly*, 43, on women who called themselves actresses.

47. Logan, *Apropos of Women and Theatres*, 147; Comstock cited in Lesser, *Enchanting Rebel*, 206. See Richard C. Johnson, "Anthony Comstock: Reform, Vice and the American Way" (Ph.D. diss., University of Wisconsin, 1973); Anna Louise Bates, "Protective Custody: A Feminist Interpretation of Anthony Comstock's Life and Laws" (Ph.D. diss., State University of New York at Binghamton, 1991).

48. Dion Boucicault explained this shift in what was permissible when in 1887 he wrote, "Fifty years ago the dancer wore skirts reaching to her ankles—no revelation of her limb was tolerated—but on the other hand the language in the plays was decollete. Now a word susceptible of a double meaning is revolting—while women strip themselves to the skin" (cited in Richard Fawkes, *Dion Boucicault: A Biography* [London and New York: Quartet Books, 1979], 233). The greater ease of policing the verbal as opposed to the visual is attested to by developments in England, where theatrical material was subjected to censorship by the Lord Chamberlain. Tracy Davis notes that much suggestive onstage behavior, including the notorious can-can, escaped censorship precisely because it was not part of the written script (Davis, *Actresses as Working Women*, 117–18). Note, too, that Anthony Comstock spent much more time and energy on obscene literature than on live performances (Johnson, "Anthony Comstock"; Bates, "Protective Custody"). On Degas, see Eunice Lipton, *Looking Into Degas: Uneasy Images of Women and Modern Life* (Berkeley and Los Angeles: University of California Press, 1986), chap. 2.

49. For sour grapes, see "Reply to Olive Logan's Letter," *New York Times*, 30 May 1869. Kellogg's tour with Forrest in Gertrude Kellogg Diaries, February and March 1872, Kellogg Family Papers. Quote from a review of Bulwer-Lytton's *Money*, clippings file, Kellogg Family Papers. The review is undated and the reviewer is not identified, but Kellogg's diary entry of 1 Feb. 1870 says she is the subject of a "most cutting criticism" in the *Tribune*, and the entry of 4 Feb. identifies Winter as the hostile reviewer.

50. Kellogg Diaries, Sept. 1870–March 1871, Kellogg Family Papers; Skinner, *Footlights and Spotlights*, 138; [Dora Ranous Knowlton], *Diary of a Daly Debutante* (New York: Duffield, 1910).

51. Wills, "Riddle of Olive Logan," 196 – 205.
52. Data on occupations in 1870 are from Johnson, *American Actress*, 50 – 51.

CONCLUSION: LOOKING AT WOMEN

1. In this way, theatre work resembled child care: however much women's work in those two realms was forced to conform to men's priorities and powers, each contained intrinsic satisfactions rare indeed in modern marketplace society. See T. J. Jackson Lears, "Making Fun of Popular Culture," *American Historical Review* 97 (December 1992): 1417 – 26 for a sensible critique of purely functionalist explanations of popular culture.

This bibliography is divided into the following sections: Manuscript Collections, Periodicals, Plays, Books and Articles: Primary Sources, Books and Articles: Secondary Sources, Dissertations.

Selected Bibliography

MANUSCRIPT COLLECTIONS

Beekley, N. Diary. American Antiquarian Society, Worcester, Mass.

Benjamin, Park. Collection. Columbia University Library, New York.

Billy Rose Theatre Collection. New York Public Library for the Performing Arts.

Cadwallader Family Papers. Historical Society of Pennsylvania, Philadelphia.

Cushman, Charlotte. Papers. Library of Congress, Washington, D.C.

Daly, Augustin. Papers. Folger Shakespeare Library, Washington, D.C.

Dramatic Museum Collection. Columbia University Library, New York.

Duffy and Forrest Account Book. Rare Books and Manuscripts, New York Public Library at Forty-second Street, New York.

Ford, John Thompson. Papers. Library of Congress, Washington, D.C.

Harvard Theatre Collection. Pusey Library, Cambridge, Mass.

Hill, Benjamin Thomas. Papers. American Antiquarian Society, Worcester, Mass.

Keene, Laura. Papers. Library of Congress, Washington, D.C.

Kellogg Family Papers. New-York Historical Society, New York.

Kemble, Frances Anne. Papers. Library of Congress, Washington, D.C.

Matthews, Brander. Collection. Columbia University Library, New York.

Playbills Collection. Library Company of Philadelphia, Philadelphia.

Rare Book Collection. Boston Public Library, Boston.

Southworth, Henry Clay. Diary. New-York Historical Society, New York.

Stanton, Elizabeth Cady. Papers. Library of Congress, Washington, D.C.

Selected Bibliography

White Family Papers. American Antiquarian Society, Worcester, Mass.
Wister Family Papers. Historical Society of Pennsylvania, Philadelphia.

PERIODICALS

Fine Arts, 1872.
Ladies' Companion, 1834–44.
New York Clipper, 1864–70.
New York Mirror, 1823–57.
Spirit of the Times (New York, N.Y.), 1831–66.
Theatrical and Literary Journal (Philadelphia), 1830.

PLAYS

The most exhaustive collection, nearly 11,000 titles, is found in the Readex microfiche series *American Plays of the Nineteenth Century* and *English Plays of the Nineteenth Century.*

BOOKS AND ARTICLES: PRIMARY SOURCES

Bernard, John. *Retrospections of America, 1797–1811.* Edited by Mrs. Bayle Bernard. 1887. Reprint. New York: Benjamin Blom, 1969.

Blake, Charles. *An Historical Account of the Providence Stage.* 1868. Reprint. New York: Benjamin Blom, 1971.

Brown, T. Allston. *A History of the New York Stage, from the First Performance in 1732 to 1901.* 3 vols. New York: Dodd, Mead, 1903.

Butler, Pierce. *Mr. Butler's Statement.* Philadelphia: J. C. Clark, 1850.

Clapp, Henry Austin. *Reminiscences of a Dramatic Critic.* Boston and New York: Houghton, Mifflin, 1902.

Clapp, William W., Jr. *A Record of the Boston Stage.* Boston and Cambridge: James Munroe, 1853.

Clarke, Mrs. Mary. *A Concise History of the Life and Amours of Thomas S. Hamblin as Told by Elizabeth Blanchard Hamblin.* Philadelphia and New York: n.p., n.d.

Clemens, Samuel L. *Mark Twain's Travels with Mr. Brown.* Edited by Franklin Walker and G. Ezra Dane. New York: Alfred A. Knopf, 1940.

Clement, Clara Erskine. *Charlotte Cushman.* Boston: James R. Osgood, 1882.

Cowell, Joseph. *Thirty Years Passed among the Players in England and America.* 1844. Reprint. Hamden, Conn.: Archon Books, 1979.

Creaghan, John. *The Life of Laura Keene.* Philadelphia: Rodgers, 1897.

Daly, Joseph Francis. *The Life of Augustin Daly.* New York: Macmillan, 1917.

Davidge, William. *Footlight Flashes.* New York: American News, 1866.

Dewey, Mary E., ed. *Life and Letters of Catharine Maria Sedgwick.* New York: Harper and Bros., 1871.

Drew, Louisa Lane. *Autobiographical Sketch of Mrs. John Drew.* 1899. Reprint. New York: Benjamin Blom, 1971.

Dunlap, William. *History of the American Theatre.* 2nd ed. 1832. Reprint. New York: Burt Franklin, 1963.

———. *Memoirs of a Water Drinker.* 2nd ed. 2 vols. New York: Saunders and Otley, 1837.

Ford, Thomas. *A Peep Behind the Curtain by a Supernumerary.* Boston: Redding, 1830.

Gilbert, Anne Hartley. *The Stage Reminiscences of Mrs. Gilbert.* New York: Charles Scribner's Sons, 1901.

Howells, William Dean. "The New Taste in Theatricals." *Atlantic Monthly*, May 1869, 635–44.

Hutton, Lawrence. *Plays and Players.* New York: Hurd and Houghton, 1875.

Ireland, Joseph N. *Records of the New York Stage from 1750 to 1860.* 2 vols. 1866. Reprint. New York: Benjamin Blom, 1966.

James, Henry. *A Small Boy and Others.* New York: Charles Scribner's Sons, 1913.

Jefferson, Joseph. *Autobiography.* New York: Century, 1889.

Kemble, Frances Anne. *Journal.* 2 vols. London: John Murray, 1835.

———. *Journal of a Residence on a Georgian Plantation in 1838–39.* Edited by John A. Scott. Athens, Ga.: University of Georgia Press, 1984.

———. *Further Records, 1848–1883.* 2 vols. London: Richard Bentley and Sons, 1890.

———. *Records of a Girlhood.* New York: Henry Holt, 1879.

———. *Records of a Later Life.* New York: Henry Holt, 1882.

Leavitt, M. B. *Fifty Years in Theatrical Management.* New York: Broadway, 1912.

Leman, Walter M. *Memories of an Old Actor.* 1886. Reprint. New York and London: Benjamin Blom, 1969.

Logan, Olive. *Apropos of Women and Theatres.* New York: Carleton, 1869.

———. *Before the Footlights and Behind the Scenes.* Philadelphia: Parmalee, 1870.

———. "The Leg Business." *Galaxy* 4 (August 1867): 440–44.

Ludlow, Noah. *Dramatic Life as I Found It.* 1880. Reprint. New York: Benjamin Blom, 1966.

Maeder, Clara Fisher. *Autobiography.* New York: Dunlap Society, 1897.

Matthews, Brander. *These Many Years: Recollections of a New Yorker.* New York: Charles Scribner's Sons, 1919.

Morgan, Helen M., ed. *A Season in New York, 1801.* Pittsburgh: University of Pittsburgh Press, 1969.

Morris, Clara. *Life on the Stage.* New York: McClure, Phillips, 1901.

Murdoch, James E. *The Stage; or, Recollections of Actors and Acting.* Philadelphia: J. M. Stoddart, 1880.

Nason, Elias. *A Memoir of Mrs. Susanna Rowson, with Elegant and Illustrative Extracts from Her Writings in Prose and Poetry.* Albany, N.Y.: Joel Munsell, 1870.

Nevins, Allan, ed. *The Diary of Philip Hone, 1828–1851.* New York: Arno, 1970.

Nevins, Allan, and Milton Halsey Thomas, eds. *The Diary of George Templeton Strong.* 4 vols. New York: Macmillan, 1952.

Northall, William Knight. *Before and Behind the Curtain; or, Fifteen Years' Observations among the Theatres of New York.* New York: W. F. Burgess, 1851.

Phelps, Henry P. *Players of a Century: A Record of the Albany Stage.* 1880. Reprint. New York: Benjamin Blom, 1972.

Price, W. T. *A Life of Charlotte Cushman.* New York: Brentano's, 1894.

Ransome, Eleanor, ed. *The Terrific Kemble: A Victorian Self-Portrait from the Writings of Fanny Kemble.* London: Hamish Hamilton, 1978.

Rede, Leman Thomas. *The Guide to the Stage, With Additional Information Applicable to the American Stage.* Edited by Francis C. Wemyss. London, 1827. New York: Samuel French, 1858.

Reignolds-Winslow, Catherine Mary. *Yesterdays with Actors.* Boston: Cupples and Hurd, 1887.

Ritchie, Anna Cora Mowatt. *Autobiography of an Actress.* Boston: Ticknor, Reed and Fields, 1854.

———. *Mimic Life; or, Before and Behind the Curtain.* Boston: Ticknor and Fields, 1855.

Skinner, Maud, and Otis Skinner, eds. *One Man in His Time: The Adventures of H. Watkins, Strolling Player, 1845–1863.* Philadelphia: University of Pennsylvania Press, 1938.

Skinner, Otis. *Footlights and Spotlights: Recollections of My Life on the Stage.* Indianapolis, Ind.: Bobbs-Merrill, 1923.

Smith, Sol. *The Theatrical Journey-Work and Anecdotal Recollections of Sol Smith.* Philadelphia: T. B. Peterson, 1854.

———. *Theatrical Management in the West and South for Thirty Years.* New York: Harper and Bros., 1868.

Stebbins, Emma. *Charlotte Cushman: Her Letters and Memories of Her Life.* Boston: Houghton, Osgood, 1878.

Stone, Henry Dickinson. *Personal Recollections of the Drama; or, Theatrical Reminiscences.* 1873. Reprint. New York and London: Benjamin Blom, 1969.

Vandenhoff, George. *Leaves from an Actor's Notebook.* New York: D. Appleton, 1860.

Wallack, John Lester. *Memories of Fifty Years.* New York: Charles Scribner's Sons, 1889.

Wemyss, Francis C. *Theatrical Biography; or, The Life of an Actor and Manager.* Glasgow: R. Griffin, 1848.

———. *Twenty-Six Years of the Life of an Actor and Manager.* New York: Burgess, Stringer, 1847.

White, Richard Grant. "The Age of Burlesque." *Galaxy* 8 (1869): 256–66.

Whitman, Walt. *Prose Works, 1892.* Edited by Floyd Stovall. 2 vols. 1892. Reprint. New York: New York University Press, 1963.

Whitton, Joseph. *Wags of the Stage.* Philadelphia: George H. Rigby, 1902.

Willard, George O. *History of the Providence Stage, 1762–1891.* Providence, R.I.: Rhode Island News, 1891.

Winter, William. *The Press and the Stage.* New York: Lockwood and Coombs, 1889.

———. *Vagrant Memories; Being Further Recollections of Other Days.* New York: George H. Dorian, 1915.

Wister, Fanny Kemble, ed. *Fanny, the American Kemble: Her Journals and Unpublished Letters*. Tallahassee: South Pass Press, 1972.

Wood, William B. *Personal Recollections of the Stage*. Philadelphia: Henry Carey Baird, 1855.

Wright, Mabel Osgood. *My New York*. New York: Macmillan, 1926.

BOOKS AND ARTICLES: SECONDARY SOURCES

Agnew, Jean-Christophe. *Worlds Apart: The Market and the Theatre in Anglo-American Thought, 1550—1750*. Cambridge and New York: Cambridge University Press, 1986.

Allen, Robert C. *Horrible Prettiness: Burlesque and American Culture*. Chapel Hill: University of North Carolina Press, 1991.

Auerbach, Nina. *Ellen Terry: Player in Her Time*. New York and London: W. W. Norton, 1987.

———. *Private Theatricals: The Lives of the Victorians*. Cambridge, Mass.: Harvard University Press, 1990.

———. *Woman and the Demon*. Cambridge, Mass.: Harvard University Press, 1982.

Bank, Rosemarie K. "Theatre and Narrative Fiction in the Work of the Nineteenth-Century American Playwright Louisa Medina." *Theatre History Studies* 3 (1983): 55—67.

Barish, Jonas. *The Antitheatrical Prejudice*. Berkeley and Los Angeles: University of California Press, 1981.

Barker, Barbara. "Maria Bonfanti and *The Black Crook*, New Orleans, 1872." *Theatre Journal* 31 (1979): 88—97.

Bobbé, Dorothy. *Fanny Kemble*. London: Elkin, Mathews and Marot, 1932.

Booth, Michael R. *English Melodrama*. London: Herbert Jenkins, 1965.

———. *Theatre in the Victorian Age*. Cambridge and New York: Cambridge University Press, 1991.

Bost, James S. *Monarchs of the Mimic World*. Orono, Maine: University of Maine Press, 1977.

Brockett, Oscar G. *History of the Theatre*. 4th ed. Boston and London: Allyn and Bacon, 1982.

Brooks, Peter. *The Melodramatic Imagination*. New Haven, Conn.: Yale University Press, 1976.

Buckley, Peter G. "The Culture of 'Leg-work': The Transformation of Burlesque after the Civil War." In *The Mythmaking Frame of Mind*, edited by James Gilbert, Amy Gilman, Donald M. Scott, and Joan W. Scott, 113—34. Belmont, Calif.: Wadsworth Publishing Co., 1993.

Butler, Judith. "Performative Acts and Gender Constitution." *Theatre Journal* 40 (Dec. 1988): 519—531.

Butsch, Richard, ed., *For Fun and Profit: The Transformation of Leisure Into Consumption*. Philadelphia: Temple University Press, 1990.

Case, Sue-Ellen, ed. *Performing Feminisms: Feminist Critical Theory and Theatre.* Baltimore: Johns Hopkins University Press, 1990.

Chinoy, Helen Krich, and Linda Walsh Jenkins, eds. *Women in American Theater.* Rev. ed. New York: Theatre Communications Group, 1987.

Coad, Oral Sumner, and Edwin Mims, Jr. *The American Stage.* New Haven, Conn.: Yale University Press, 1929.

Davies, Robertson. *The Mirror of Nature.* Toronto: University of Toronto Press, 1983.

Davis, Tracy. "The Actress in Victorian Pornography," *Theatre Journal* 41 (Oct. 1989): 294–315.

———. "Actresses and Prostitutes in Victorian London." *Theatre Research International* 13 (1988): 221–34.

———. *Actresses as Working Women: Their Social Identity in Victorian Culture.* London and New York: Routledge, 1991.

———. "Sexual Language in Victorian Society and Theatre," *American Journal of Semiotics* 6 (1989): 33–49.

Donahue, Joseph W., ed. *The Theatrical Manager in England and America.* Princeton: Princeton University Press, 1971.

Dormon, James H., Jr. *Theater in the Antebellum South.* Chapel Hill: University of North Carolina Press, 1967.

Dorson, Richard M. "Mose the Far-Famed and World-Renowned." *American Literature* 15 (1943–44): 288–300.

Falk, Bernard. *The Naked Lady.* Rev. ed. London: Hutchinson, 1952.

Ferris, Lesley. *Acting Women: Images of Women in Theatre.* New York: New York University Press, 1989.

Fisher, Judith L., and Stephen Watt, eds. *When They Weren't Doing Shakespeare: Essays on Nineteenth-Century British and American Theatre.* Athens, Ga.: University of Georgia Press, 1989.

Flynn, Joyce. "Melting Plots: Patters of Racial and Ethnic Amalgamation in American Drama Before Eugene O'Neill." *American Quarterly* 38 (1986): 417–38.

Furnas, J. C. *Fanny Kemble: Leading Lady of the Nineteenth-Century Stage.* New York: Dial Press, 1982.

Garber, Marjorie. *Vested Interests: Cross-Dressing and Cultural Anxiety.* New York and London: Routledge, 1992.

Grimsted, David. *Melodrama Unveiled: American Theater and Culture, 1800–1850.* Chicago: University of Chicago Press, 1968; University of California Press, 1987.

Halttunen, Karen. *Confidence Men and Painted Women: A Study of Middle-Class Culture in America, 1830–1870.* New Haven and London: Yale University Press, 1982.

Harris, Laurilyn J. "Extravaganza at Niblo's Garden: *The Black Crook.*" *Nineteenth Century Theatre Research* 13 (Summer 1985): 1–15.

Hawes, David S. "Much Ado about John Brougham and Jim Fisk," *Midcontinent American Studies Journal* 8 (1967): 73–89.

Henneke, Ben Graf. *Laura Keene.* Tulsa, Okla.: Council Oaks Books, 1990.

Hughes, Glenn. *History of the American Theatre, 1700–1950.* New York and London: Samuel French, 1951.

Johnson, Claudia. *American Actress: Perspective on the Nineteenth Century.* Chicago: Nelson-Hall, 1984.

———. "That Guilty Third Tier: Prostitution in Nineteenth-Century Theatres." *American Quarterly* 27 (1975): 575–84.

Kaplan, E. Ann. *Women and Film: Both Sides of the Camera.* 1983. Reprint. New York and London: Routledge, 1988.

Kasson, John F. *Rudeness and Civility: Manners in Nineteenth-Century Urban America.* New York: Hill and Wang, 1990.

Kasson, Joy. *Marble Queens and Captives: Women in Nineteenth-Century American Sculpture.* New Haven and London: Yale University Press, 1990.

Kent, Christopher. "Image and Reality: The Actress and Society." In *A Widening Sphere*, edited by Martha Vicinus, 94–116. Bloomington: Indiana University Press, 1977.

Kornfeld, Eve. "Women in Post-Revolutionary American Culture: Susanna Haswell Rowson's American Career, 1793–1824." *Journal of American Culture* 6 (Winter 1983): 56–62.

Leach, Joseph. *Bright Particular Star: The Life and Times of Charlotte Cushman.* New Haven and London: Yale University Press, 1970.

Lesser, Allen. *Enchanting Rebel: The Secret of Adah Isaacs Menken.* Philadelphia: Ruttle, Shaw and Wetherill, 1947.

Levine, Lawrence W. *Highbrow Lowbrow: The Emergence of Cultural Hierarchy in America.* Cambridge, Mass.: Harvard University Press, 1988.

Lott, Eric. "'The Seeming Counterfeit': Racial Politics and Early Blackface Minstrelsy." *American Quarterly* 43 (June 1991): 223–51.

McArthur, Benjamin. *Actors and American Culture, 1880–1920.* Philadelphia: Temple University Press, 1984.

McConachie, Bruce. *Melodramatic Formations: American Theatre and Society, 1820–1870.* Iowa City: University of Iowa Press, 1992.

McConachie, Bruce, and Daniel Friedman, eds. *Theatre for Working Class Audiences in the United States, 1830–1980.* Westport, Conn.: Greenwood Press, 1985.

McCullough, Jack W. *Living Pictures on the New York Stage.* Ann Arbor, Mich.: UMI Research Press, 1981.

———. "Model Artists vs. the Law: The First American Encounter." *Journal of American Culture* 6 (Summer 1983): 3–8.

McGlinchee, Claire. *The First Decade of the Boston Museum.* Boston: Bruce Humphries, 1940.

Mammen, Edward. *The Old Stock Company School of Acting.* Boston: Trustees of the Public Library, 1945.

Mates, Julian. "The Black Crook Myth." *Theatre Survey* 7 (May 1966): 31–43.

Matlaw, Myron, ed. *The Black Crook and Other Nineteenth Century Plays.* New York: E. P. Dutton, 1967.

Meisel, Martin. *Realizations: Narrative, Pictorial and Theatrical Arts in Nineteenth-Century England.* Princeton: Princeton University Press, 1983.

Meserve, Walter J. *An Emerging Entertainment: The Drama of the American People to 1828.* Bloomington, Ind.: Indiana University Press, 1977.

Miller, Tice. *Bohemians and Critics: American Theatre Criticism in the Nineteenth Century.* Metuchen, N. J.: Scarecrow Press, 1981.

Myers, Norman J. "Josephine Clifton: 'Manufactured' Star." *Theatre History Studies* 6 (1986): 109–23.

Odell, George C. D. *Annals of the New York Stage.* 15 vols. New York: Columbia University Press, 1927–1949.

Poggi, Jack. *Theater in America: The Impact of Economic Forces, 1870–1967.* Ithaca, N.Y.: Cornell University Press, 1968.

Postlewait, Thomas, and Bruce A. McConachie, eds. *Interpreting the Theatrical Past.* Iowa City: University of Iowa Press, 1989.

Quinn, Arthur Hobson. *A History of the American Drama from the Beginning to the Civil War.* New York and London: Harper and Bros., 1923.

Reynolds, David S. *Beneath the American Renaissance: The Subversive Imagination in the Age of Emerson and Melville.* Cambridge, Mass.: Harvard University Press, 1989.

Rinear, David L. *The Temple of Momus: Mitchell's Olympic Theatre.* Metuchen N.J.: 1987.

Robinson, Alice, Vera M. Roberts, and Milly Barranger, eds. *Notable Women in the American Theatre.* New York and Westport, Conn.: Greenwood Press, 1989.

Rourke, Constance. *American Humor: A Study of the National Character.* New York: Harcourt, Brace and Co., 1931.

Schofield, Mary Anne, and Cecilia Macheski, eds. *Curtain Calls: British and American Women and the Theater, 1660–1820.* Athens: Ohio University Press, 1991.

Seller, Maxine, ed. *Ethnic Theatre in the United States.* Westport, Conn.: Greenwood Press, 1983.

Senelick, Laurence. "The Evolution of the Male Impersonator on the Nineteenth-Century Popular Stage." *Essays in Theatre* 1 (Nov. 1982): 31–44.

Senelick, Laurence, ed. *Gender in Performance: The Presentation of Difference in the Performing Arts.* Hanover, N.H.: University Press of New England, 1992.

Sennett, Richard. *The Fall of Public Man.* New York: Random House, Vintage Books, 1978.

Swift, Mary Grace. *Belles and Beaux of Their Toes.* Washington, D.C.: University Press of America, 1980.

Toll, Robert C. *Blacking Up: The Minstrel Show in Nineteenth Century America.* New York: Oxford University Press, 1974.

———. *On With the Show: The First Century of Show Business in America.* New York: Oxford University Press, 1976.

Weil, Dorothy. *In Defense of Women: Susanna Rowson.* University Park, Pa.: Pennsylvania State University Press, 1976.

Wilson, Garff B. *History of American Acting.* Bloomington, Ind.: Indiana University Press, 1966.

Zellers, Parker R. "The Cradle of Variety: The Concert Saloons." *Educational Theatre Journal* 20 (1968): 578–85.

DISSERTATIONS

Baines, Jimmy Dalton. "Samuel S. Sanford and Negro Minstrelsy." Ph.D. diss., Tulane University, 1967.

Buckley, Peter. "To the Opera House: Culture and Society in New York City, 1820–1860." Ph.D. diss., State University of New York at Stony Brook, 1984.

Gintautiene, Kristina. "*The Black Crook*: Ballet in the Gilded Age, 1866–1876." Ph.D. diss., New York University, 1984.

Humble, Alberta Lewis. "Matilda Heron, American Actress." Ph.D. diss., University of Illinois, 1959.

Merrill, Lisa. "Charlotte Cushman: American Actress on the Vanguard of New Roles for Women." Ph.D. diss., New York University, 1985.

Moses, Marilyn A. "Lydia Thompson and the 'British Blondes' in the United States." Ph.D. diss., University of Oregon, 1978.

Shank, Theodore J. "The Bowery Theatre, 1826–1836." Ph.D. diss., Stanford University, 1956.

Taylor, Dorothy Jean. "Laura Keene in America, 1852–1873." Ph.D. diss., Tulane University, 1966.

Turner, Willis Lloyd. "City Low-Life on the American Stage to 1900." Ph.D. diss., University of Illinois, 1956.

Whitehead, Barbara. "Fancy's Show Box: Performance in the Republic, 1790–1866." Ph.D. diss., University of Chicago, 1976.

Wills, Robert J., Jr. "The Riddle of Olive Logan." Ph.D. diss., Case Western Reserve University, 1971.

Yeater, James Willis. "Charlotte Cushman, American Actress." Ph.D. diss., University of Illinois, 1959.

Numbers in *italic* indicate pages with illustrations.

Lightning Source UK Ltd.
Milton Keynes UK
UKOW02f1402280716

279434UK00001B/68/P